River Song

Naxiyamtáma (Snake River-Palouse) Oral Traditions
from Mary Jim, Andrew George, Gordon Fisher,
and Emily Peone

Collected and edited by
RICHARD D. SCHEUERMAN & CLIFFORD E. TRAFZER

Foreword by
CARRIE JIM SCHUSTER

Color Plates by
JOHN CLEMENT

Washington State University
Pullman, Washington

Washington State University Press
PO Box 645910
Pullman, Washington 99164-5910
Phone: 800-354-7360
Fax: 509-335-8568
Email: wsupress@wsu.edu
Website: wsupress.wsu.edu

© 2015 by the Board of Regents of Washington State University
All rights reserved
First printing 2015

Reproduction or transmission of material contained in this publication in excess of that permitted by copyright law is prohibited without permission in writing from the publisher.

Library of Congress Cataloging-in-Publication Data

River song : Naxiyamtama (Snake River-Palouse) oral traditions from Mary Jim, Andrew George, Gordon Fisher, and Emily Peone / collected and edited by Richard D. Scheuerman and Clifford E. Trafzer ; foreword by Carrie Jim Schuster.
    pages cm
  Includes bibliographical references and index.
  ISBN 978-0-87422-327-9 (alk. paper)
 1. Paloos Indians--History. 2. Paloos Indians--Biography. 3. Paloos Indians--Folklore. 4. Snake River Plain (Idaho and Or.)--Folklore. 5. Indians of North America--Washington (State)--Folklore. 6. Indians of North America--Idaho--Folklore. 7. Oral tradition--Northwest, Pacific. I. Scheuerman, Richard D., editor. II. Trafzer, Clifford E., editor. III. Title: Naxiyamtama (Snake River-Palouse) oral traditions from Mary Jim, Andrew George, Gordon Fisher, and Emily Peone.
  E99.P22R58 2015
  979.7004'97--dc23
                                                        2014036204

Cover image, "Palouse River Canyon," and color photographs on pages xiii, 1, 59, 71, 86, 137, and back cover are courtesy of John Clement, www.john clementgallery.com

For Carrie Jim Schuster,
Ione Martel, and Susie Weaskus,
and in memory of
Mary Jim, Andew George, Gordon Fisher, and
Emily Friedlander Peone

Contents

List of Maps	viii
Foreword by Carrie Jim Schuster	xi
Preface	xvii
Notes on Lineages and Spelling	xxiii
Introduction	1
PART I/*Náxc*: Mary Jim/Xínstanik	45
"Calling for Our Land"	47
"How Coyote Learned to Fish"	59
"The Creatures of Cloudy Mountain"	62
The Tiłqawayks (Wolf) and Chowawatyet (Jim) Families	66
PART II/*Nápt*: Andrew George/Tipiyeléhne Xáyxayx	71
"Nature is Our Teacher"	73
Chief Cleveland Kamiakin	77
"Salmon Man and the Wolf Brothers"	87
"Why Coyote Made the Palouse Hills"	93
The Kamíakin Family	95
PART III/*Métad*: Gordon Fisher/Yoosyóos Tulikécin	103
"Take Care of Mother Earth"	105
"How Beaver Brought Fire"	113
"The Origin of Palouse Falls"	116
The Póyakŭn/Billy Andrews and Páween Families	120
PART IV/*Pínapt*: Emily Friedlander Peone/Q'uomolah	127
"Too Many Memories"	129
Mary Owhi Moses/Sanclow	134
"*Yámuštas*—Elk's Abode at Steptoe Butte"	137
"The Two Sisters and Star Brothers"	139
The Sulkstalk'scosm/Moses Family	144
PART V/*Páxad*: Landscapes of Beaver and Coyote	149

Appendix A: A Naxiyamtáma Lexicon of Animal and Plant Terms	163
Appendix B: Historic Era Naxiyamtáma Village and Place Names	171
Appendix C: Atinapam-Johnley Stories	177
Selected Bibliography	190
Index	195

Maps

The Snake River–Palouse Region and Northwest Indian Reservations	x
Snake River–Palouse Tribal Area	173

"That is where I should be, at Snake River. My river sings to me. That song is my Snake River."

—MARY JIM

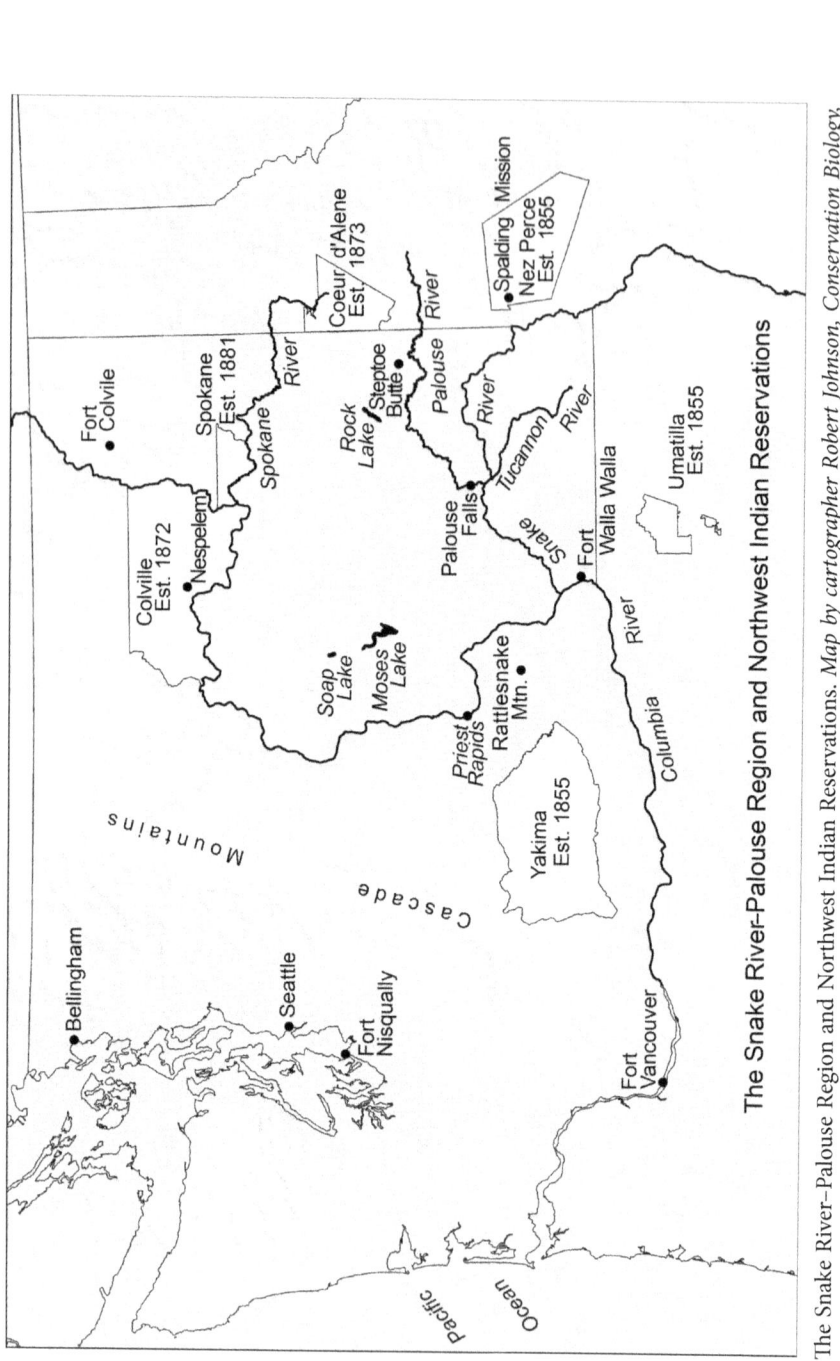

The Snake River–Palouse Region and Northwest Indian Reservations. *Map by cartographer Robert Johnson, Conservation Biology, University of California, Riverside*

Foreword

Carrie Jim Schuster

Oral histories and literature like the ones in this collection that my mother, Mary Jim, and others—like Andrew George and Gordon Fisher—shared over the years have long been told to create awareness in young and old alike about our place in the world. The lives of all creatures are beautifully woven in the fabric of life, from the tiniest insects, butterflies, and moths to the larger creatures like beaver and salmon. The water and earth they inhabit is also here to sustain us.

Our tribal elders reminded us of the old prophecies and warnings about what will happen if we neglect our responsibilities as stewards of the land. Today we experience some of the consequences of this neglect. My mother and the Fishers, Georges, and others like them faced shared challenges because we grew up living freely in our ancestral lands. Only later in life were families like ours confined to the reservation, long after I had begun my education from my parents, aunts, uncles, and other elders.

I was raised in camps along the Snake River as our ancestors had lived for generations, with the bounty of the river and land sufficient for all our needs. Only with the flooding of our home after the building of Ice Harbor Dam were we forced to move to the reservation. Through the courage and faith of elders like my mother we made a new life, but our hearts are still back home and we return there every year.

Having that natural world cut off was a great sorrow, and the elders sought each other's presence to deal with the loss of the life we knew. They remembered the cruel way in which so many older ones had left this life, but found strength in the words of our prophets at Priest Rapids—Yúyuni, Šmuhalla, and on back in time. After humanity's fall in the ancient time the people repented and our prophets told us how to follow the Creator's way by honoring the sacred foods—water, roots, salmon, berries, venison. He fashioned their images in the petroglyphs along the Snake River and at Priest Rapids as instruction for the people. Those stones are sacred so we did not touch them.

Our prophets taught us not to waste the Creator's gifts but to honor them in order to sustain the people. They fasted at sacred places like Rattlesnake Mountain for visions and strength, and we learned the stories of such places:

In the time before the Animal People,
    Áan—Sun, had four wives
        as was customary back then.
His wives were Rattlesnake Mountain and three sisters—
    Mt. Adams, Mt. St. Helens, and Mt. Hood.
Rattlesnake Mountain was Sun's favorite wife.
As sunrise appeared each morning in the east,
    he first loved her.
At that time she was as tall and beautiful
    as the great Cascade peaks,
        and cast a shadow upon the other mountains.
The four sisters grew jealous of Sun's attention,
    and wanted him to spend more time with them.
They talked it over and decided to destroy his favorite.
One day after Sun had passed overhead
    they attacked Rattlesnake Mountain
        and pounded her down in a terrible fight.
When Sun arose the next day,
    and saw what had happened,
        he mourned the loss of his beloved
            and rain fell upon the earth for many days.
Sun gathered Rattlesnake Mountain's remaining hazel and pine nuts,
    her camas roots and huckleberries,
        and spread them around his remaining wives.
But Sun still loved his disfigured wife,
    and left around her beautiful stands of balsamroot

and lupine for the coming people,
    and *piyaxí, anipä´c, sawítk*,
        and some roots that only grow there.

The lessons taught to us by elders like my mother, Andrew, and Gordon are not only about our people's covenant with the Almighty. They are also offered as a guide to others who care about our world because this natural law takes precedence over the commercial exploitation of resources given to us by the Creator. If we follow our elders' examples as stewards of the land then our children and grandchildren will benefit. But misuse threatens their future through contamination of our water, air, and land, which affects everyone's food and health. There is so much pollution and noise today that

Carrie Jim Schuster and Rattlesnake Mountain. *John Clement*

young people do not recognize the sound of the earth and what it is telling us.

Back on the Snake River where I was raised we lived with the fish and animals. There were lots of beavers living all over. They made pools in the streams to cleanse the water, trees grew along the river banks and cooled the water for the salmon, and we had safe places to play. The animals were put here to do these things and to teach us. But now our rivers and streams have become nothing but lifeless reservoirs and concrete canals. These are the kinds of things my mother, Andrew, and Gordon would mourn. They remembered the days of no dams on the river and no paved roads across our lands—the way God had made it.

Gordon was wise because he listened to his grandparents who told about their everyday experiences in the Palouse and on the Snake River before their life on the reservation. He also learned from them to be a man of peace. When he was young he lived for a time with Cleveland Kamiakin and his wife, Alalumt'i, in Nespelem and learned from them and others like Charlie Williams about the old ways. Gordon attended the Longhouse with the men and he would listen to them talk. Cleveland and Charlie and Camille Williams would tell about Chief Kamiakin and Chief Joseph. He also spent time with his Fisher grandparents, Sam and Helen, at the old village of Palús on the Snake River.

Andrew George was a Longhouse spiritual leader, and the first time I saw him was when he was visiting with Robert Burke from Umatilla at Wówniyu's place, where we stayed after coming to the reservation. They loved smelt and fresh muffins so I worked to make them just right—the smelt rolled in corn meal and everything cooked on a wood stove. Andrew went on to also become a leader in the All-Tribes Church. He knew the spiritual truths that form the foundation for the well-being of children and grandchildren. No whip-man was needed when Andrew was around. He was a disciplinarian but never needed to execute his power! Everyone respected him.

We were trained to be silent in the elders' presence and to listen—no playing the radio or making noise. They taught us to be still—something they learned from their parents during the war times, and they passed that on down to us. Our elders knew the beautiful life we all once shared, and at the center of that beauty was the family. We learned how our families were related from the time we all lived together along the river. These are relationships that go back many generations.

My hope is that young people will benefit from these teachings, and will avoid thinking that unlimited exploitation and technology bring only progress. May they benefit from the lessons of those who inhabited this land since time immemorial, and understand that rivers and trees and animals also have their place in the circle of life. Appreciation and respect for this knowledge represent real hope for our shared future.

Carrie Jim Schuster
Parker, Washington

Carrie Jim Schuster and Mary Jim, 1980. *Richard Scheuerman*

Preface

In the fall of 1980, Snake River-Palouse elder Mary Jim walked along a small dirt trail near her home at Parker, Washington. Two young men, we had driven halfway across the state of Washington to learn from this elder-teacher. As she walked along with us Mary Jim pointed to a nearby irrigation ditch, saying "That is not my Snake River." She stated emphatically, "I love my Snake River. That is where I should be, at Snake River. My river sings to me. That song is my Snake River." For many generations, Mary Jim, her family, and their ancestors lived in their villages along Snake River, traveling each spring to begin their seasonal round from early root grounds to fishing areas to hunting landscapes. In the early twentieth century, the Snake River-Palouse and other tribes moved across the Columbia Plateau on horseback from Snake River to Badger Mountain and back to the river to fish before hunting in the Blue Mountains of Oregon.

During the twentieth century, Mary Jim, Andrew George, Emily Peone, and Gordon Fisher lived free and open lives on the Columbia Plateau. They lived in the old way by hunting, fishing, and gathering. Like their ancestors, they interacted and intermarried with Indians from a vast region in the Northwest, and their stories are rich in content, interpretations, and nuances. Our interviews with them spanned many years, from the 1970s into the 2000s, and enriched our histories and our lives. Their words and stories offer unique historical sources that cannot be found in written documents left by newcomers. Their voices, shared in the oral tradition, provided new and critical sources that significantly influenced the writing of our books and articles. Although we have interviewed numerous tribal elders since then, the oral histories of these four elders stand out as extraordinary. They were passionate about the history and culture of their people as well as the importance of family and faith—especially faith tied to their homelands of the inland Northwest, commonly known as the Great Columbia Plateau.

We (Clifford and Richard) came together as a research team in 1978 at Washington State University (WSU) and within a short time agreed to co-author *Renegade Tribe: The Palouse Indians and the Invasion of the Inland Pacific Northwest* (1986), which drew on the oral interviews we conducted in the 1970s and 1980s. The book was honored with a Washington State Governor's Writers Award, but we gained much more than book and award through our associations with Mary Jim, Andrew George, Emily Peone, and Gordon Fisher—people we respectfully consider our teachers and elders. Through this partnership we came to know Mary Jim and her family, good people who opened their homes, memories, knowledge, and histories to us so we might know more about the Snake River-Palouse Indians and others of the Columbia Plateau.

On one of our excursions to the Yakama Indian Reservation in 1980, we gave a presentation on the importance of oral histories in our academic work. Tribal elders attending our formal talk informed us that we could not possibly research and write a book on the Snake River-Palouse without learning from Andrew George, who was born on Snake River shortly after the turn of the twentieth century. We had heard of Andrew George many times before from tribal elders living on the Colville, Nez Perce, and Umatilla reservations, but were never able to meet him. He was a spiritual leader and healer, a man always on the move to help others. We explained this to the elders on the Yakama Reservation, and they informed us that Andrew was currently on the reservation, staying with his daughter. They gave us directions to his daughter's home as the family had no telephone.

With Lee Ann Smith—Cliff's future bride—we followed the directions into the Yakima Valley, down a canal road, and ultimately found three homes. We drove to the third house, went to the door, and knocked. It was November and a cold wind had kicked up as the sun began to sink quickly into the west over the Cascade Mountains. Two young girls answered the door and we asked to speak to Andrew George. They left the door open and ran off laughing. Shortly thereafter, Andrew walked out of the hallway to our left. As we tried to explain who we were and why we were there, he reached out to take each of us by the arm and brought us into his home. Symbolically, we had entered his world. Andrew taught us through stories about the time of creation and the exile of his family to Indian Territory, *Eekish Pah*—the Hot Country—where the United States had exiled the Nez Perce and Palouse bands after the 1877 Nez Perce War. Portions of Andrew's narratives and teachings are included here as well as those of Palouse and Nez Perce tribal elder Gordon Fisher.

We worked with Gordon during a Palouse Indian conference and gathering at WSU. In addition, we each met separately with him at his home on the Nez Perce Reservation, on Snake River, and later when he was confined to a hospital at Lewiston, Idaho, and asked to continue our meetings. Like the other elders, Gordon had a remarkable memory of his life and that of his people. Collectively, their stories reached back into the eighteenth century, and the elders also possessed very clear knowledge of the nineteenth and early twentieth centuries. All of them shared freely about a wide range of topics, knowing that we would use their voices in our scholarly work as teachers and researchers. Their voices taught us invaluable lessons about Native American history and specifics about the history and culture of Indian people of the Great Columbia Plateau. Most significantly, they taught us the power of faith and family among their people.

For thousands of years, Plateau Indians lived off the bounty of the earth as they gathered fruits and vegetables, hunted many diverse animals, and fished the great rivers of the region. All of the tribal elders featured here emphasized the close and spiritual relationship of their people to the environment that gave them sustenance. The elders spoke of the economic collapse that occurred in their homeland when the United States, American settlers, and states of Washington, Oregon, and Idaho destroyed the Native American economies based on hunting, gathering, and fishing. Once Native economies on the Columbia Plateau collapsed, men, women, and children turned to wage labor in order to survive, working on farms, ranches, and towns while still doing limited traditional food-gathering. Still, the people never surrendered their sacred obligation to offer prayers of thanksgiving and to celebrate the first catch or harvest with First Food feasts that continue today.

In the spring of 1981, we traveled to the Yakama Reservation to learn more from Mary. When we arrived at her home, several members of her extended family greeted us and shared their oral histories. They invited us to remain at the house and join them for dinner. The dinner proved to be a First Feast ceremony, officiated by Charlie Jim, who rang a large school bell and began the service with prayer and songs. During the ceremony we shared a pinch of cooked salmon, eating it in communion. We each took a small draft of water, and drank in unison, praising the water, fish, and the Creator who made the ceremony—and life—possible. Mary's family taught us by example, and we shared far more than a meal that day. The ceremony taught us about the depth of spirit that provided a powerful factor in their history and culture.

All of the tribal elders featured in this work participated in First Feast ceremonies many times throughout their lives, and they taught the younger generations to continue the gatherings of thanksgiving. Their people had learned to give thanks during First Feasts through traditional oral narratives, shared from one generation to the next. They learned through ancient stories, such as those about Coyote, chief among the old characters that taught by example, and continue to teach humans today.

Mystic Coyote provided examples of behavior for humans, sometimes acting as culture hero and sometimes as buffoon. But the stories found in this work are not just "fairy tales" or quaint Indian stories for children. The oral narratives are sacred texts that contain many levels of meaning, which tribal elders shared with community members as life lessons. Andrew George once explained that when he was a child, his elders told the same stories year after year. But one winter night, while everyone gathered in a large mat lodge, an elder asked Andrew to tell a specific story. Andrew tried but he "had listened with only one ear" and did not tell the story correctly. So the elder told the story and had Andrew repeat the story until he got it right. Andrew explained that he learned many lessons in the oral tradition in the manner described here. When he met with us, he used this Native methodology to educate us, sharing his knowledge and life experiences. In this way, he allowed us to enter his Native world and his way of thinking about the past and present.

Mary Jim, Gordon Fisher, and other tribal elders shared in the same manner, teaching us about historical events that occurred years, even centuries before, but have meaning today. Through the oral tradition, we learned. This collection is an attempt to write in that tradition, offering you, the reader, an opportunity to share in the stories and narratives provided by these knowledgeable elders. These narratives are significant for the reader who wishes to know more about Native Americans of the Great Columbia Plateau and the Native universe in general. The stories found here are not children's stories, but children can benefit greatly by reading, studying, and thinking about them.

We feel honored to have known and learned from Mary, Andrew, Emily, and Gordon. They and other tribal elders shared their knowledge and lives with us so that we could get the story right. Yellow Wolf, Chief Joseph's nephew, once explained that white people who had told their versions of Native American history had often "told it to please themselves." We have used non-Indian and Native American sources to inform our understandings, and here we share some of our sources. We are especially indebted to each of the tribal elders, and to their families. We owe a special appreciation to Carrie Jim Schuster, Albert Redstar, Michael Finley, Susie Weaskus, and Tanya Tomeo.

We are changed people and more thoughtful scholars as a result of our work with the elders. As you read this work, we ask you to think deeply about them. We ask you to be silent, quiet your mind, and listen to these words so that you might know the voices of these honored elders and other storytellers from among the Plateau tribes. Mary, Andrew, Emily, and Gordon always spoke in a slow and purposeful cadence, measuring each word and idea so that listeners could understand. They did not attempt to confuse or impress. They wished to communicate effectively so that we might know more about their cultures and histories.

Many others also helped to make this work possible and we are especially grateful for support over the years from Sahaptin scholar Bruce Rigsby at the University of Queensland in Brisbane, Australia; Colville Confederated Tribes Business Council chair and historian Michael Finley; and Rob McCoy, professor of history at Washington State University. The scholarly work of ethnographers Eugene Hunn, University of Washington, and Rodney Frey, University of Idaho, have also informed our understandings of Plateau Indian culture. At Seattle Pacific University, we are indebted to School of Education dean Rick Eigenbrood and professors Kristine Gritter, Mícheál Roe, and Arthur Ellis. At the University of California, Riverside, we wish to acknowledge the support of the Rupert Costo Endowment, California Center for Native Nations, and the Department of History. Work on this project could not have been conducted without the abiding support of UC, Riverside, Chancellor Kim Wilcox, dean Stephen Cullenberg, assistant deans Katherine A. Kinney and Shaun Bohler, chair Randolph Head, and professors Rebecca Kugel, Michelle Raheja, Jacqueline Shea-Murphy, and Stella Nair. In addition, Michelle Lorimer, Kevin Whalen, and Elvia Rodriquez have helped us with research and sources, providing professional assistance around every corner. Our thanks also to WSU Press staff members Ed Sala, Robert Clark, Beth DeWeese, Nancy Grunewald, Kerry Darnall, and Caryn Lawton.

Family members Lois Scheuerman, Mary, Karl, and Leigh; and Lee Ann Smith Trafzer, Louise, Tess, Hayley, and Tara, have given us time to work, and we thank them for the continued assistance and encouragement. Finally, we extend sincere appreciation to all the tribal areas of Washington, Idaho, Oklahoma, California, Nevada, and Arizona who have shared their oral traditions and added to the understanding of the larger world of Native American culture and history.

Richard Scheuerman, Seattle Pacific University
Clifford Trafzer, University of California, Riverside

Notes on Lineages and Spelling

Following the oral histories and stories from each of the elders featured in this book are detailed family lineages. Family associations significantly inform personal identity in any culture, and our understandings have been enhanced by oral histories we have conducted over the years and by those recorded by others whose similar questing preceded ours. We have followed trails taken in times past by historians like W. C. Brown and Cull White on the Colville Indian Reservation, Andrew Splawn and L. V. McWhorter in the Yakima Valley, and by Robert Ruby and John Brown among the Umatilla and Nez Perce people. We acknowledge here the debt we owe to these individuals and the many tribal oral historians with whom they consulted.

Invariably the wisdom generously related by the elders spoke of the essential roles family members have long served to enrich succeeding generations. In this way, our own parents have passed down stories of our grandparents' travels in difficult times, uncles have shown us favored places where their fathers hunted, and women have shared tales of overcoming personal adversity and of those who succumbed to the odds. Usually such stories come with names attached that put flesh and breath to someone else's experience.

In the course of a recent publishing project, we encountered the challenge of attempting to reconstruct the remarkable saga of a Native American family prominent in the history of the region and nation. Early into the work we realized that, as with most any large clan, no one group or single repository existed that held the scope of available memory and documentation necessary to assemble the fullest account possible. Yet each resource contained highly relevant information. While seeking to glean this knowledge through patient conversation and the examination of notes and official records, we found ourselves assembling a substantial collection of related materials we thought might be of cultural value and historical interest to family members and others.

Nineteenth-century dates of birth and death are based on census reports, enrollment documents, probate proceedings, and other public records and oral history transcripts found at the National Archives and Records Administration, Seattle, and in regional university archives and libraries. The Columbia Plateau was divided linguistically between southern Sahaptin-speaking tribes including the Yakama, Palouse, and Nez Perce, and such Interior Salish peoples to the north as the Wenatchi, Moses Columbia, and Spokane. Although these two language families were mutually unintelligible, many inhabitants of the region were bilingual due to intertribal family associations and seasonal travel patterns. Individuals throughout the area, therefore, sometimes had names in more than one language and whenever known, the additional names are given. Names in Native American cultures are often hereditary, with origins in the ancient past. To better distinguish between individuals sharing the same name, designation by roman numerals (I, II, etc.) begins with the first person identified in the oral or written record bearing the name.

In any language, terms and names exist for which there are no true equivalents in other languages. Indian names translated into English by non-Indians in historical documents can have different connotations and sometimes misrepresent the original word or expression. Moreover, among the Plateau peoples, names traditionally change over time, marking growth from infancy to adolescence and adulthood. Whenever known, an individual's adult name is used in the lineages.

Many individuals and non-reservation families in particular opposed participating in federal censuses during the nineteenth century, so vital statistics are limited in some cases for those who did not later relocate to reservations where agency records were maintained to various degrees. Because ages are listed in censuses and some probate documents rather than dates of birth and death, those dates followed by abbreviations for such documentation (see below) may vary in accuracy by at least one year. Children from marriages are entered from the left; spouses are placed to their right. Birth order is from top to bottom, though children who died in infancy are generally not listed.

The use here of birth (b.), circa (c.), death (d.), and question mark (?) varies slightly from common practice. Circa (c.) is used to indicate uncertainty about a date when only general information has been provided (e.g., "When he died in 1930, he was about sixty years old."). A question mark (?) indicates that differing dates are provided by the sources. This most common contradiction occurs when oral histories state one year, but census records indicate a different one. In these instances, the year supplied in family accounts is used, but a question mark is added. Birth (b.) and death year (d.) are used only when one or the other, but not both, is known, and a question mark might also relate to these circumstances.

Most of the letters for spelling personal names and terms in the appended lexicon appear in Standard English, but several symbols and diacritical marks shown in the following key are used to indicate some sounds in Sahaptin and Interior Salish unfamiliar in English. Among speakers of these indigenous languages there may be several ways to spell the same word since they have only recently been rendered in written forms and individuals and families maintain distinct phonetic structures. We acknowledge the contributions of Emily Peone, Isabel Arcasa, Virginia Beavert, Carrie Jim Schuster, Gordon Fisher, Margaret Gore, Bruce Rigsby, and Noel Rude for systematizing the alphabet and lexicons of these languages.

á	short "a," as in "arise"
áa	long "a," as in "pay"
k'	closing throat glottal stop, pronounce "k"
q'	closing throat glottal stop, pronounce "q"
c	"ts" sound, as in "hits"
č	"ch" sound, as in "church"
š	"sh" sound, as in "shape"
t'	closing throat glottal stop, pronounce "t"
ú	short "u," as in "look"
úu	long "u," as in "true"
ł	"lh" sound, as in "philharmonic"
´	phonemic accent
x̣	gutteral "kh," as in German "ach"
i̵	unstressed "eh," as the "a" in "accept"

Lineage Abbreviations

AA: Albert Andrews (with R. Scheuerman), Moses Lake, WA, 2005.

AB: Agatha Bart (with M. Finley), Nespelem, WA, 2005.

AD: Agnes Davis (with R. Scheuerman and M. Finley), Pullman, WA 2006.

AG: Andrew George (with R. Scheuerman and C. Trafzer), Toppenish, WA, 1980.

AJS: Andrew J. Splawn, *Ka-Mi-Akin*, 1917.

AMA: Alice Andrews (with Robert Ruby), Nespelem, WA, 1961.

APK/AO: Annie Paween Kamiakin and Annie Owhi (with Verne Ray), Nespelem, WA, 1971.

AS/BR: Alex Saluskin (with Bruce Rigsby), Yakima, WA, 1966.

AT: Arthur Taylor (correspondence with R. Scheuerman), Moscow, ID, 2009.

ATK: Arthur Tomeo Kamiakin (with R. Scheuerman), Nespelem, WA, 1972.

BR: Bruce Rigsby Papers, University of Queensland, Graceville.

CAC: Colville Agency Federal Censuses (Moses Columbia and Nez Perce Bands), 1885, 1887, 1890, 1891, 1892, 1894, 1896, 1897, 1898, 1899, 1900, 1910.

CAR: Colville Agency Records (National Archives, RG 75).

CJS: Carrie Jim Schuster (with R. Scheuerman), Toppenish, WA, 2006.

CK: Cleveland Kamiakin (with Cull White), 1957, Manuscripts, Archives, and Special Collections (MASC), Washington State University Libraries, Pullman.

CS/MS: Cecelia Sam, Mollie Si-een-wat (with L. V. McWhorter), Yakima, WA, 1922.

CTC: Colville Tribal Council Minutes, 1911, Relander Collection, Yakima Public Library.

CW: Cull A. White Papers, MASC, WSU Libraries, Pullman.

EB: Ernie Brooks (with Michael Finley), Nespelem, WA, 2006.

EC: Edward S. Curtis, The North American Indian (7), 1911.

EP: Emily Peone (with R. Scheuerman), Nespelem, WA, 1981.

ES: Eagle Seelatsee (to R. Blakely), Yakima, WA, 1974, Ellensburg Public Library.

FA: Frank Andrews (with M. Finley and R. Scheuerman), Nespelem, WA, 2006.

FW: Flora Wasis (with R. Scheuerman), Mission, OR, 1984.

GF: Gordon Fisher (with R. Scheuerman), Lapwai, ID, 2006.

GG: Geraldine Gabriel (with M. Finley), Nespelem, WA, 2006.

IC: Inez Cleveland (with R. Scheuerman and M. Finley), Seattle, WA, 2007.

IP: Isaac Patrick (with R. Scheuerman) Mission, OR, 1981.

JB: John Brown Papers, Wenatchee Valley Museum Archives, Wenatchee, WA.

JD: James L. Davis Collection, Museum of Arts & Culture (MAC), Spokane, WA.

JeT: Jeff Thomas Papers, Puyallup, WA, 2011.

JY/LN: Josephine Yemowit (with L. V. McWhorter), Yakima, WA, 1912.

LC: Lucy Covington (with Cull White), Nespelem, WA, 1961.

LVM: Lucillus V. McWhorter Papers, MASC, WSU Libraries, Pullman.

MCJ: Mary Jim and Carrie Jim Schuster (with R. Scheuerman and C. Trafzer), Parker, WA, 1979.

MF: Michael Finley Papers, Inchelium, WA.

MK: Mary Kamiakin, 1916.

MKl: Matilda Kalyton, 1918.

MM: Mary Moses (with W. C. Brown), Nespelem, WA, 1918.

NA/FH: Family Histories, RG 75.291.1, National Archives, Seattle.

NA/GC: General Correspondence (Inheritance), RG 75.107.2, National Archives, Seattle.

NR: Noel Rude, "Sahaptin Personal Names," n.d. (c. 1990).

RJ: Rose Jack (with R. Scheuerman), Mission, OR, 1984.

RR: Robert Ruby Papers, MAC Archives, Spokane, WA.

SF: Sam Fisher (MF), 1917.

SHM: Sacred Heart Mission (marriage and baptismal records, 1860-1900), Desmet, ID.

SR: Sharon Redthunder (with R. Scheuerman), Nespelem, WA, 2006.

SW: Sophie Wak-wak Williams (with C. Relander), Yakima, WA, 1951.

TA: Tom Billy Andrews (with Bruce Rigsby), Nespelem, WA, 1964.

TK: Tomeo Kamiakin (with W. C. Brown), Nespelem, WA, 1928.

TT: Tanya Tomeo (with R. Scheuerman), Yakima, WA, 2006.

UAC: Umatilla Agency Federal Censuses (Walla Walla, Cayuse, and Umatilla Bands), 1892, 1893, 1896, 1898, 1901, 1903, 1913, 1918, 1930.

UAR: Umatilla Agency Records (National Archives, RG 75).

WCB: William C. Brown Papers, MASC, WSU Libraries, Pullman.

WW: Wilson Wewah Jr. (correspondence with R. Scheuerman), Warm Springs, OR, 2006.

YAR: Yakama Agency Enrollment Records, Ellensburg Public Library, various years.

Palouse Hills Blue. *John Clement*

Introduction

WRITING IN THE ORAL TRADITION

During the winter months on the Columbia Plateau, snow and ice often cover the earth. Before the twentieth century, Snake River-Palouse Indians used this time to meet in A-framed tule-mat lodges or tipis to tell stories and learn the history, culture, language, and traditions of their people. Elders taught children to listen carefully to the stories and to be courteous toward their teachers. As storytellers spun the tales, children listened in warmth and comfort, tucked under blankets as winter weather swirled about outside the lodge. Thick fog sometimes obscured the terrain and enveloped the landscape in a dense cloud. Just as quickly as winter cold consumed the land, warm, wild Chinook Wind might blow across the Plateau from the west, sweeping aside the fog and melting snow and ice.

The contributions presented here in *River Song* serve the same purpose as Chinook Wind, clearing the academic landscape of misunderstandings and misinterpretations, exposing Native American truths told by Naxíyampam (Snake-River Palouse) elders who lived during the twentieth century. Elders Mary Jim, Andrew George, Gordon Fisher, and Emily Peone offer first-person accounts of their lives, people, and culture. Used in part in *Renegade Tribe* (1986) and *Finding Chief Kamiakin* (2008), those narratives are presented fully in *River Song*.

The accounts provided by these four remarkable persons are reminiscent of traditional oral narratives of death and rebirth. Plateau tribes have versions of the same story motif that describe a time when the North Wind Brothers, or Arctic Wind, covered the Northwest with snow and ice. The warm Chinook Wind, represented by Young Chinook, broke the power of the North Wind Brothers and their allies, the Five Wolf Brothers. Young Chinook Salmon defeated these creatures, but the sister of the Wolf Brothers returned each winter with a milder version of her brothers' severe weather. The contest between Young Chinook and the North Wind Brothers set forth the *tamánwit* "law" of creation, which established that every year there would be a time of winter but a promise of spring, when Young Chinook and the Chinook Wind would clear the land of its winter covering and allow life to sweep over the land once more.

We have written this work from the oral tradition with the hope that it will illuminate elements of Northwestern Indian history and culture. Mary Jim, Andrew George, Gordon Fisher, and Emily Peone offer oral histories of a personal, familial, and tribal nature. They are an important part of American and Northwestern history. Like Chinook Wind, their voices clear the academic landscape and make visible specific topics and truths based on their cultural experiences and knowledge.

Sharing Indigenous Knowledge

We have visited tribal elders and teachers since the 1970s. We have also spent over three decades researching libraries, archives, and special collections for additional documents and oral histories produced by earlier scholars. The elders presented in *River Song* willingly shared their voices to inform, interpret, and inspire those interested in learning more about the Snake River-Palouse and other indigenous peoples of the Columbia Plateau. The accounts and traditional stories they provide here are at once ancient and contemporary.

Mary Jim, Andrew George, Gordon Fisher, and Emily Peone related this knowledge so we might know more about Northwestern tribal history. They also expected us to share their voices with wider audiences, including young American Indian people, so they might come to know about Native American life during the twentieth century, a difficult transitional era. These four individuals lived through the period when most Indians had to surrender their free lives and move onto reservations. They felt that if they did not relate details of their tribal and familial histories themselves, indirect and incorrect versions of their history might be presented. Thus, by telling us their stories they attempted to teach us American Indian history in a traditional manner. We have responded to their gifts of knowledge by writing our past and present works in the oral tradition.

We interviewed more people than those included in this work, but the ones featured in *River Song* provided the most detailed and pertinent information. They all had ties to leadership families among Plateau people, and they were among the oldest people we interviewed. They had lived the old ways of the life-sustaining seasonal round, traveling across the Columbia Plateau to gather, hunt, and fish. They grew up around horses, breeding, breaking, training, and riding roans, sorrels, bays, and Appaloosas. By horseback, buggies, wagons, and automobiles, they traveled extensively during their lives. Traveling was a way of life for these elders, and Gordon even traveled far overseas to fight in Vietnam for his country and people. He earned the old family name Yoosyóos Tulikécin (Blue Man), taken from a great warrior who had fought Blackfeet, Shoshone, and Paiute.

Andrew George told us much about Palouse horses grazing south of the Snake River, and how men drove them across the water and up canyons to the north. Mary Jim mentioned the men who broke horses before traveling to early spring root grounds. Gordon remembered how his grandfather fancied Appaloosa ("a Palouse") horses and made medicine so his mares would produce spotted colts and fillies.

We have arranged *River Song* into four parts with three sections each. Each part features an elder's oral history, followed by one or more traditional creation stories, and then by genealogies of Snake River-Palouse families. The book offers several major themes that emerge from the oral histories and sacred narratives: spirituality tied to the environment; the power of language and oral tradition; the importance of material culture and ceremony; and deep respect for history and ancestors.

Wáshat and Spirit

First and foremost, each person interviewed demonstrated a pervasive spirituality tied to the Creator and their environment. Their narratives and oral stories illustrate that Plateau Indian culture emphasized the spiritual and human relationship between indigenous people and the animals, plants, and places of their homeland. The Naxíyampam are inextricably linked to sacred obligations and holy kinship with nature. These are not New Age philosophies but the heart of ancient Plateau Indian culture and the lives of traditionally oriented Native Americans.

The elders featured in this volume participated in the ancient *Wáshani* religion and believed in the traditional teachings of their elders and spiritual leaders. They had been raised to honor the Creator through First Food ceremonies, and they gave thanks for the natural bounty that fed the two-leggeds and the four-leggeds, and other creatures of the air and water. The subjects of *River Song* had close relationships with the lands of the Columbia Plateau of Washington, Oregon, and Idaho. In addition, they had knowledge of the Cascade, Bitterroot, and Blue Mountains where they hunted and gathered, sometimes traveling beyond the Cascades to the Pacific Coast and east into Montana and the Great Plains.

These Naxíyampam narrators lived all or most of their lives in the Northwest, and shared a deep and abiding connection to the earth, landscape, and life of their ancient homeland. They often spoke about these treasured lands marked by historic and sacred sites, and grew wistful when mindful of their relocation. This is one of the hallmarks of this volume, a journey into the homeland of thousands of indigenous people who love this portion of the earth.

The intimate relationship of the Snake River-Palouse people with the natural world created a sustainable economy for thousands of years before European ships sailed up the Pacific Coast, or Lewis and Clark's Corps of Discovery traveled down Snake River, and continued even after removal to reservations. But this relationship is not simply based on exchange and livelihood. It is a spiritual relationship in which the people give thanks to the Creator for the earth's bounty and to the plants, animals, and water for sustaining human life. Indian spiritual beliefs are not new philosophic inventions, but are born of ancient concepts passed down for generations by Plateau people. Naxíyampam spiritual beliefs are alive in every reservation Longhouse and Wáshat Ceremony practiced today.

According to the spiritual beliefs and teachings of Plateau peoples, humans have a sacred obligation to treat the earth, plants, and animals in a respectful manner, taking only what is needed for consumption and trade, and not exploiting resources for material gain. In fact, Naxíyampam elders say that the desire to take more than is needed actually harms people, groups, and nations. Thus, the health of human communities is intimately tied to the health of the environment and the way humans interact with plateaus, valleys, plains, forests, streams, rivers, beaches, mountains, and oceans. Traditional law, or *tamánwit*, requires humans to be in balance with their environment and aware of their sacred relationship with the earth, animals, and plants—all gifts of the Creator.

Through their oral testimonies, Mary Jim, Andrew George, Gordon Fisher, and Emily Peone teach how we rely on Mother Earth for sustenance. They recognize that the environment is fragile and susceptible to exploitation through over-production, excessive gathering or grazing, fishing and hunting, and mining. According to traditional beliefs, humans are a part of nature and must interact with the landscape to understand their place on earth. Traditional stories explain this relationship and the place of animate and inanimate elements within the Northwestern environment.

Language, Culture, and *Tamánwit*

One may find this concept of connection with the land embedded within the Northern Sahaptin language of the *Naxíyampam*. The use of family names and bands are derived from the locative Sahaptin suffix "*-pam*," meaning "people of," with indigenous geographic place names. Thus, people identified themselves by principal winter villages, and other Indians understood that person was from a specific geographical site known for certain ancient events or power. Mary Jim was born at *Samyúya* and raised at *Tyáwtaš* along the lower Snake River, while Andrew George grew up at *Palús*, the ancient crossing place at the confluence of the Palouse and Snake rivers, where the Wolf Brothers killed giant Beaver in the time of the Animal People. The creature's petrified heart in the river's mouth nearby was an abiding visual reminder of this event. Gordon Fisher spent many summers of his youth at *Palús* with his grandparents, Sam and Helen Fisher, the last permanent residents of the village. With them he often visited other *Naxíyampam* who still clung to the old homeland at the upriver villages of *Alamótin* (Almota) and *Wawáwi* (Wawawai). Emily Peone lived most of her life on the Colville Indian Reservation, but some of her Kamiakin family relatives like Tesh Palouse and Pete Bones lived for much of the twentieth century at *Palús*.

At an early age and through the oral tradition, people learned *tamánwit*, or *tamánwas*. These are the sacred laws or rules of creation, taught to the first people on earth. They learned to take care of themselves and others in specific ways. They learned to be stewards of the earth. The Snake River-Palouse were stewards—not owners—of certain regions of creation. They learned of *ahtów*, or the covenant relationship and sacred trust to protect and preserve the landscape, which was entrusted to them by the Creator at the beginning of time. The physical, mental, and spiritual health of river people depended on how they acted in relationship to their environment. Traditional stories provided the "laws" for human habitation on the Plateau, and the people carefully followed these traditional ways to maintain health and happiness.

People absorbed this relationship through oral stories and songs, cultural information given to each child among Palouse people when they lived in their villages. Each person presented in *River Song* grew up learning these lessons and each of them practiced their *ahtów* with the Plateau environment.

ORAL LITERATURE AND HISTORY

Another significant element of Naxíyampam culture is found in the testimony and oral narratives of the featured elders. Words contain special force implicit in sounds associated with natural forces, life forms, and landscapes. Storytelling fosters understanding in entertaining and compelling ways. Tribal elders transmitted knowledge through oral narratives—stories, tales, lore, laws, and history. People learned the practical and symbolic meaning of plants, animals, people, and places through songs and stories that also conveyed cultural values and beliefs. These means of communication helped develop moral sensibilities and respect for people and environment. Stories, like those offered in this work, taught Snake River-Palouse people concepts of cooperation, cleanliness, stewardship, reciprocity, and hospitality. Tribal stories emphasized sharing and condemned selfishness. Storytellers championed the virtues of generosity and obligations to others.

The selections from Snake River-Palouse oral literature presented here are formatted with conventions that attempt to express in writing the distinctive personal style and nuances of words passed down by word of mouth through many generations. Masterful Plateau storytellers offered these ancient tales with wonderfully varied dimensions of rhythm, intonation, and emphasis. We have benefitted from the work of anthropologist Rodney Frey of the University of Idaho, whose work with Columbia Plateau elders Lawrence Aripa, Tom Yellowtail, and others led to his formulation of various conventions to guide this genre's formatting so the texts resemble poetry more than prose. Frey identifies core aspects of this approach as verses, scenes, and word intonations. Verses are word phrases ("morpheme clusters") in which the narrator's dramatic pauses vary from brief to extended as indicated by a range of commas, semi-colons, periods, or ellipses. A scene is a plot component associated with a particular place and characters that is set off by double spacing. Word intonations are voiced inflections indicated by italicized words. In the case of the unpublished Atinapam-Johnley texts taken down by Melville Jacobs in 1930 on the Umatilla Reservation (see Appendix C), the formatting is based on retellings of the stories by contemporary Naxíyampam storytellers.

Material Culture and Ceremony

Oral stories represent one of many art forms known to Snake River-Palouse Indians. The people also earned a reputation for artistic accomplishments and aesthetics in their everyday tools, including mats and nets, gaffs and fishhooks, bows and arrows, axes, knives, tipis, and an array of other utilitarian items. In addition, Naxíyampam became well known for making leather clothing, dance outfits, drums, gloves, belts, and distinctive beadwork. Their exquisite cornhusk bags were made from corn grown on their farms along the Snake River, which, documented as early as the 1840s, were among the first farms noted anywhere on the Plateau.

Snake River-Palouse Indians, including the people featured here, decorated material objects with motifs associated with their uses, place of origin, personal power, and symbols of familial identity, particularly those images and symbols attached to sacred power. Winter gatherings, family naming ceremonies, powwows, and tribal gatherings foster appreciation for these special designs.

In his autobiography, *Yellow Wolf: His Own Story*, Nez Perce warrior Yellow Wolf recounts how materials in the environment called out to him. When the spirit of a tree identified itself to him, he created a war club from its wood. This wood contained power that was transmitted to the young warrior. Yellow Wolf believed his war club, eagle bone whistle, and personal power enabled him to survive the Nez Perce War. Men like Andrew George, Gordon Fisher, and Cleveland Kamiakin taught boys and men how to make quivers, bows and arrows, shields, and other items associated with hunting

Traditional Plateau beadwork, cornhusk bags, bone work, and baskets. *Carrie Jim Schuster collection*

and ceremonies. Like their grandmothers, aunts, and other relatives had done for them, Mary Jim and Emily Peone taught young girls and women how to cut, sew, and bead a variety of objects, including women's and men's clothing. Tribal elders taught young people the arts, some of which are now displayed at the Smithsonian's National Museum of the American Indian in Washington, D.C.

Snake River-Palouse have often worn intricately beaded clothing at sacred and popular ceremonies and celebrations, events of extreme significance to all Plateau people. Andrew George served as a leader of the *Wáshat* religion, or Seven Drums faith, but safeguarded details about the spiritual gatherings, songs, dances, and rites. In a letter to the authors, Andrew provided some information on *Wáshani* beliefs, but explained that he could not divulge specific details because to do so was contrary to the teachings of his faith. Nevertheless, Snake River-Palouse and other Plateau Indians have invited us to participate in Longhouse ceremonies of the Seven Drums religion, where we ritually partook of the prayers and foods while listening to the songs and drumming. The old faith lives today on many reservations, and the leadership today remembers the contributions made by the four tribal elders represented in *River Song*.

The elders presented here participated often in the Seven Drums of *Wáshat*. Each sang songs of thanksgiving and ate sacred native foods. These ceremonial presentations of the First Foods reveal the obligations man has to a sustainable environment and spiritual connections. The ceremonies demonstrated the hierarchy of creation and the creature chiefs of the Columbia Plateau, including life-sustaining *kus* or water, *núsux̣* or salmon (fish), *yámaš* or venison (animals), *piyax̣í* or bitterroot (plants), and *wíunu* or huckleberries (fruits).

Songs, feasts, rites, and other ceremonies commemorate relationships among people, and those of people with plants, places, and animals. Some ceremonies commemorate the relationship of the living with the dead. Andrew George described how his family would gather each year to lament the passing of their relatives killed during the 1877 Nez Perce War and in subsequent exile, when Palouse, Cayuse, and Nez Perce had to leave the graves of their loved ones in Indian Territory, the future territory and state of Oklahoma. Ceremonies among the Snake River-Palouse also reinforce the connectedness of large, extended families and past generations. These connections, regularly honored at ceremonies, developed between people from many tribes, bands, and families. Each year they meet to celebrate life and renew relationships.

ADAPTATION, CYCLES, AND BLOOD MEMORY

Mary Jim, Andrew George, Gordon Fisher, and Emily Peone held onto many of their tribal traditions, the language of the people, and their ancient spiritual beliefs. However, they represented the ability of Snake River-Palouse people to change and adapt over time. They balanced their traditions with innovations of a modern world where newcomers dominated the landscape, economy, and politics. The elders knew of the destructive history between newcomers and indigenous people; they knew about the American invasion of the Northwest, treaties, reservations, war, disease, and theft of indigenous resources. They witnessed malnutrition, new illnesses, and death. They felt the sting of racism against Native Americans, but not one of them held onto bitterness against non-Indians. In fact, Andrew George felt sorry for newcomers who did not have a close relationship with nature, and regretted that newcomers had never heard Snake River sing.

The tribal elders presented here spoke dialects of the Sahaptin language, but they also learned and used English. Andrew George taught himself to write English so he could communicate, but he never abandoned his native tongue. *Naxíyampam* elders believed that some elements of change had enhanced Indian life and the well-being of humans within the natural world system. They well understood that tribal people had many conflicts and differences with the dominant society, but focused on the higher needs of Indian people. They were pragmatic and demonstrated their ability to resist and adjust to the world. This theme resonates in their narratives.

Like the Plateau Indian leaders of old, the elders practiced their own religion, but many accepted the teachings of Christian missionaries.

Chief Kamiakin, for example, a leading Plateau *míyowax* (chief), invited Oblate missionaries into his lands and learned from them, as they did from him. He also saw advantages from farming and adopted agricultural and pastoral innovations brought by newcomers. Kamiakin and other leaders adopted the planting of grains, crop irrigation, and selective breeding of livestock. Spiritual leaders, or *twati* (Nez Perce: *tooat*), like Kotaiaqan and Smohalla, preached the family and brotherhood of all mankind, and they believed in limited technical progress within the limits of moral obligations toward creation.

These Snake River-Palouse elders learned to be pragmatic from their leaders and to act to benefit Indian people as they were taught in the old narratives about heroes. They believed in the continuity of culture within an ever-changing world. They had learned from their own elder-teachers the importance of adaptation and change, acculturating some aspects of non-Indian peoples while maintaining their own culture and identity as Native Americans. The testimony of the tribal elders speaks to their own ability and that of their families to cope with the modern world while maintaining their identity as Plateau Indians. In this way, these four individuals speak to the youth of today, using their lives and experiences as examples of living with non-Indians but holding on to the rich culture of the Columbia Plateau.

The accounts found in *River Song* address the Native American belief in cyclical time through which physical and spiritual experiences reoccur in cycles that transcend time and circumstance. Indian time is not bound by linear progression but a belief that people, places, and events move in a cyclical way. Time exists in a dimension beyond the course of chronological incidents. Thus, the retelling of creation stories, like those found in this volume, brings events to life again in the mind.

When the Palouse speak of historical people, such as Sam and Helen Fisher, Fishhook Jim and Millie, and Cleveland and Alalumt'i Kamiakin, such figures appear again and can affect the dealings of humans living today. Personal qualities of persons from former generations sometimes reveal themselves in dreams or the songs and sounds of nature. These can influence the contemporary experiences of the living. The elders believed in blood memory, a concept in which a living person has memories of past events, people, and experiences that influence the way they deal with the contemporary world.

The people recorded many events through the oral tradition, but they also had another system by which they kept historical accounts. During the lives of the four Snake River-Palouse elders, they saw tribal people keep *ititamat,* or balls made of hemp string that served as "counters" of days for the year. The balls were tied with tiny markers of colored stones, bones, beads, and cloth as mnemonic devices to record significant events. Many Palouse and Plateau people buried their loved ones with their *ititamat.* Just as events from an individual's season might touch upon another person from a different time and place, so humanity's wisdom and experience may intersect through the power of a sacred word, story, record, creature, or event.

Tribal Elders as Historical Treasures

Knowing and working with the elders presented in *River Song* has personally enriched our lives. Snake River-Palouse elders not only invited us into their homes and lives, but they opened their hearts and minds to the work of teaching us about Naxíyampam culture and history. We spent many hours traveling to visit the elders on Northwestern reservations and in their old homelands. These wise souls rewarded us with a wealth of information that changed the way we conducted research and presented histories. The information provided by the elders could not be found in any secondary or primary sources available to us, because the stories they offered were original and one-of-a-kind. They had not often shared their histories with other scholars, although members of their families knew the stories and their importance. Some of the information we collected dates to the time of creation, and is about people and historical events from the eighteenth century and before. These oral histories have profoundly influenced our interpretations of the past and present.

We have framed *River Song* so readers may enter the world of Plateau Indian culture through the words of four elders. Later in this introduction is a survey of several major events, including the signing of the 1855 Walla Walla Treaties and subsequent wars that involved families of the principal figures presented here. Mary Jim, Andrew George, Gordon Fisher, Emily Peone, and their relatives participated in many of these historical and watershed events. The elders and their families lived through the transitional era of American Indian history, including wars, forced removal, and life on the reservations. Through indomitable persistence, some—like the Jim family—still retain title to aboriginal Snake River lands as a result of the nineteenth-century Indian Homestead Act.

Many Palouse and other Plateau Indian people tried hard to hold onto their traditional lands and ancient cultures. In the long run, the people had to change in order to survive. Many Indians faced death by gunfire if they remained free upon the Plateau, so many moved from their homelands to resettle on one of the Northwest reservations. Both Mary Jim and Andrew George remembered their forced removal from their villages along Snake River. Mary recalled the day when archaeologists, armed with federal authority, robbed her grandfather's burial place, stealing his canoe coffin, body, and grave goods. Non-indigenous grave-robbers also desecrated Chief Kamiakin's grave at Rock Lake within a year of his passing "for scientific purposes." To date, neither the authors nor the chief's family have been able to locate and repatriate Kamiakin's skull. These tragedies remain very sensitive matters, and for good reason some Naxíyampam elders remain suspicious of outsiders' intentions.

ORAL HISTORIES

The core elements of this text are the oral histories we conducted with Mary Jim, Andrew George, Gordon Fisher, and Emily Peone. For many years local historians and scholars have written about the Indian people of the Columbia Plateau, but only a few of them, primarily anthropologists and linguists, spent time learning from tribal elders.

Few outsiders interviewed and learned from these four remarkable individuals. With us, they shared personal stories, culture, and spiritual beliefs. They told us about themselves, their people, and special places. Through their oral histories, the elders actively and affirmatively participated in acts of survival, giving details of Native American history that can be found nowhere else except in these pages. By sharing their stories, these traditional Native American scholars have preserved a precious part of Plateau Indian history.

These Palouse present their knowledge about a host of topics, including sacred narratives, the ancient *tamánwit*, and joint land use through seasonal rounds. They provide details about the importance of plants and animals, the significance of family, village life, war, treaties, gold, and materialism. They speak about Native American prophets, religion, and ceremony. Elders tell us about mountains, brides of the Sun, and *Yámuštas*—"Elk's Abode" at Steptoe Butte. The elders speak of their families and lineages. Each interview offers personal, historical, and cultural information.

Mary Jim

Mary Jim shared about fishing, roots, and berries. She emphasized the importance of *Wáshat* and protection of graves at Snake River villages. This sacred word, from the Sahaptin term *wásha* ("dancing"), relates to the rhythmic movement associated with Longhouse, or Seven Drum, religious activities and beliefs. (The word *Wáshani* is sometimes used in reference to its adherents.) Mary Jim cried every time she told us about non-Indians invading the Snake River cemetery and the theft of her grandfather. She recalls Chief Wolf Necklace and his attempt to live free on the land. She also tells us about Indian allotments and the expropriation of Indian lands, including her homeland on Snake River. "Money is not worth land," she said. Mary sang and prayed in the Longhouses of the Northwest, especially at Priest Rapids on the Columbia River where she took her children to be taught by Smohalla's nephew, Pakayatút ("Birds Circling to Feed," Johnnie Buck).

Andrew George

Andrew George led many ceremonies in the Longhouse and elsewhere throughout the Northwest Plateau. He was a healer and medicine man, calling on the healing power of the universe to help others. When he first met us, he asked if we were from the university where they studied plants and animals. When we told him we were, he said, "I feel sorry for those people. They have never spoken with plants and animals, and they have never heard their songs. I have seen things they have never seen and heard things they may never hear. I have heard their songs and stories."

Andrew emphasized that the traditional *Wáshat* faith is similar to teachings found in the Bible, particularly the respect for the Creator and creation. He urged humans to honor clean water, salmon, deer, roots, and berries. Andrew spoke to us about the sacred way of life, saying that nature is the great teacher of human beings. In an extract from a recently discovered oral history by Chief Cleveland Kamiakin, which is included in Part II, Andrew's revered relative tells how Coyote taught humans to conduct sweat lodge ceremonies by his own creation of the sweat lodge and use of it. The river people believe the sweat lodge to be a deity, a sacred portal between the earth and the Creator.

Gordon Fisher

Gordon Fisher tells about the first Yoosyóos Tulikécin, or Blue Man, a warrior during the eighteenth century, whose native name Gordon shared. Related to Chief Joseph and Chief Kamiakin, Gordon grew up with Palouse-Nez Perce grandparents, Sam and Helen Fisher. Sam was a medicine man whose power was Rattlesnake, a topic Gordon details along with Sam's love of Appaloosa horses. Gordon talks about Steptoe Butte and Cricket power, the Palouse fights with Colonel Edward Steptoe and Colonel George Wright, and Húsis Kute and Kamiakin's father, Čiyái. Gordon had a great appreciation of history and the role his families had played in the great drama of Pacific Northwest history.

EMILY FRIEDLANDER PEONE

Emily Peone also had a deep sense of regional Indian history, and counted a host of leaders within her family. Emily was related to two women who had traveled to the stars and married two star men, creating a great leader, Chief Wiyáwiikt (Weowicht). She was related to Chief Moses and Chief Kamiakin's youngest wife, Colestah. In addition, she was a direct descendant of Chief Moses of the Columbia-Sinkiuse, Yakama leader Chief Aúxai (Owhi) and Owhi's famous son, Qáhlchŭn (Qualchan). Owhi and Qualchan entered the American camp of Colonel George Wright in 1858 under a white flag of truce, only to be seized. Wright ordered Qualchan hanged while his father looked on. Not long afterward, near present Starbuck, Owhi tried to escape unarmed and an army sergeant shot him to death.

In 1978, we traveled to Spokane to hear Emily's sister, Lucy Friedlander Covington, talk about Indian rights. For many years, Lucy Covington had served as tribal chair of the Colville Tribe, and she saved her tribe from the federal government's termination policy that would have ended the government's formal relationship with the Colville Confederated Tribes. During the lecture, Covington explained that every time she visited the city, "my heart hits the ground because in 1858, the Army hanged my relative, Qualchan, and shot and killed Chief Owhi. They were my relatives." Lucy's great aunt and Qualchan's sister, Mary Moses, who lived well beyond the century mark, helped raise Emily and Lucy and imparted much family history. Mary helped bury Qualchan on the banks of Latah (Hangman) Creek and endured the tragedies of post-war exile from the family's Yakama homeland after the 1850s. Emily's interview provides information about the Snake River-Palouse holy man Húsis Kute, family historian Tomeo Kamiakin, and other topics important to the history of the Naxíyampam and Plateau people.

Family Genealogies

Mary Jim, Andrew George, Gordon Fisher, and Emily Peone were related to significant historical characters in Northwestern Indian history, as seen in the genealogies following their narratives. The elders were also related to each other in the "Indian way," which means they were brothers and sisters who practiced *Wáshat* and shared a profound love of the earth, bounty of creation, and ceremonies celebrating creation. The people highlighted in the genealogies taught the four Palouse elders the sacred ways of Plateau Indians, including the ancient stories that explained relationships between the plant and animal "people" as well as human beings.

Oral Narratives and Lexicon

We offer a few of the traditional stories told to us, so readers might come to appreciate their significance to our Palouse subjects and Native American history of the Northwest. These oral narratives inform us of the laws of creation, and the way the Creator formed the world of Plateau Indians. In addition, in Part V, we offer a discussion of the various landscapes found on the Columbia Plateau and touch on early human habitation sites at the Marmes Rockshelter on the Snake River and in Kennewick, Washington. We also provide a lexicon of animals and plants as well as an analysis of Naxíyampam villages.

By providing the interviews, family genealogies, and sacred narratives, we seek to retrace the adventures of Salmon Man and Young Chinook. We hope that our unique contribution will act as one means of survival and continuance of Native American history and culture. Through this book, the voices of Mary Jim, Andrew George, Gordon Fisher, Emily Peone, and other tribal elders speak to the present generation, especially children and young adults. Just as they taught us, their words and stories will teach readers about various elements of Northwestern Indian history. Through their oral narratives, the four Snake River-Palouse elders will live again and teach us through their words, stories, and experiences.

When we first conducted the oral histories, each of these elders knew of our research for writing books and articles. Some of the elders and members of their families read portions of manuscripts before publication, just as we have shared this present work with family members before we completed this study. The original four elders understood the purpose of our work, and each of them gave their stories and knowledge to us so that we could use them in our historical research and teaching. The families of these four Palouse elders remain in contact with us, and they have encouraged us to share this work. We had permission from the elders to use their stories, and we did not pay them for their knowledge. Instead, they shared their knowledge freely so that we might know and grow, just as we share their stories with you.

Northwest Indian History

To place this work in perspective, we offer an overview of Northwest Indian history to help readers understand the context of these four featured elders and their relatives. Like ancient stories of the first creation, this collection opens with a sacred oral narrative that represented to the four elders Indian history, not mythology. By retelling this version of the story, they understood that the story would live again, just as this tiny portion of creation comes alive again to teach those who would be silent and allow the words to enter their minds and melt into meaningful understanding.

Sustainable Lives

Mary Jim, Andrew George, Gordon Fisher, and Emily Peone shared a deep respect and spiritual relationship with their Creator, the earth, and all that exists on the Columbia Plateau. The tenets of their religion provided the foundation of their being and guided their lives. These elders came from a long line of Indian people who had lived sustainably for generations without newcomers from Europe, Asia, or Africa. They were born sovereign and they died sovereign people. Although their families fought horrific battles with the Americans, they stepped forward into time and survived.

They never forgot they carried an obligation to look forward, but with a deep understanding of their heritage.

Members of their families met Meriwether Lewis and William Clark, and they actively interacted with fur trappers, missionaries, soldiers, and other representatives of the United States government. Some negotiated with Americans and fought the United States Army and territorial volunteers during the 1855-58 Plateau Indian Wars and the Nez Perce War of 1877. The elders tell ancient stories related to their body of traditional spirit and law—*tamánwit ku sukat*. The stories that they share in this work offer fundamental cultural understandings of Plateau Indians, a history that begins with oral narratives of the time of creation.

Significance of Creation Stories

Several American Indian tribes of the Great Columbia Plateau believe that there were two periods of creation. During the first era of creation, the earth, planets, sun, moon, plants, and animals came into being. Before the time of humanity, the Creator and the first "people" on earth established *tamánwit* or the natural laws about the universe, earth, and relationship of plants, places, and animals to each other. They established the first laws and prepared the earth for people who emerged in the second period of creation. Many Plateau Indians, included the Palouse, share common stories about this time of Native American history. Although details often vary, certain stories offer similar motifs and meanings. Consider, for example, the story of Salmon Man.

The Five Wolf Brothers opposed Salmon Man's marriage to their sister so they plotted to destroy him. Unwilling to confront Salmon Man directly, they persuaded Rattlesnake to bite Salmon Man, who then fell and was cut to pieces by the Wolf Brothers. But before the magnificent creature perished, a small piece from inside him dropped into the river and floated all the way to the Great Water. Life stirred within it and Young Chinook soon grew into a smolt. Eventually he was large and strong enough to return to his natal water and bring the Chinook wind to warm the region's cold valleys and plains.

Young Chinook swam up the Columbia and Snake Rivers where he met the Animal People. He learned about Coyote's fishing places and helped Sandpiper, who warned him about Rattlesnake. Young Chinook was then able to defeat the serpent who then became his confederate in order to help defeat the Wolf Brothers. In this way, the hero Young Chinook learned and restored the law of creation, directing the Salmon People to travel upriver to spawn. Young Chinook destroyed the Wolf Brothers and restored the warm wind. He made the law right again.

The Naxíyampam and other Indians of the Pacific Northwest know this story and relate to Salmon Man and the challenges of returning to one's native land. Indigenous history of the region began with creation, and the stories remain meaningful to tribes today. These ancient accounts are not fairy tales or "fish tales that grow with the telling," as one reviewer once commented. Traditional people, like Andrew George, say the old stories are history and Native American truths. In addition to history, the first oral narratives of Plateau Indians offer the first literature, law, geography, and drama of the indigenous peoples of the region. Tribal elders say the stories are alive with meaning, offering contemporary people understanding and direction based on the ancient knowledge of the first peoples of the Northwest.

Indigenous Sovereignty and *Tamánwit*

For thousands of years, American Indians of the Great Columbia Plateau shared their knowledge through the oral tradition. In formal and informal settings, the people told ancient narratives that explained their place on earth and their relationship with their environment. Tribal sovereignty emerged from the original culture of Plateau people, not from the treaties and laws of the United States. Long before Vikings or Spaniards arrived in the Western Hemisphere, Native Americans had established rich cultures that survived for generations without the influence of Europeans, Asians, or Africans.

Traditional oral narratives and songs of Plateau people provide evidence of their aboriginal sovereignty. The stories taught the people their relationship with the Creator, mountains, rivers, plants, and animals. The stories taught the people *tamánwit* for proper conduct among each other and with newcomers. During a discussion about Northwestern Indian fishing rights, Andrew George once explained that the first concern of all people should be the preservation of the salmon people because this was traditional law. To illustrate the point, he told a story about a time when man took too many salmon:

> After the arrival of human beings on earth, the law came to pass that human beings would fish and eat salmon. Spilyai, Creator Coyote, had broken the fish dam on the Columbia River and became a Salmon Chief himself, guiding the salmon upriver and designating which routes they would take to their spawning grounds. If certain tribes were generous to Coyote, he would direct the fish toward their villages, but if they proved too stingy, Coyote guided the salmon in new directions away from the people, forcing them to travel to harvest the salmon.
>
> Early in the history of people here, some people became greedy and took too many salmon. They violated *tamánwit* so the Salmon People met in council to discuss their course of action. During their deliberations, they concluded that they needed power to remind humans of the law. Someone suggested the Salmon People needed power like that of Rattlesnake, since humans avoided Rattlesnake. Salmon Chief agreed and traveled the river looking for Rattlesnake. He found the snake basking in the sun on a large, flat basalt rock. Salmon Chief explained his dilemma to Rattlesnake and asked for his power to use against greedy humans.
>
> When Rattlesnake refused to part with any of his power, Salmon Chief used his powerful tail to beat the snake's head. He beat Rattlesnake hard and then requested some power. Rattlesnake refused, so Salmon Chief repeated the beating five times. Salmon Chief beat it so hard that the snake's head flattened. Reluctantly, Rattlesnake gave Salmon Chief some of his poison power, which the chief shared with all Salmon People. To this day, salmon have the ability to bite fishers and put poison into their bodies, a reminder not to abuse their fishing rights.

The story above explains a tribal law regarding fishing rights and the responsibility of people to care for the fish to ensure continued salmon runs. This is one of countless stories shared by Plateau Indian people who lived in villages along the major rivers of the inland Pacific Northwest. The stories and songs provided a body of laws presented in story form to explain how to act and be a citizen of Plateau Indian communities.

During an interview on July 19, 2008, Nez Perce scholar Josiah Pinkham said *tamánwit* was "divine principle" that provided "cultural norms" for Plateau people. He felt people should "dream back to traditional ways" and be at rest with and guided by *tah* (spiritual) power. In this way, contemporary Plateau Indian people could "be in accord" with the temporal and spiritual world around them. "What is in your mind, directs your life," so *tamánwit* must be foremost in the lives of the people so that life will be good in spite of set-backs and tragedy. "When Coyote went up the river" bringing the Salmon People, "he had to think good things, positive thoughts."[1] Creation of positive things, such as the first foods of the Plateau, resulted from his good thoughts. The four Snake River-Palouse elders always emphasized positive thinking and action, contributing to the continuance of the sacred way.

Regardless of where the people lived, tribal elders and holy people taught the people to follow *tamánwit*. Its spiritual and philosophical tenets have guided the Palouse and Plateau people for thousands of years, since the time of creation. *Tamánwit* is also associated with certain special or sacred places on the Plateau where the people eventually settled. For example, once the Naxíyampam hunters and warriors killed Giant Beaver at the mouth of Palouse River at Snake River. Beaver died and his heart turned to stone near the tribe's principal village of *Palús*. The story of Giant Beaver chewing up the landscape on the Palouse River that flows through the Plateau, the bravery of the warriors seeking to protect the people, and the great rock that is Beaver's petrified heart, are woven into the fabric of *tamánwit*.

Such places, including village sites, are constant reminders of traditional Indian laws. Plateau people have strong ties to such places and to stories associated with these sites. The oral interviews presented in this volume attest to their teachings and places. The elders often mention them. Plateau people identified with these sites and with their former villages located in these regions. Although various Plateau peoples understood their tribal differences, they shared common knowledge of *tamánwit* and places mentioned in the ancient stories.

In the past, tribes did not conceive of themselves as nation states, certainly not in the way of European nations or the United States. Villagers who shared common languages and cultures grew to view themselves as tribal nations in the twentieth century, interrelated with other Indian people, villages, and tribes. Plateau people generally organized themselves into villages along the Columbia, Snake, Palouse, Clearwater, and other major rivers of the region. As a result of their marriage laws, they intermarried with and had kin among tribes throughout in the Northwest. Many people were multilingual, and some knew languages of tribes in the Rocky Mountains and Great Plains. Many people knew sign language and Chinook Jargon, a trade language often used along the Pacific Coast and in the Puget Sound.

Sahaptin-speaking people like the Snake River-Palouse, Nez Perce, and Yakama learned the Chinook language of the Wasco and Wishram as well as the Interior Salish language of the Spokane, Pend Oreille, and Coeur d'Alene. Most people of the Columbia Plateau had relatives among other tribes. Palouse Indians, for example, intermarried with Cayuse, Nez Perce, Yakama, Umatilla, Wanapum, Spokane, Coeur d'Alene, Wishram, Wasco, and other Indians with whom they had cordial relationships.

Plateau people rarely married Shoshoni, Paiute, Bannock, or Blackfeet people, as they were traditional enemies of Plateau Indians. Although the various tribes of the Columbia Plateau inhabited the same geographical region, they knew a great diversity of people, places, and cultures within their larger domain. Plateau Indians inhabited, traveled, and used every part of the Northwest. They intimately knew the region's topography, from the Pacific Coast east to the Bitterroot Mountains, and from the Canadian Plateau south into Central Oregon. They traded south into California, and they hunted buffalo on the Great Plains of Wyoming, Idaho, and Montana.

SACRED WAYS

Although they traveled, traded, and hunted widely, Plateau people viewed the Inland Pacific Northwest, drained by the Columbia River, as a special place. The landscape lived in the hearts of Plateau Indian people. It still does. In fact, Indian people say the landscape of the Columbia Plateau is sacred, or as Young Chief proclaimed at the Walla Walla Council of 1855: "God placed me here. The Earth says that God tells me to take care of the Indians on this earth; the Earth says to the Indians that stop on the Earth feed them right. God named the roots that he should feed the Indians on; the water speaks the same way. God says feed the Indians upon the earth. The grass says the same thing; feed the horses and cattle…God placed me here to produce all that grows upon me, the trees and fruits. The same way the Earth says, it was from her man was made. God on placing them on the Earth desired them to take good care of the earth and do each other no harm."[2] Years later in the twentieth century, Yakima Valley rancher and historian L. V. McWhorter wrote about the spiritual relationship of Plateau people and their landscape: "Their religion is the earth, and the earth is their religion."[3]

HOLY PLACES OF POWER

Strong spiritual beliefs characterize the Naxíyampam and their Plateau neighbors. Spiritual power provides the alpha and omega of traditional Plateau Indians. It is tied to creation of the universe, solar system, earth, and Plateau. The people know of this spiritual power through their stories and songs, both of which provide lessons about power and its positive and negative uses by mankind. The people believe that spiritual power is both general and specific, and is found in various sacred places on the Plateau. They believe that all people may access some amount of power, and medicine people can access and use that power to a much greater degree. Power exists in many forms and can manifest itself in various ways. Animate and inanimate objects may contain power, and both places and objects are often personified.

In her foreword to this volume, Carrie Jim Schuster tells of a time in human history when the people went against the laws, but repented and followed the holy ways of the Creator "by way of honoring the sacred foods." To remind the people of their spiritual training, the Creator "fashioned their images in the petroglyphs along the Snake River and at Priest Rapids." Traditional Indians of the Plateau believe the "stones are sacred so we do not touch them." Carrie Jim and the other Native American testimony presented in this volume identify Rattlesnake Mountain, Steptoe Butte, Rock Lake, Mount Adams, and Priest Rapids among their sacred places, but these represent only a few of the holy sites found on the Plateau.

Power exists in many places found on the landscape of the Columbia Plateau, and over many years, Indian people sought power at these places. Parents, grandparents, aunts, and uncles once took children to these places to seek visions. Children had to remain in a specific area for several nights without food or protection. According to Indian accounts, various spiritual entities visited the children during their vision quests, including birds, voices, clouds, bones, snakes, and bears. In his autobiography, Chief Yellow Wolf reported that a yellow wolf came to him, rose up into the air, and sang to him. His central power, however, became White Thunder, which protected him throughout the Nez Perce War.

A Wenatchi woman named Tehánap spent several days and nights in the Wenatchee Mountains where water spiders skirted about, and she received healing power that was so strong, it paralyzed her legs. Along the Columbia River, Tehánap's father conducted a healing ceremony with five fires that brought her healing power under control and restored her ability to walk. Tehánap's daughter said of her mother: "Mama done pretty good healing people!" Chief Kamiakin found his buffalo power high on the fierce slopes of Tahoma (Mount

Rainier). In this collection, Gordon Fisher shares some details of his vision in the Bitterroot Mountains and the cricket power he carried with him when he fought in the Vietnam War.

Spiritual Power and *Wáshat*

Twati spiritual leaders among the many tribes of the Columbia Plateau taught the people how to use and control personal power. They instructed the people about the *tamánwit* of their people, and encouraged them to use their power in positive ways to help people, not harm them. Carrie Jim pointed out the "prophets taught us not to waste the Creator's gifts but to honor them in order to sustain the people." They taught the people ceremony, ritual, song, and doctrines associated with spiritual power and life on earth.

The Wanapum prophet Smohalla, one of many Indian prophets, taught the people to follow the Creator's path. He revitalized the sacred *Wáshat* dance, and added songs and formality to the old religion. It was the old faith, but the people today commonly refer to the religion as Seven Drums or Longhouse. In the twentieth century, Andrew George was a prominent spiritual leader of the Seven Drums religion, and he helped people on several reservations on the Plateau, Puget Sound, and Coast. As a prophet, healer, and ceremonial leader, Andrew sang *Wáshat* songs and led gatherings of the drums, including wakes and First Food ceremonies.

For these ceremonies, cooks prepared a variety of Native foods, including salmon, venison, camas, and huckleberries. Often young people delivered the food to participants, carefully bringing each dish separately to the table in ritual fashion. Andrew George prayed for water first and after some time in prayer, everyone drank water in unison. He then instructed everyone to take a small piece of cooked salmon. After another prayer of thanksgiving, everyone ate the small piece of salmon in unison. In this way, the people prayed through the communion with their Creator and his gifts. During the ceremony, men sang loudly to the rapid and loud beat of large hand drums or bells, sharing the ancient melodies of the Columbia Plateau. The drums create a great sound that vibrates off the walls and leaves a song and sound planted deep into the brain, which is the point of the force found in this ceremony.

Andrew George and his relatives kept the Seven Drums alive, and the faith continues today among Plateau Indians from every part of the region. Seven Drums has become synonymous with the landscape of Indian country on the Plateau, just as the love of the lands and culture continues today. Plateau Indians love the land of their ancestors, a love based on their familial and spiritual beliefs about the earth. To them, land was not about real estate, possessions, or money. Land is a holy gift. The landscape is at the heart of this belief system. At the time of creation, many wondrous things happened on the landscape that marked the sites as Native. The arrival of newcomers from Europe and the United States marked the beginning of the seizing of land and resources from Northwestern Indians.

COYOTE AND CUSHO

In April 1921, L.V. McWhorter recorded a story about the loss of Indian lands on the Plateau. At the time, McWhorter hunted with a group of Plateau Indians in the mountains west of the Yakama Reservation. According to the story, Coyote owned a "big book" that contained the names of people (representing lands) deserving to be chief of particular groups of people (resources) in specific areas. Whenever a village or tribe needed a new leader, Coyote consulted the big book, which indicated who was next in line for leadership. By and by, a new person (non-Indian) came to the Columbia Plateau. Indians called the newcomer Cusho. In Northwest Sahaptin, Cusho means a pig-like creature. Once Cusho saw the beautiful lands and resources of the Plateau Indians, he wanted the lands and resources Indians possessed. So he tricked Coyote, chief of the Plateau Indians, into a contest representative of gaining the Native American estate.

Cusho invited Coyote to a contest to see who could remain awake for five days. Coyote agreed to the challenge, believing he was a better man than Cusho. But Coyote did not know that Cusho had five younger brothers, all of whom looked exactly like the eldest.

So they began their contest, but each evening, Cusho stepped out of his lodge. When this happened, one of his brothers took over for Cusho. Coyote did well for four days and four nights, but he fell into a sound sleep during the fifth night. Cusho and his brothers used this opportunity to steal Coyote's big book. In this way, Cusho stole "the big laws for himself, then he have plenty, everything. Cusho eat all; eat everything he sees. Coyote then get poor, him broke. Always broke, Coyote." The storyteller explained, "I guess Cusho was white man. Both alike, Cusho and white man. Take everything, eat up everything. Always rooting for more. Indian like Coyote, lose out, all. Everything white man takes from Indian."[4]

Lewis and Clark and Early Fur Trade

The first white men to visit the Pacific Northwest came to explore, map, and trade. The English, Spanish, Russians, and Americans all had economic designs on the region. Meriwether Lewis, William Clark, and their Corps of Discovery explored the Columbia Plateau in 1805-1806, making note of many natural resources and stating that the area would be ideal for American settlement. They reported on the wealth of peltries in the mountains and along the Pacific Coast. The possibility of making substantial economic gain from the fur trade enticed non-Indians to the region. While the Russians exploited the resources of Alaska, the British and Americans formed companies to take furs in the Northwest. The Northwest Company, American Fur Company, and Hudson's Bay Company operated across the Columbia Plateau, establishing trading posts that brought manufactured goods into the hands of Plateau Indians. Native Americans adopted guns, ammunition, knives, cloth, beads, and many other items, and some grew dependent on manufactured material items.

Christian Missionaries, Measles, and War

By right of discovery, the British and Americans claimed the Northwest, even though the Indian tribes had aboriginal rights to all the land and resources. During the 1840s, Presbyterian ministers and

Catholic priests moved into the Northwest to establish their mission systems to bring Christianity and "civilization" to Native Americans. Marcus and Narcissa Whitman established their work among the Cayuse at Waiilatpu, the Place of the Rye Grass, while Henry and Eliza Spalding built a mission at Lapwai, the Place of Butterflies. Catholic priests started missions among the Umatilla, Yakama, and Wenatchi. Some Indians converted to Christianity while many others held onto their traditional beliefs. Some did both. In any case, the arrival of non-Indians with new trade items and new religions created divisions among families, villages, and tribes. These divisions grew worse after Americans settled permanently on the Columbia Plateau and travelers on the Oregon Trail unintentionally brought with them infectious diseases.

In 1847, a measles epidemic swept the Indian communities of the Columbia Plateau, especially those living near the Oregon Trail. An old man among the Snake River-Palouse proposed to find out if Dr. Whitman was poisoning Indian people and thereby causing the measles. The elder took medicine from Dr. Whitman at Waiilatpu and contracted measles, eventually dying. Today we understand the measles virus and how it spreads, but in the 1840s, Plateau Indians and others had no idea about viruses, bacteria, and the spread of contagions. Native Americans believed Whitman had caused the measles epidemic and subsequent deaths, and the Cayuse told the Whitmans to leave their lands. Mary Jim recalled stories of entire villages decimated by epidemics, leaving only a few bewildered children.

When the Whitmans refused to leave, a few Cayuse attacked the mission, killing the missionary couple and others. This triggered the first war between Plateau Indians and non-Indians on the Plateau, which ultimately involved Snake River-Palouse people. The war strained relations between the two peoples as more and more Americans migrated into the Oregon Territory and claimed Indian lands as their own. Americans also brought territorial government to Oregon, which set in motion a series of events that significantly altered the lives of all Plateau Indians. We chronicled these events in the book *Renegade Tribe*.

Some of our Snake River-Palouse consultants told us their people were "renegades" and we sometimes used their term in our descriptions. We received some criticism for the use of the word "renegade" with the peace-loving Naxíyampam. To be sure, many remained pacifists throughout the cataclysmic period of the nineteenth century Plateau wars. But patriot leaders like Kamiakin, Tiłqawayks (Tilcoax), and Húsis Kute rose to defend the river people when they were threatened with annihilation by government leaders and attacked by territorial militias. The army's initial investigation of events leading to the outbreak of hostilities in 1855 led U.S. Army Commander of the Pacific, General John Wool, to rebuke civilian authorities for their management of Indian affairs. The criticism led to protracted efforts by Washington Territorial Governor Isaac Stevens and others to oust Wool, who was replaced by Newman Clark in 1856.

Palouse warriors are often mentioned in military reports of the time as "renegades," especially devoted to their families and lands, and willing to defend them. Even after the wars of the 1850s and 1870s, substantial numbers of Naxíyampam stubbornly remained at traditional Snake River-Palouse village sites at *Téksas·pa*, *Wawyuk'má*, *Pínawáwi'*, *Alamótin*, *Wawáwi*, and *Alpáwa*. Some like the Jims and Kamiakins persisted against substantial bureaucratic and cultural challenges to navigate through procedures required to acquire legal title to their ancestral properties at *Palús* and elsewhere under the terms of the 1887 Indian Homestead Act. They were helpfully guided in these efforts by families like the McGregors and Pettyjohns. Relations were generally peaceful with local residents of the frontier river towns that derived their names from some of these camps—Penawawa, Almota, Wawawai, and Alpowa. In the few instances after the Nez Perce War when violence did take place in the area, Indians were almost always the victims.

TREATIES AND WAR

The Snake River-Palouse elders of *River Song* refer to many cultural and environmental changes that took place as a result of the American takeover of their former domain. Some of them mention contact and change directly, while others address the topics more generally. In spite of the arrival of non-Indians, Native Americans considered themselves the holders and stewards of all lands on the Northwest Plateau. Americans did not view their presence in the region in the same way. Non-Indians believed that humans could divide and own parcels of land, which was contrary to ways of Indian ownership of real property. In 1854, the United States split the Oregon Territory, creating a new Washington Territory. President Franklin Pierce named Isaac I. Stevens governor of the new territory as well as the superintendent of Indian affairs.

Superintendent Stevens and his Oregon counterpart, Joel Palmer, set out to extinguish aboriginal title to lands through treaties. After negotiating agreements with tribes on the Pacific Coast and Puget Sound, Stevens met with several leaders of the Plateau tribes in the Walla Walla Valley in May and June 1855. At the Walla Walla Council, Stevens and Palmer presented their proposals for treaties, reservations, civilization, and commerce. The Indians responded by explaining that the Creator had given them their lands and they had obligations to care for the earth, plants, and animals. As Yakama Chief Owhi explained to Stevens and Palmer: "God looked one way then the other and named our lands for us…I am afraid of the laws of the Almighty." Owhi then asked, "Shall I steal this land and sell it? Shall I give the lands that are part of my body and leave myself poor and destitute? I cannot."[5] But representatives of the United States ignored the views of Owhi, Young Chief, and Peopeo Moxmox. Their views fell on deaf ears, and the Americans composed three treaties, which they directed the Indian leaders to sign.

After much discussion within the camps, many Indian leaders signed the Yakama, Nez Perce, and Cayuse-Umatilla-Walla Walla treaties that created a formal relationship between some tribes and the United States. Tribal leaders secured for themselves a small portion of their former lands, but those tribes that did not make an agreement received no lands recognized by the government. The Naxíyampam did not secure a reservation in their river homeland.

Their vast aboriginal domain was divided through the Yakama, Nez Perce, and Umatilla treaty cessions. The Walla Walla Treaties provided the catalyst for the largest Indian war on the Columbia Plateau between 1855 and 1858.

The 1855-58 Plateau Indian War and Reservations

When white miners discovered gold in the Colville district northeast of present-day Spokane, a rush began from coastal communities across the Plateau. Yakama, Snake River-Palouse, and other Indians reported miners stealing horses and cattle. Responding to reports of miners assaulting Indian women, leaders instructed warriors to hunt down and kill the perpetrators. The Plateau exploded into war after a few Indians murdered Indian Agent Andrew Jackson Bolan. The elders featured in this book understood the great cost of the Plateau Indian War, which claimed the lives of many Indians, including several central leaders among the tribes. Relatives of the people offering their oral testimonies in *River Song* died during the war or conflicts that emerged after the war.

Some Plateau Indians moved to reservations after the Plateau Indian War, but others remained free on the "public domain." Treaties liquidated Indian title to millions of acres, but could not end the spiritual relationship of the Palouse to their homelands. Most Snake River-Palouse people did not move to reservations for many years after 1859 when the Senate of the United States ratified the three treaties. Some Palouse and Yakamas under Chief Kamiakin lived in Montana in the aftermath of the war and then relocated about 1860 to the Palouse River between present-day Endicott and St. John, Washington. Kamiakin subsequently moved to Rock Lake where he died in 1877. His family buried him there far from reservations.

Many non-reservation Indians feared for their lives and those of their families during and after the Plateau Indian War because government officials considered them hostile and dangerous. Emily Peone, an elder from the Colville Indian Reservation, mentions this fear in her oral history, and her sister, Lucy Covington, often mentioned that the Army under Colonel George Wright had killed her relatives, Chief Owhi, his son, Qualchan, and others. Owhi's daughter and Chief Moses' wife, Mary Owhi Moses, survived the ordeal of this time when many Native women with small children were left to fend for themselves. She lived to great age in the household of her grandnieces Emily and Lucy, and made sure they did not forget the sacrifices of their ancestors, and how "all our good fighters" were "hunted down." The war and its aftermath proved dark days for Plateau Indians whether they lived on or off the reservations as the government attempted to control Indian people, regulate Native American social and commercial intercourse, and claim most of the land and resources of Columbia Plateau Native Americans.

The Thief Treaty and 1877 Nez Perce War

Most Nez Perce did not engage significantly in the Plateau Indian War, but in 1860, Elias Pierce and ten miners discovered gold on the Nez Perce Reservation, triggering another gold rush. Without regard for Indian rights and treaty boundaries, non-Indian miners flooded onto the reservation, digging gold and establishing towns and businesses on Indian lands. The Army and Indian Office did nothing to prevent the invasion. In fact, a new treaty expropriated nearly 7,000,000 acres from the original Nez Perce Reservation. The Nez Perce, Palouse, Cayuse, and their neighbors refer to the new agreement as the Thief Treaty of 1863.

In 1855, Nez Perce leaders had negotiated the first treaty in good faith, but nearly every Nez Perce leader refused to sign the Thief Treaty. Only Chief Lawyer and fifty-one followers signed the agreement, which the Senate ratified and President Abraham Lincoln signed into law. Many non-treaty and non-reservation Snake River-Palouse, Nez Perce, and Cayuse did not recognized the Thief Treaty and continued to live free on the Plateau. But the Sioux Wars of the 1870s brought the issue of non-compliance with the Thief Treaty into focus. The Army began demanding the forced removal of non-reservation Indians onto reservations, especially in the wake of the Lakota, Cheyenne, and Arapaho victory at the Little Big Horn Battle of 1876. After Colonel George Custer and more than five hundred men lost the battle and their lives, General William Tecumseh Sherman ordered his district commanders to round up non-reservation Indians and force them to the reservations.

In the Pacific Northwest, General Oliver O. Howard received Sherman's directive. Sherman ordered Howard to bring non-treaty Nez Perce, Snake River-Palouse, Cayuse, and others onto reservations. He especially focused on the Nez Perce, including Chief Joseph's band from the Wallowa Valley of northeastern Oregon. Gordon Fisher, one of the narrators in this collection, was a member of Chief Joseph's family through his grandmother Not-ta-mo-le-kaset (Helen Waters Fisher) who grew up hearing stories about her father and the Nez Perce War. Joseph opposed removal to the Nez Perce Reservation in Idaho, and he used all his persuasion to prevent relocation. During the 1876 and 1877 Lapwai Councils, Joseph and other leaders made their case against removal. A medicine man named Toohoolhoolzote told Howard about the "chieftainship" of the earth and explained *tamánwit*, the law of his people that directed them not to divide and sell the earth.

Toohoolhoolzote and the Palouse leader Húsis Kute explained at length their spiritual obligations to the earth. "You white people get together, measure the earth, and then divide it," the Nez Perce observed. Toohoolhoolzote represented the views of other river people by explaining, "Part of the Indians gave up their land. I never did. The earth is part of my body, and I never gave up the earth." He told General Howard that the United States was "trifling with the law of the earth." Howard exploded, telling the leader and the people that they had no choice but to move to the reservation. Howard threatened to lead his Army against them and force them. Toohoolhoolzote spoke defiantly to Howard, and the general ordered his soldiers to seize and jail him. As Joseph later recalled, "We were the deer. They were like grizzly bear." The Nez Perce, Snake River-Palouse, and Cayuse either had to agree to move or fight. They chose to move to the Nez Perce Reservation in Idaho.[6]

American versus Indigenous Views

General Howard, known as the "Christian General," had earlier in his career dealt honorably with Chief Cochise and Chiricahua Apaches. But he did not approve of the religious beliefs of the traditionalists among the Nez Perce, Snake River-Palouse, Cayuse, and other Plateau Indians. He wrote about them in pejorative terms. "The dreamers," Howard wrote, "among other pernicious doctrines, teach that the earth being created by God complete, should not be disturbed by men, and that any cultivation of the soil or other improvements to interfere with its natural productions, any voluntary submission to the control of the government and improvement in the way of schools, churches, etc., are crimes from which they shrink."[7]

Howard was only partially correct in his representation of the Plateau people since some cultivated the earth and accepted Christianity. But many of them also opposed American education, large-scale development, injury to the earth, and suppression of their traditions—all of which Indians knew would come with American occupation of their homeland. Howard wrote to an American, largely Christian audience, and he wrote with a purpose to sway American views about his forced removal of free Indians to the reserves. But those who participated in the Lapwai Councils left feeling the United States was forcing them to surrender their beloved land, the earth that held the bones of their loved ones.

In April 1879, Chief Joseph gave an interview to an editor of the *North American Review*. Joseph expressed many views representative of Snake River-Palouse, Cayuse, and other Plateau Indians. For the first time, he addressed a large American audience, and explained the way the United States bought his land by telling this story: "Suppose a white man should come to me and say, 'Joseph, I like your horses, and I want to buy them.' Joseph responded, 'No, my horses suit me, I will not sell them.' Then the white man goes to a neighbor and says, 'Joseph has some good horses. I want to buy them, but he refuses to sell.' The neighbor responded, 'Pay me the money, and I will sell you Joseph's horses.'" The white man returns to me and says, 'Joseph, I have bought your horses, and you must let me have them.' If we sold our lands to the government, this is the way they bought them."[8]

In spite of this logic, the United States recognized the Thief Treaty as the supreme law of the land, and Howard demanded the forced removal of non-reservation bands to the Nez Perce Reservation in Idaho. This included Snake River-Palouse camps of Hatáhlekin (Red Echo) and Húsis Kute (Bald Head). After the Lapwai Council of 1877, the Indians returned home to prepare their move to the reservation. For Chief Joseph, the trip from northeast Oregon to Idaho proved fateful.

PATRIOTIC WAR AND EXILE

While traveling from the Wallowa Valley to Lapwai, a few young men triggered the Nez Perce War by killing several white men who had harassed and harmed the people. Once the war began, the Nez Perce fought a series of battles in Idaho before a council of leaders discussed their next move. Some Snake River-Palouse and Cayuse families followed the Nez Perce during the war. Most of the bands chose to follow Looking Glass, and reluctantly, Joseph joined the withdrawal from Idaho into Montana. Snake River-Palouse fought with the Nez Perce and Cayuse, including Hatáhlekin and Húsis Kute. The Nez Perce, Palouse, and Cayuse fought several campaigns in Montana on their way to Canada, but the Army cut off their march northward by attacking them at the Bear Paw Mountains, forty miles from the border.

The Naxíyampam family of Andrew George fought with the Nez Perce, and General Sherman ordered the Army to exile the Palouse, Nez Perce, and Cayuse to *Eekish Pah*, the "Hot Place" or Indian Territory (in present-day Oklahoma). From 1878 to 1885, the people lived in Indian Territory on the Quapaw and Ponca reservations. In their narratives, Andrew George and Emily Peone mention the tragedy of the Snake River-Palouse and Nez Perce whose remains rest today near the former Quapaw and Ponca agencies as well as Fort Leavenworth, Kansas, where the Army initially held them as prisoners of war.

The Palouse warrior Páxalawasq'ísit (Five Shades), a veteran of the fighting and exile known later to whites and Mary Jim as Star Doctor, was so determined to return to his Snake River homeland that he managed to escape from Kansas and walk virtually the entire way back to his northwestern homeland. University of Washington anthropologist Melville Jacobs found him in the 1930s residing on the Umatilla Reservation and the two collaborated on an extensive lexicon of Snake River-Palouse terms. For years, however, he remained wary of divulging his experience to others for fear he would be arrested, imprisoned, and perhaps executed.

Free and Reservation Palouse

After the Nez Perce War, some Naxíyampam still ranged freely on the Plateau, hunting, fishing, and gathering. During the first half of the twentieth century, several bands lived by engaging in a seasonal round, traveling to different areas to gather food, conduct ceremony, intermarry, and trade. After removal to the reservation, the Naxíyampam and their relatives among extended Plateau tribes adjusted to living away from their homelands and under the surveillance of government agents and Christian missionaries. The government forced the Palouse to adapt to new ways of life on the Colville, Coeur d'Alene, Warm Springs, Nez Perce, and Yakama reservations—far away from the landscapes and sacred places of their native rivers, canyons, and hills.

Policies of the United States severely damaged the traditional economies of the Snake River-Palouse and other Plateau Indians. Wars and forced removals of Palouse families drove them from their homelands, which opened lands to non-Indian settlers. The newcomers were citizens of the territories and nation, unlike the Palouse and other Plateau Indians, who had no political power or voting rights in Washington, Oregon, or Idaho territories. As Indians vacated their former lands to seek food, protection, and familial ties on the reservations, newcomers encroached on those lands. Various companies took possession of former Indian lands, in particular the railroads, which received generous government subsidies in cash and land.

Hard-working farmers and ranchers, eager for new opportunities, transformed the Native landscape into farms, ranches, and productive businesses. In the process, the newcomers destroyed Native root grounds, hunting areas, fishing places, and berry patches. As Mary Jim experienced firsthand, whites often blocked Indians from entering their former places and threatened them with guns. On other occasions county sheriffs and federal marshals prevented Indians from traveling off the reservations. Indian agents discouraged Indians from leaving the reservation to fish, hunt, gather, and trade, yet the United States provided few work opportunities for reservation Indians.

Survival through Work

During the late nineteenth and early twentieth centuries, the traditional Native American economy of the Columbia Plateau collapsed, although many Indians have continued to hunt, fish, and gather to supplement their diets to the present day. However, people could no longer sustain themselves on their sacred foods, which they continued to honor in First Food ceremonies. Although the Indian people did not end their relationship with these foods—salmon, deer, roots, and berries—they could no longer feed all their people on traditional foods alone.

In order to provide food, the reservation Snake River-Palouse accepted some commodities and they worked for a living, bringing home cash to buy food at stores. These cultural changes brought on an epidemic of diabetes and obesity that plagues Plateau tribes today. The epidemic, like the malnutrition and infant mortality of the past century, resulted in part from the government's destruction of Indian economies. War, removal, reservations, and neglect through the lack of budgets for Indian health have resulted in disease, depression, and death.

Education for Extinction

Government officials believed that it would be a waste of time and money to assimilate adult and elder Indians, so they separated

Native American children from their extended families to plant American knowledge, ideas, and values into the hearts and minds of the young. They sent Plateau Indian children to government- and mission-run day and boarding schools, where administrators and teachers attempted to strip them of their history, culture, language, religion, and ways of being. The federal government used reservations and boarding schools as vehicles to "tame," "civilize," and assimilate Indian people, strategies considered by many to be cultural genocide.

In spite of these setbacks, the Naxíyampam survived the physical, mental, and spiritual assault of state and federal policies. The schools did great harm to culture, but they also provided knowledge that future people used to advance their individual and tribal sovereignty.

The river people lost many aspects of their former lives, but they did not lose their spiritual compass and relationship with the earth, animals, and plants. They did not abandon their love of their landscape and rivers that flowed through their former homeland like the blood of the earth. In spite of their physical separation from their homelands, the Naxíyampam retained a profound spiritual attachment to sacred places and territory drained by the great rivers and their tributaries.

Ethnogenesis of the Snake River-Palouse

Many Naxíyampam and their neighbors found it difficult to adjust to modern Euro-American culture. Some people, like Chief Kamiakin and members of his extended family, lived away from the reservations as free people. Others moved onto one of the reserves or traveled back and forth from the reservation to their former lands. In both cases, the people struggled with a world turned upside down by white resettlement of Indian lands, the market economy, development of transportation systems, and reservation management where agents and missionaries exerted significant influence and power. Reservation Indians had little food and less opportunity.

The people made the transition as best as possible. They acculturated, wore Western clothing and cowboy hats, engaged in new labor, participated in a foreign economy, and lived under the thumb of the

Army and Office of Indian Affairs. They contracted new diseases and lost their children to schools operated by non-Indians. The Snake River-Palouse watched as Indian agents made deals to sell Indian lands, water, and other resources. However, the people did not capitulate to the new world order but fought back in many ways. They especially held onto their traditional religion, oral literature, and ceremonies. They sang and danced in the Longhouse. They drummed and prayed. The ancient *Wáshat* ways continued, and were manifested in the Seven Drums religion, which honored the Creator, creation, and the foods planted by Coyote at the beginning of time.

The Naxíyampam continued their familial lives and lineage associations, traveling great distances on horseback and by automobile to visit friends and relatives living on and off the reservations. Families intermarried with other tribal people, and soon the river people's blood lived on in many of the Northwestern reservations on the Columbia Plateau. Other Snake River-Palouse married people living west of the Cascade Mountains or east of the Bitterroot Mountains. Mary Jim's son, Tom Estama, married Jennifer Mike, a Chemehuevi woman and member of the Twenty-Nine Palms Tribe of California. Tom remembered his mother taking him to Priest Rapids to learn from Johnnie Buck, a leader of the Seven Drums religion.

Mary Jim insisted her children grow up learning Naxíyampam language and culture. Mary wanted them to worship in the old way and to remember to give thanks at First Foods ceremonies. After the 1960s, Mary lived on the Yakama Reservation, but she had spent the early part of the twentieth century as a free Snake River-Palouse woman, living with her family on the Snake River and raising her family on fish, eels, venison, roots, and berries. She and her children lived much of the old life until the "law" forced them from her land.

NAXÍYAMPAM VOICES

During our several meetings with Mary Jim, the elderly, white-haired lady with poor eyesight and unique dialect of English would reminisce about her life "on Snake River," a personal characterization suggesting kinship. In her mind, Mary would travel back to the sandy shores of her family's old village site to smell and hear the song of the river flowing through the landscape dotted with greenery and timeworn shoreline boulders. She remembered the smell of salmon, split on sticks and roasting slowly by a smoldering fire. Mary's personal account offers an unusual voice in Native American history, a voice she shares in this work.

By 1978, Richard Scheuerman already knew Mary Jim and her daughter, Carrie, and he took Cliff Trafzer to the Yakama Reservation to meet them. They made that trip several times, crossing the Columbia Plateau and arriving at Mary's small white clapboard home near Parker, Washington, where they often found her preparing Native foods. One time they found Mary outside her house with her hand in a large bowl of biscuitroot dough, which she squeezed in the palm of her hand to make small, oblong biscuits. The two young men ate some of the dried biscuits, savoring the nutty flavor. They took a few handfuls of the biscuits home and shared them with students at Washington State University. For many years, Trafzer kept one biscuit in a small box to show to his classes in American Indian history.

The biscuit bore the impression of Mary Jim's fingerprints, left there when she had squeezed the fibrous batter. Like the five fingers printed on the biscuitroot, Mary left an indelible impression on the minds of two academics who share here some of her knowledge—and that of Andrew George, Gordon Fisher, and Emily Peone. Their lives are intentionally tied to the vast span of Northwestern history from the arrival of Lewis and Clark to the twenty-first century. Elements of their lives appear in the pages of *River Song*, an original work the compilers hope will enchant and delight. The history and culture of Snake River-Palouse deserves further study and greater understanding, and these voices deserve to be heard.

Notes

1. Josiah Pinkham, oral history recorded by Clifford E. Trafzer, July 19, 2008, Oklahoma City, Oklahoma.
2. Documents Relating to Ratified and Unratified Treaties, National Archives, Record Group 75, Microfilm T494. Proceedings of the Walla Walla Council

and all the Treaty Councils of the Northwest in "Report on Sources, Nature and Extent of Fishing, Hunting, and Miscellaneous Related Rights of Certain Tribes in Washington and Oregon." Portland: Bureau of Indian Affairs, No Date. Hereafter cited as Walla Walla Treaty Proceedings, 1855.
3. L. V. McWhorter, McWhorter Collection, MASC, WSU Libraries, Pullman.
4. In 1921, L.V. McWhorter recorded this story by a Native American storyteller in a typescript manuscript. See the published version in Clifford E. Trafzer, editor, *Grandmother, Grandfather, and Old Wolf: Tamanwit Ku Sukat and Traditional Native American Narratives from the Columbia Plateau* (East Lansing: Michigan State University Press, 1998), 132-133.
5. Walla Walla Treaty Proceedings, 1855.
6. Toohoolhoolzote's comments are found in Oliver O. Howard, *Nez Perce Joseph* (Boston: Lee and Shepard, 1881), 64-66; the comments by Chief Joseph are found in his interview published as Young Chief Joseph, "An Indian's View of Indian Affairs," *North American Review* 128 (1879), 57.
7. Report of the Commission...to Nez Perce Indians, Annual Report of the Secretary of the Interior, 1877, 607-609.
8. Young Chief Joseph, "An Indian's View of Indian Affairs."

Part I/*Náxc*

Mary Jim/Xínstanik

Mary Jim Chapman, Parker, Washington, 1980. *Richard Scheuerman*

Oral History

"Calling for Our Land"

Our longtime friendship with the Jim family began in 1977 after Richard was introduced to Mary and her daughter, Carrie, by Wanapam elder Rex Buck Sr. This account is compiled from interviews we conducted with Mary at her home in Parker, Washington, on May 1, 1977; April 1-2, 1979; November 10, 1979; November 17, 1979; August 12, 1980; and February 21, 1985. We always visited with Mary at the family home on the Yakama Indian Reservation. She usually spoke in English but often used Palouse Sahaptin terms that Carrie translated. Sometimes other family members, including Tom Estama and Charlie Jim, helpfully participated in our conversations.

The text includes minor edits for fluency. For example, when asked about locations along the river, Mary would usually refer to a place being "on Walla Walla side," for which we have substituted "south." Terms in parentheses are obtained from other elders and published sources; those in brackets are from Sahaptin language scholar Dr. Bruce Rigsby of the University of Queensland, who interviewed Harry Jim and other Columbia Plateau elders on the Umatilla, Nez Perce, and Yakama reservations in the 1960s. Recordings of our interviews with Mary Jim were transcribed by Marjorie Grunewald and Cindy DeGrosse. Mary Jim died in Toppenish, Washington, in 2000.

Mary Jim: My grandfather was Cawa-w'tiak ["Hanging Up to Dry"]—Fishhook Jim [1835?-1922] and my grandmother was Amtalút, also called Wha-lits-pah. Her father was Xímtyutsá'kin; means "Shot in the Mouth."[1] My grandpa was raised by Levey on Snake River. He was a kind man; he'd get ready on Saturday for service on Sunday, and on Monday close them up. He was always taking care of his life, serving the Creator all the time. My father was Thomas Jim, Alíwiya [b. 1879]. It is a Nez Perce name. My mother was Liplíptkwin,

47

also known as Annie Jim. Her parents were Táwiway and Xaluwáyx. My grandma was raised at Priest Rapids, and Táwiway was from above Richland.

Harry Jim at his family's Snake River camp (1956). *Roger Chute photograph, Washington State Historical Society*

By Richland was *Táalapaypia*, the place where North Wind Brothers had their big fight with Chinook Wind. Grandma was related to Yuyúni and Šmúxala (Smohalla). My father had two sisters—Annie Jim (Tu-yu-tu-yet) and Agnes Jim. Their brother was Harry Jim [1894-1968], Indian name Xímtyutsá'kin, also Fú-ta-kin. They didn't want to go to the reservation. Indian people lived all up and the down the river. We were Snake River and Palouse Indians and Naxíyampam and Palúspam,[2] and Wanapams and Yakamas and Nez Perce. Yes, all mixed up!

I was born long time ago [c. 1910] at *Samyúya* on Snake River. In the old days it was a big village on that [south] side. The Indians used to live in mat houses along the river, mostly on the north side. There were four or five big houses in the main villages. They used willow traps there to catch fish and eels. We lived at *Tyáwtaš* ["drying shed"] on that [north] side of the river at *Shapanúk* ["put in the water," opposite present Charbonneau Park].

There in the river on the south side by the dam is *Pápts'aq* ["piled"] where Áan (Sun) piled up Indian heads and where people later fished. Up from there at Ash was *Wa-núk-ša*. It means "water gushing out."

My father used to catch a lot of sturgeon, great big ones. We watched the old people swim and then swim ourselves. Later we lived up the river by Levey; we called it *Sooksa*, which means "pointing in." Just up from there on the south side was *Twinátsas*. That means "making rope" and is where Coyote learned how to make a hemp net. Annie Johnson (Wówniyu), Táwiway's sister, made rope that way. We used to stay there all the time, my sister Helen and me. We used to camp with the old man, Uncle Harry Jim, every summer.

Three islands are upstream from Levey. One is *Nch'i-'imá* [Big Island] where Fishhook Jim caught salmon and where the graveyard was. Another was *Šiik-šiik* which means like "joint grass" that grows along the river there [from *šaykwšáykw*, "horsetail fern"]. The other one is *Siipa* [piled "rubble" rock]. On the south side of the islands and upstream was *Wawiyúkma*. Big village named for *wawiyik'k* [the bird poorwill] that warned the people when the Snake Indians came to capture horses long ago. *Wawiyik'k* called out to warn the people, "*Wawiyik! Wawiyik!*" And they took the horses and children onto the island to save them! The men they stayed and fought them.

Up from there was *Šaxshax-mí* ["of the kingfisher"] and Eel Place at *Láwlikas*. Coyote made his boat out of rock with a high one in the middle where the eels would gather. He made it for the Indian people because he knew they were comin'. He made lots of places there and over here, and went with his brothers over to *Palús* and where Nez Perces live. Went all over to make things for the people. At *Láwlikas* we would dry eels and salmon to trade for blankets and shawls and things. On the north side was *Tamáyp-ła* ["wind against the river]. Harry Jim had a place there. Fishhook Bend was about five miles upstream from the three islands where Fishhook Jim stayed. He took care of another big graveyard there. He stayed to keep people from digging the graves. He was buried on the island. The village was called *Tásiwiks*, means "like a whirlpool"; was on the north side. Page Ferry was near there.

Wintertime was *Wáh-šot* when we lived on Snake River, means "Cold Time," then *Tsin-bik*. Next is *Áah-mi*, when "Crows Come," and *Hiš-hiš*, when "Insects Come." Then *Wo-ših-tash*, "Moving Out Time" in March and April, and *Ika-taš* in fall ["Fishing Time"]. In spring we would go by horseback to Soap Lake, dig certain kinds of roots. We used to dig *sk'okul*, *xmaaš* [camas], and some other roots. We used a *kapon* [root digger] and *tá-khon-ta* [root bag]. Takes two or three days to cook the roots. Then we would move to Badger Mountain by Waterville and Douglas, and all over that big hill, Badger Mountain. And we used to stay there at *Tá-puš* [Pine

Tree Place]. That's where people used to gather, play stick games, dance the *Wáshat*, the Seven Drums religion.

The First Foods Feast shows the Creator's way. Start with water [*kúš*], then the chiefs of the creatures: salmon [*núsux*] for fish and venison [deer/*yáamaš*] for animals, then the plants [bitterroot/*piyáxi*] and fruits [huckleberries/*wíwinu*]. We do this each season. The land was our religion; given to us by the Creator. The earth is our Mother because it provides us all food. *Imepship* [the Great Spirit] placed us on our *Imephsha* [Earth Mother] who gives us roots and berries. The Great Spirit created the deer, antelope, and elk, and these animals share the earth with us.

We used to race horses by Badger Mountain. Then more and more fences up and can't get in. One time a fellow had a gun and told us no more digging there. We also went to Ephrata—*Haup-haupt*, "Cottonwood Place" and Soap Lake—*Wa-tám*, Medicine Lake. When we were done there, we moved back to Snake River, last of May maybe. We called that time *Ah-e-weena-e-noo'-sakh*. It means "New Salmon Come" because the salmon came up Snake River. We fished and got all kinds of fish. Yea, we got salmon and put it away. We used to dig a hole, big hole, and put bunchgrass all around it, then boards, then sticks. We buried that and nothing would happen. That's for the spring salmon and eels and other kinds of fish—sturgeon. We used to sell sturgeon. We caught all kinds of fish and we kept the fish. There was no [government] law at that time. You couldn't tell my grandpa, "You're going to get out of the fishing place. It's our law." We didn't have that law.

We caught lots of eels in June and dried them just like salmon. They would catch them at night with two men in a boat. One would hold up a torch and the other one fished. They also caught beaver that way at night. We would dig a pit and heat the rocks, wrap *sawícht* [bunchgrass] around the beaver and put it in the pit and cover it over for two or three hours. My father trapped beaver. They were going to arrest him but he had the title to that land and he showed it to them so they let him go. And they don't put him in jail because it was on his own land, because that was our home.

In the fall we went over to Walla Walla to dig *kouse*. That's where we used to camp and dig and hunt. Get lots of deer and dry the meat and put it away for winter. Then we went up toward the Blue Mountains to dig other kinds of roots and gather *wíwinu*, huckleberries. We always prayed over the First Foods, and also did this with the berries. The first to ripen are *khá-nen* [currants] and *woo-wán*, which are little white berries, so these are prayed over. We also gathered raspberries, chokecherries, and blackberries. You baked some of the roots which turned black, almost like wild onions, but different. Then we cooked tree moss, *kunch*, and we baked it and ground it. We camped near *Palinywash* ["Lost Mountain"], *Wátniwash* ["Spirit Mountain"], and *Tehám-tehám*. We called that place "Cloudy Mountain" and you were not to climb it [see "The Creatures of Cloudy Mountain"].

It's hard work to take hair off three or four deer hides in a day. After that you soak them two or three days in salmon brains. Then it takes two or three hours to rub the hides and make them soft. You need about three to make a man's shirt, and maybe five for a woman's dress. It takes about a week to make a shirt or dress. I can make a pair of moccasins without beads in half a day. We traveled a lot. Yea, you ought to have seen them horses: packing, packing, packing. No car at that time! We all went to Walla Walla. We got a wagon there, and we loaded that stuff and then moved back to Snake River, almost fall time.

And still they used to go fishing at Wallowa and Winahah. Way up on top of the canyon, Kooskooskie Canyon. We gathered there, just like on Badger Mountain. They used to race and used to *Wáshat*. They gambled, played ball. We had different kinds of games long ago. It's wheat farm there now; it was a long time ago we stayed up there. We also went over to Kamiah and up to that big plateau to dig and bake. They said young women and men used to come from far away, clear from Montana. They'd get married, different bloods.

We used to go up the Snake River in the fall time after we worked the corn. There was *Páyčaš* ["standing at the edge"] and *Palús*,[3] where Skalumkee Kamiakin and Tamayatut [Charlie Williams] lived, and then *Tékšeš* ["mouth of the (Tucannon) river"] and *Almáta* [Almota].⁴ *Ka-náp-kin* had two daughters, Tootsie and Alice, and they all lived at *Palús*. *Pa-luš-sa* is "something stickin' in the water," a big rock there. We were related to Ka-nap-kin and used to ride up to their place at horse round-up time. There were lots of Appaloosa horses up there. We would also cut wood and get fresh water for the old ones. I knew Young Charley. His Indian name was Wáptas Timani, it means like "Feather Written" [Painted]. Star Doctor—Haslou [George Lucas, 1850?-1938?] was Páxalawasq'ísit [Five Shadows].⁵ He led *Wáshat* feasts and burial dances. Kay-yee-wach [Hiyouwath], his last name was Kamiakin [Pete Bones, 1895?-1954]. He was crippled and was a hunchback. Alalumt'i Kamiakin [1885-1977] was our relative. She was Cleveland's [1870-1959] wife. I knew Waughaskie; the whites called him Chief Old Bones [1827?-1915]. Sam Fisher [Yoosyóos Tulikécin, 1866-1944] was buried in Nespelem. His name is Nez Perce and means something like "Covered with Blue." His nephew was Carter Fisher who lived on the river. Once when we were up there we went to the graveyard and got some beads, and a whipping! We would then come back home to get ready for *Ah-num-ka-pás*, "Winter Cold Time."

My grandpa's brother, his name was Ish. He was caught by the soldiers when he was a boy during all that fighting with the white people.⁶ They want to come fight, and they took that little boy away and they gave him that name "Thomash" [Thomas]. His parents and everybody were all scared off so the soldiers took him to Walla Walla. Thomash was smart and he went to school in Walla Walla and learned, but he ran away. That doctor [Whitman] was killing them. I heard my grandma say when they went along the river there'd be a whole village, nobody alive but maybe a child wandering around alone. All dead from disease. Thomash run away to the Snake River. He had no folks, just the brother. After that they came with the law and they sent people to the reservation. They are going to have the land, they thought we were going to give them land.

Thomash had everything and he said he can answer them in English. And his brother told him, "We don't want to leave this

Lyons Ferry on the Snake River, near the confluence of the Snake and Palouse Rivers and Pálus village, c. 1950. *Colville Tribal Museum*

fishing place; we don't want to leave this graveyard; we don't want to leave. How would we keep our horses?" They had lots of horses. Then he was a chief and he told the white people, "You're not going to take my people; no, no reservation. My people want to keep their background. They want to stay here." And they took him to jail, they put him in jail [in 1878].[7] Pretty soon they tell him, "Thomash, you've got a big head. You don't want to move no place. Now you take your people back, and they are going to get a homestead, and nobody's going to bother them."[8] And they came down and got a homestead [in 1884] on the other side of Ice Harbor. That's why we got that land. They wouldn't give it up. They never enrolled in the reservation. That's why my mother didn't have no [reservation] land, and my father the same way.

Yea, we had lots of horses there—everybody had lots of horses, and the soldiers killed those horses. And Chief Wolf [Necklace] went to Washington, D.C., and then they [whites] here stole his money. They made his son [David Wolf] go and collect all his money. He went to sleep, he said to me, and then they stole it. There's only one more left, Gina [Wolf] in Pendleton, and we are close relatives.[9] We didn't want to leave our buried people, and where we grew up. We didn't want to leave our fishing rights because that was important to catch and dry the fish and put it away for winter.

We were over the other side of Pasco to pick strawberries. We were there about two or three days and we see somebody comin'. He says, "You know what? There's a tent on your island. Somebody's digging." So we went down there, and I said, "I'll give you this red handkerchief, and you just keep waving it, like that." And he stood by the sand and he waved and waved, because we didn't have no boat or nothing. And finally they come across and they talk to us. They said, "We're from the college and we're doing this, we like to find for people how long they been livin' here, and we're checking on those graves." We asked help from the agency. I said, "I wished they'd quit digging our graves up." But they says, "We can't do nothing. We can't do nothing." They didn't help us.

Then one morning when Carrie was a girl and Anna, she was small: "Wake up, Mom, wake up! They took our grandpa!" Now they took him. They went across and they took that grave. He was buried in a canoe. They dug a hole and we hollered at him. Charlie Jim went out to tell them to stop. We waved red handkerchiefs at them, telling them, "Stop!" Then some kinda' [amphibious] car went through the water and on the ground, too. We didn't know how to chase them or where they went. We reported this to the agency but nothing happened. It costs to hire attorneys, and gas money. Help one another. I'm doing it myself all the time. We do our own, what we have a little we do.[10]

My mother and grandmother are under that water, and my brothers and father are under that water. They took everything. They took the salmon. We pray for Snake River. God gave the fish and land; taken away by the dams. I didn't sign no papers to sell my land. There's no sign there unless they lied to me. I never signed no paper. I'm sellin' my things to get by. The government sent $500. I didn't keep it.[11] I don't want it because I know they are sellin' our land even if I can't read the papers. I don't want that money. That's just awful for me to sell my graveyard.

I respect the dead because they came here first and lived here. God put them here to live and they had the land and everything, all kinds of food—salmon and deer and all kinds of things what they use for themselves. They even used these tules and plants to make houses. Now they flood the area and I didn't know all the time they were stealing my land. We had to send the kids to school [in 1959] when they built the dam.[12] The first thing covered up was where we used to have a tipi. First thing the water come up there. We were there that last year and we was fishin'. And the next year it was water all over. We lost our shed, and didn't get paid for that shed and sacks and canvas and stuff like that. So we moved here to the [Yakama] reservation.

We came here to my "grandpa" on my mother's side. His name was Yai-nach-shaw, and this is his allotment. Used to be a big Longhouse here in Parker, like Priest Rapids.[13] We had an old house across there; that's where we used to stay, and they had to go to school. They enrolled us here but don't give us any land. They took me one time to a meeting here. I got there and I was sitting there listening to them talking about this land, the [reservation] land here. They say, "It's your turn to talk now." I told them, "I am not from here. I can't lie to you. These hills, I know nothing about it, all those things. I could go to find roots and berries and things like that. But here, I don't know nothing about it."

I'm calling for our land and everything else to pray and ask Him. And my own self, my body is going to be healed and feel good. I like to reach out for my children, and their children, because some children now have no homes. They have to go around all over. And our land just wastes away without us. Sometimes I cry, feel sorry. Fishhook Jim has maybe two or three hundred children [descendants]. Many young ones, and they don't know what to do. They got no place to stay, they got no background, they got no land. That's why we would like to have a piece of our background and have our homes again.

Notes

1. According to Harry Jim (B. Rigsby), Xímtyutsá'kin ("Shout in the Mouth") was born in the Dayton area and was hung at Walla Walla for involvement in the 1847 Whitman killings.
2. *Naxíyampam* translates in the Northeast Sahaptin language of the Palouse and Wanapam as "Lower River People," a form of the Sahaptin root *Naxíyam*, "Lower (Snake) River." According to Sahaptin linguist Bruce Rigsby, the words appear related to the Nez Perce term *Lexéyu*, or "Sahaptin People" (e.g., Palouse, Wanapam, Yakama) through a common ancient cognate. The Nez Perce word for the Snake River is *Pik'úunen*, or "Big River," perhaps the origin of the name "Ki-moo-e-nim" for the river recorded by Lewis and Clark. The explorers noted the presence of "Snake Indians" residing along the upper stretches of the river who were likely Shoshone, and the name came into common use for the main course later in the nineteenth century. Some historians contend the Shoshone S-shaped hand sign for salmon was misinterpreted by frontiersman which contributed to the association of a serpent for the river's name. See B. Rigsby to R. Scheuerman, October 15, 2011; H. Aoki, 1994:1133-34, and G. Fisher, oral history, 2008. Rigsby's 1960s field studies with Charley Kamiakin Williams, Tom Billy Andrews, and Palouse-Nez Perce elders indicate that the word "Palouse" is derived from the Northeast Sahaptin name for the village of *Palús* (sometimes pronounced *Pelús* by Snake River-Palouse descendants). The term is derived from the rock monolith prominent in tribal mythology at the mouth of the river formed with Palouse Sahaptin prefix, *pa–* ("placed upright") and the root, *–lú* ("be in water"), plus the diminutivized mediopassive suffix –s.
3. *Páyčaš* (Pichias) was at present Jim Boat Island. "Harry Jim visited when he was a little boy; there were graves here; the resident population was about one hundred; a river crossing where one could swim horses across; jumping off point for travels north and west in spring for root digging, as far as Moses Lake by way of White Bluffs. One large and three small islands choked the channel in the river bend here" (B. Rigsby). Skalumkee ("Snake River") Kamiakin (1867-1949) was the son of the Yakama-Palouse leader Chief Kamiakin (1800?-1877), a leading figure in the Columbia Plateau Indian wars of the 1850s. Charlie Williams (1879-1969) was the son of Chief Kamiakin's son, T'siyak. Both men eventually relocated to the Colville Indian Reservation and served as the last traditional chiefs of the Colville Palouse band. Their lives are profiled by Richard D. Scheuerman and Michael Finley in *Finding Chief Kamiakin* (Washington State University Press, 2008).
4. *Tékšeš* was a fishing site located at the frontier settlement of Riparia and the namesake of the "Texas Road" that crossed the Snake River at the point and crossed the western Palouse Country. The name "Tucannon" is from *Tkwanamá*, the name of a village located near Starbuck about ten miles up the Tucannon from its confluence with the Snake. *Almáta* is present Almota.
5. Five Shadows ("Star Doctor") fought in the 1877 Nez Perce War but escaped from exile in Oklahoma by walking all the way back to the Pacific Northwest. He was the nephew of *Palús* residents Felix and Palouse Jack.

6. Thomas Cornelius was the commander of the Oregon Territorial Volunteers who attacked lower Snake River villagers in March 1856. In a fight near *Tásiwiks* they killed four Indians and took a small boy captive whom they later named Thomas after Cornelius. He eventually returned to his people and became a revered religious leader and headman. See Trafzer and Scheuerman, *Renegade Tribe*, 69-70.
7. Thomash's arrest by Fort Walla Walla trader Andrew Pambrun is described in Pambrun's memoir, *Sixty Years on the Frontier*, 128-29. Accusatory accounts of the "Dreamer Chief Thomas" frequently appear in the *Walla Walla Statesman* and other pioneer press accounts of the period.
8. The Jim family Indian homestead was filed by Fishhook Jim in 1884 and originally consisted of 116 acres on the Walla Walla side of the river. At the same time Thomash filed on 124 acres on the north side of the river at Fishhook Bend. Today the property is divided by the Snake River in Franklin and Walla Walla counties and covers the east half of Section 4, Township 9 North, Range 32 EWM. Although most of the land was flooded by the Ice Harbor Dam reservoir, at least forty acres remain above the water line. The property is about four miles southwest of present Fishhook Park.
9. Gina (Eugena) Wolf's father, David Wolf (1868-1901?), and Matilda Kalyton (b. 1873) were siblings. Matilda's son was Mary Jim's husband, Alex Jesse Chapman (1907-1957). The theft of Chief Wolf's hoard while he was in Washington, D.C., is told by Click Relander in *Drummers and Dreamers* (1956), 107-09.
10. Archaeological excavations of Indian burials in the Ice Harbor Dam area were conducted by members of the Mid-Columbia Archaeological Society and faculty and students from Washington State University's Department of Anthropology during summer field schools in the 1950s. See Richard Daugherty and Roderick Sprague, *Archaeological Excavations in the Ice Harbor Reservoir* (1959). In 2006, nearly two decades after the enactment of the Native American Graves Protection and Repatriation Act and following extensive litigation by Columbia Plateau tribes, 150 lower Snake River burial remains from Washington State University and University of Idaho were reinterred on a bluff near Page.
11. This may have represented the Corps of Engineers condemnation settlement for Jim family property that was flooded by the Ice Harbor Dam reservoir.
12. The *Tri-City Herald* (July 9, 1959) reported that Harry Jim and Mary Jim were living on 42-acre Fishhook Island in a crude shelter made from driftwood, cardboard, and burlap with four of Mary's children. Harry once caught four to five hundred salmon per year but was now seeking several acres for a garden and employment because of the construction of Ice Harbor Dam at Five Mile Rapids. The Army Corps of Engineers was preparing a condemnation suit for lands flooded by the reservoir. The dam's first concrete footings had been poured in June 1957 and in May 1959 a coffer dam was built on the north side of the river. Harry Jim worked with members of the Priest Rapids Wanapam band to relocate Chief Wolf's log cabin near Fishhook Bend to the grounds of the Grant County Historical Society's Pioneer Village in Ephrata. The thirty-mile reservoir began filling in late November 1961 and the area behind the dam, named Lake Sacajawea, completely filled by April 1962. The dam was dedicated

on May 9, 1962, by Vice President Lyndon Johnson and in April 1965 the Corps, in cooperation with the Yakama, Warm Springs, Nez Perce, Umatilla, and Colville tribes, unveiled an enormous pictograph commemorating the area's flooded graves. The Jim family did not participate.

13. The Yakama village of *Pákiut* was located at present Parker where the *Wáshani* leader Kooatyahhen (1837-1899) led Longhouse services. The activities of Kooatyahhen, son of Yakama Chief Showaway, were strongly opposed by reservation agents James Wilbur and Robert Milroy throughout the 1880s. Kooatyahhen's grandson, Alba Shawaway (1902-1968) and his wife, Nettie (Túnshpam, 1902-2003), longtime friends of the Jim family who also lived at Parker, were leading figures in twentieth-century Yakama traditionalism. Thirteen *Wáshani* Longhouses presently function on reservations in Washington, Oregon, and Idaho.

The annual nineteenth-century runs of several million salmon had dwindled to approximately 8,000 spawning Chinook in 1995. In the 1950s, Bureau of Reclamation Commissioner Floyd Dominy had remarked, "People can live without salmon, but I don't think they can live without beans and potatoes." A generation later, Commissioner Dan Beard wrote that restoration of the Snake River salmon runs represented "the most complex natural resources problem in America."(Both quotes from Marc Reisner, "Begin the Fight for Reclamation," *High Country News*, March 20, 1995.)

"How Coyote Learned to Fish"

Retold by Mary Jim Chapman (1980)

Apútaput (Palouse Falls and Palouse Canyon, Coyote's Sons/Castle Rock at top left of falls). *John Clement*

Coyote and his older brother lived at *Twinátsas*;[1]
  his older brother lived upstream on the other side.
Younger Spilyaí had five sons
  so was always working to feed them.
He would look across the river
  and see his brother with lots of salmon,
    but he couldn't catch any….
He wanted to find out how to get them.
One day he said to his youngest son,
  "Go over and ask your uncle,
    'How are you catching all those salmon?'"
So his son went over to where his uncle was fishing,
  and he asked him about it.
The older Spilyaí said,
  "I'm using *kaamúukii!*[2]

---

[1] "Rope Making Place," near present Levey.
[2] A heavy brown string made from processed milkweed hemp.

I gather it from the prairie,
   and weave it into a net,
      and catch the salmon in it."
Little Coyote ran home to tell his father,
   but he went so fast he fell down
      and hit the ground so hard
         he forgot what his uncle was using.

So next day Spilyaí gathered all his five sons,
   And says to his oldest,
      "Ask your uncle what he is using
         to catch all those salmon.
And if something happens so you forget,
   one of your brothers can carry the message."
So Coyote's children took off in a line;
   they crossed the river
      and went to their uncle's fishing camp.
The oldest brother asked him about the salmon
   and he told them the same thing:
      "I am using *kaamúukii*."
So all five sons ran and crossed the river,
   heading towards home saying over and over
      "*Kaamúukii, kaamúukii, kaamúukii!*"
One fell down but the rest kept going;
   They repeated, "*Kaamúukii, kaamúukii!,*"
      and kept falling all over each other
         until the youngest one got back home.
He ran up to his father and said,
   "*Kaamúukii!*"
Spilyaí said, "Ah, that's what I was thinking."

So Coyote and his sons went up along the plains;
   they gathered *kaamúukii* to make into twine.
Then Spilyaí wove it into a net and said,
   "The people will soon come here and need a fishing place,

    they will catch salmon along here."
Coyote could hear them coming far away,
  and Hawk could see them in the distance.
Coyote went with his sons up to Palouse Falls,
  and dipped his net into the water.
He caught a beautiful salmon
  and told his children to make a fire.
He roasted the salmon on the fire and said,
    "Now we are ready; this is the First Salmon,
      share it with each other."
Spilyaí then called that place "Repeater,"
  because the sound echoes back.
He turned his five sons into stone,
  and placed them near the falls
    where people can see them.

Swirling Heights. *Richard Scheuerman*

"The Creatures of Cloudy Mountain"

Retold by Mary Jim Chapman (1979)

Two boys traveled with their families in the fall time
    to pick berries and hunt down in the mountains.
One morning they got ready to gather huckleberries
    among the pines of Kooskie Canyon.
The boys asked their fathers
    if they could go hunting instead.
Before leaving, they were told,
    "Don't climb up *Tehám-tehám*,[1] Cloudy Mountain."
Cloudy Mountain was a mysterious place,
    different than all the other mountains,
        a forbidden high place.

The boys had seen it in the distance
    when they rode their horse several days before.

---

[1] From the Nez Perce word *tehám*, "smoke, fog"; emphatic when doubled, meaning "dark, cloudy."

The top could be clearly seen in the distance
   but clouds appeared at its top when one came too close.
That was the time to go some other way!
The elders spoke of strange beings on Cloudy Mountain
   who were not of this world….
The ancient ways respected these creatures
   who guarded the mountainside.
The two walked with their bows
   in search of rabbits and other small game.
The older boy wondered
   why the mountain needed to be guarded.
"Because it is the home of the Animal People,"
   said the youngest.
But his older friend wanted to take a look.
The two boys turned from the trail
   and went toward *Tehám-tehám*.

Soon they could see it in the distance,
   great wisps of gray clouds
      forming above on the higher slopes.
After walking at length through the pines,
   They saw a slight movement in the bushes,
      So they drew their bows.
A timber rabbit appeared,
   But its body was red like ocher.
Neither boy had ever seen a red rabbit.
The older boy released his arrow
   and it seemed to head straight for the rabbit.
But it jumped in front of the bush unharmed,
   and stood up in full view of the boys.
They were so startled
   that neither reached for another arrow.
The creature sniffed with its nose,
   seemed entirely unafraid and spoke.

"You do not belong here,
       Return at once to the people."
Then it ran away.

The younger boy said he was going back.
But the older one said,
    "No warrior was afraid of rabbits!"
So they continued up the misty trail,
    into the trees and the path disappeared.
They went around around a big rock,
    and stopped in their tracks.
A white grizzly bear sat
    on the side of the trail.
Before they could run
    Tutwit'aya loudly growled another warning:
"You do not belong here!
    Turn back while you can!"
He then crawled off into the darkening mist.

The younger boy was afraid…
He said they must not go any farther.
They both started back,
    but the oldest said,
"These are only disappearing animals,
    and mean us no harm.
        We must be close to the top."
He paused,
    turned around,
        and continued up alone.

The climb became steeper with no trail,
    but the boy continued with strength from his excitement.
A stand of tall evergreens near the top
        moved with the swirling fog.

As the boy approached the trees,
   a birdman appeared from the mist
      clad entirely in blue feathers.
"You have come too far,"
   he scolded the boy,
      "and you must turn back here.
         Do not go beyond these trees!"
The creature raised his arms
   and flew off over the clearing.
But the boy had made up his mind,
   and was going to the end.
He started up again and disappeared.

When the younger boy finally returned to camp
   long after dark,
      he found their parents waiting.
He told them all that happened
   on their way up the forbidden mountain.
The elders began to weep.
His grandfather said the top of *Tehám-tehám*
   was like an entryway to the cloud world.
No one could return.
The families remained in the area for many days
   waiting and waiting.
But the other boy never came back.

Tíłqawayks (Wolf) and Chowawatyet (Jim) Families

1. Tíłqawayks (Tilcoax, Telxawey, Tilch-ko-waks, Telgawêê [DeSmet], Chil-e-wax, Til-ko-yakes [WCB]), d. 1860? m. Maggie Kalyton[1] (Kaláytun [NR], Colliten, Collidon), b. 1814 (UAC)

A. Wolf Necklace (Xáliš Wášimuxš [BR], Wolf Wearing Necklace [CS], Tilcowax (MKl), Tilcoax the Younger), 1843[2]-1914 m. (1st) I-ya-to-yik[3] (Iyatoyik, dau. of Wocatsie, *Umatilla* [WW]), b. 1848 (2nd) Sinsinq't (II), 1841-1909 (Seen-seen-tak, Nellie, dau. of Lokout, *Yakama*) (3rd) Teek-ton-nay (Ticktanonmy), *Nez Perce, Timothy-Red Wolf Band* (WCB)[4]
   (1, 1st m.). David Wolf (Old David), 1868?-1901? (MKl) m. Kel-we-son-mi (II) (Humalatakabut),[5] b. 1872 (UAC)
      (a). Rufus Wolf, b. 1892 (UAC) m. Annie Andrews (Sowecus [Su-a-cus]), 1900-1933?
   (2). Matilda (Mary, Kitty) Kaláytun/Kalyton (Ilawáwiltalatsán'may [NR], ["Water Breaking Down," CJS]), b. 1873 m. (1st) Harry Billy, b. 1870, *Walla Walla* (2nd) Billy McKay (Áwiyaw [NR]), b. 1873, *Cayuse* (3rd) Johnson Chapman, 1883-1957 (UTC), *Yakama*
      (a, 1st m.). Isaac Billy Patrick (Watashsitsláy'min [NR]), b. 1900[6] m. Ada J., b. 1905 (UAC)
      (a, 3rd m.). Alex Jesse Chapman (Nawinałá), 1907-1957 m. (1st) Ruby, *Nez Perce* (2nd) Mary Jim (dau. of Thomas Jim), 1910?-2000, *Palouse* (CJS)
      (b). Elizabeth (Kàmstikáyh? [NR]), 1909-1945 m. (1st) Isaac Hill, *Nez Perce* (2nd) Lloyd Wannassey, *Yakama* (3rd) Charley McKay
      (c). James, b. 1911
      (d). David, 1917-1918
   (1, 2nd m.). Peter Wolf (SHM) (A-la-cay) b. 1876?

B. Shap-ta-ka-win (Shaptaween [UAR], Peter Kaláytun),[7] b. 1848 m. (1st) To-yat, b.1857 (UAC) (2nd?) Wal-why-por, d. 1904 (UAR)
   (1, 1st m.). Peter Kaláytun (Pak-at-we-a-na, Little Pete),[8] 1867-1914? m. Hahomayet, b. 1868 (UAC)
   (2, 2nd m.). Joe Kaláytun (Húsis Ka-out),[8] b. 1869 m. (1st) Louise (Pe-tints), b. 1857 (2nd) Maria, b. 1872 (UAC)
      (a). Ko-laps ♂, b. 1882
      (b). Tot-son-it-son ♂, b. 1889
      (c). Agnes, b. 1898

(1, 2nd m.). A-low-ta-mup ♀ (UAR)
(2, 2nd m.). Peo-wats-som-my (UAR)

C. Wee-ash-i-wit (Weashuit, U-yes-wich) m. Quanspeetsah (niece of Chief Moses), *Moses-Columbia* (SM, CW)
    (1). Peter Dan Moses (Weashuit), 1861, Moses Coulee (RR)-1962 m. (1st) Catherine (Si-la-kia-mont), b. 1880 (2nd) Margaret Nellie Pakotas (his sister-in-law and dau. of Felix Kolockan and Nellie Sam, after Joe Moses' death [NA/GC])
        (a). Charlie Moses, 1895-1957 m. Katherine (Kittie) Jefferson Nanpooya Moses (dau. of Daniel and Amelia [Paween] Jefferson Greene), b. 1894 (RW)
        (b). Wapati, b. 1898
        (c). Annie, 1905-1989 m. Art Circle, 1900-1974 (son of Charlie Wilpocken, *Yakama* and *Alpiato*, Palouse)
        (d). Lucy Moses (II), b. 1905
    (2). Joe Moses (Quiltenenock [III], Spell-li-kulix), d. 1935 m. (1st) Quin-ho-péetsa[9] (Mary Ann, dau. of Swawilla?, d. 1929), 1879-1966 (2nd) Margaret Nellie Pakotas (SM)
        (a, 1st m.). William Quiltenenock, b. 1911 (CAC)
        (b). Addie (Thomas), b. 1912 (CAC)

D. Kel-we-son-mi (I), b. 1849 m. Chief Showaway (Sha-wa-way), 1834-1895?, *Cayuse*
    (1). Paul Showaway (Caton), 1861-1926 m. Peowatesonmi (Ida), b. 1862, *Yakama*
        (a). Wa-a-no-mox-mox-in-a ♂, b. 1884
        (b). Paul Jr., b. 1886
        (c). Abraham, b. 1890 m. Alice LaRoque, *Umatilla*
        (d). Dominic, b. 1894 m. Louise Billy, *Umatilla*
        (e). Josephine, b. 1898
        (f). Moses, b. 1905
        (g). William, b. 1908

E. Who-ko-ka-why-kin (IP)

1. Ky-yi-ky-yi, *Palouse-Wanapam* **m. Pashaspum (MF)**

A. Thomash, b. c. 1845 m. (1st) *Columbia* (2nd) Amyowit (Kistook), d. 1894? (3rd) Wawanay, d. 1908?[10]
    (1, 1st m.). Imnanonmy (Peloutspoo), d. 1887

2. To-yut'♀, *Palouse-Wanapam* **(MJ)**

3. Cawa-wátiak (BR) ("Fishhook Jim", Chowawatyet [CR]), raised near Leavy (VR), 1835?-1922, *Palouse-Wanapam* **m. Ámtalút (BR) (Whalits-pah [MJ], Millie), daughter of Xímtyutsá'kin (NR)**[11] **and K'aye'xla (VR), d. 1921**

    A. Annie Jim (Tu-yu-tu-yet, Xínway [NR]), b. 1854
        (1). Alice (Lutton)
        (2). Celia (Frank)
        (3). Maxine (McKinley)
        (4). Virginia (McKinley)
        (5). Bessie (McKinley Geary)

    B. Agnes Jim, b. 1876 (CAC)[12]
        (1). Charlie Jim (Xanáwxanáni [NR])
        (2). Helen (Sohappy)
        (3). Celia (How-to-pat)
        (4). Robert Tomalwash

    C. Thomas Jim (Alíwiya [NR], Aleeliah, Al-li-luya, Thomash), b. 1879 m. Lilplíptkwin (NR) (Annie (Lil-lipt-con [CAC], dau. of Tau-we-why and Xaluwáyx[13]), *Wanapam*
        (1). Mary Jim (Xínstanik), 1910?-2000 (CJS) m. Alex J. Chapman (Nawinałá [NR], son of Johnson Chapman)
        (2). Nancy, b. 1911? m. Harry Wyena
        (3). Henry Horn Jim, b. 1914 m. Lucy ?
        (4). Helen (Úsan'may [NR], 1915-2013 m. Wilson Sam
        (5). Lena (Mánmanix), 1910-1976 m. (1st) Shippentower (2nd) David Sampson

    D. Harry Jim (Xímtyutsá'kin [NR], Xumtu-st'aki [VR], Fu-ta-kin, Peter [CAC]), b. 1894?-1968 (CJS) m. (1st) Hatats (2nd) Madeline Moses (dau. of Joe Moses), 1898-1969, *Moses-Columbia*
        (1, 2nd m.). Agatha (Bart), b. 1924
        (2). Johnny Jim, m. Ina Thompson (dau. of Chief Tommy Thompson)

Notes

1. Since Chief Tilcoax likely had other wives whose identities are not known, the maternal affiliation of his children is not certain.
2. Wolf Necklace's year of birth is based on the 1894 Umatilla Agency census that lists "He-mean-ca-you/Old Wolf" at age 51. A son "A-la-cay" age 18 is also listed. Relander (1956) writes that Chief Wolf "was one of five brothers, his parents and the parents of Chief Moses being closely related."
3. According to Matilda Kalyton (1918), her parents separated "when I was young." Since Umatilla tribal censuses (e.g., 1898 and 1903) show two additional younger

children in I-ya-to-yik's household (Willie Wocatsie [Íɬxatwin], b. 1882, and Ke-hi-tal-set, b. 1884), they are likely her son and daughter by a subsequent marriage, and their father is identified as Wishpúsh by Noel Rude. Also note statement by Hay-Hay-Tah (Smith L. George) to W. C. Brown in 1932 that he was a nephew of "Tilcoax the Second."
4. According to Tom Andrews, Teek-ton-nay was the widow of Húsis Paween (Tom Andrews to WCB, May 1950). Maggie Kalyton/Kaláytun was the 82-year-old matriarch of the Kaláytun family residing on the Umatilla Reservation in 1896. Teek-ton-nay's sister was Wawanay, wife of the Palouse Dreamer Chief Thomash (MF).
5. Ka-lu-la-son-mi was a full sister to Wa-win-ta-la-yecht, wife of Walla Walla Chief Poker Jim (James Burke). They were the parents of Thomas, Charles, Clarence, James Jr., and Robert Burke.
6. Isaac Patrick is listed on the 1913 census as a stepson of Johnson Chapman indicating that he was Matilda Kalyton's son by a previous marriage (UAC). A 1901 Lee Moorhouse photograph shows a "Kalyton" and his younger wife, both identified as Cayuse (see S. Grafe, 2005, p. 107). In a 1981 interview, Mr. Patrick stated that he was raised by "Shep-la-kha-ween," likely Peter Kaláytun below.
7. Shap-ta-ka-win (Shaptaween, Peter Kaláytun) and Wolf Necklace as brothers stated in Colville Tribal Minutes (Peter Dan Moses and Picard), 1911 (CAR, NA).
8. Affiliations of Little Pete Kalyton, Joe Kalyton, and I-yi-to-yik are unclear in the Umatilla Reservation censuses.
9. Quin-ho-péetsa (Mary Ann Quiltenenock) was married to (1st) Whistocken, (2nd) Quiltenenock (II), and (3rd) Cash-cap-pose (Cultus Jim).
10. Wawanay and Wolf Necklace's wife, Teek-ton-nay, were siblings (MF).
11. According to Verne Ray's interview with Harry Jim (see Rigsby notes), Xímtyutsá'kin ("Shot in the Mouth") was a "Nez Perce born near Dayton, Pomeroy [and] hung [at] Walla Walla [for involvement in the] Whitman [killings]."
12. The 1916 Colville census of "Jim's Band at Fishook Bend in Snake River" lists widower Agnes Jim with three children: Ah-we-na-pa♀, b. 1908; Til-tin-sa♂, b. 1911; and Sky-wa-kon-i ♂, b. 1914.
13. When Mary Jim relocated to the Yakama Reservation about 1959, the family lived on the allotment of family elders Kúkya (Columbia Wildman [NR] c. 1867-1957) and his half-sister, Wówniyu (Annie Tamátutanik/Tu-ton-ick [NR], c. 1866-1970). Carrie Jim Schuster identified them as members of Lip-lipt-koon's family, and they may have been her siblings. Noel Rude records Kákya (Columbia Wildman) as brother to Táwiway and Wiyáynaksha, and half-brother to Wówniyu.

Part II/*Nápt*

Andrew George/Tipiyeléhne Xáyxayx (White Eagle)

Seven Drums on the Snake. *John Clement*

Oral History

"Nature is Our Teacher"

Our first opportunity to visit with Andrew George (1905-1989) came unexpectedly on November 15, 1980, on the Yakama Indian Reservation. This remarkable Palouse elder was named Washington's first "Living Treasure" by the 1989 Centennial Commission, and was related to the Kamiakin family. We met again on November 11, 1981, at the Wapato Longhouse and corresponded until his passing. The story of our first meeting is recounted in Clifford's Doubleday anthology of Native American literature, Earth Song, Sky Spirit *(1992):*

> Many times we had heard about the old Palouse medicine man who grew up the 'old way' along Snake River. Many times I had heard about Andrew George, it seemed, but I had never been able to track him down. Andrew George, it seemed, was always on the move, his services much in demand. To me, he was an Indian phantom, a spirit, a stick person from the Northwest. Sometimes I wondered if he existed at all.
>   …We walked to the front door of a house that we thought was that of Andrew George's daughter. I knocked and waited. Two little girls opened the door, and I asked, 'Does Andrew George live here?' Neither girl answered. They both giggled and ran off down a hall to the left. The door stood wide open, allowing the cold wind to swirl around the tidy living room. A few moments later an old man with long white hair emerged from the dark hallway…
>   Before I could say anything, he stepped through the open door, reached out his hands, and brought us inside. We entered his home in silence, and followed him to the kitchen table. Yes, I told myself, this is the man of my dream. I recognized him and he knew me. I know he had called me to his place to listen and learn.

Andrew George: I was born on the Palouse River and one of my earliest memories is when we were living there a big boat came to take some of us up the Snake River to the Nez Perce Reservation.

I was enrolled there [c. 1910] and spent time growin' up. I remember like a dream from long ago but I know they happened because of what my father and other friends would tell me. I remember goin' up the canyon there at Palouse Falls and seeing Beaver's claw marks in the rocks. My father [Smith L. George][1] lived all over the place—Snake River, Nez Perce, Spokane Reservation. I remember riding

Andrew George. *Matilda George*

a sleigh riding over there by Spokane! There was a small church down at the bottom of the hill.

My mother was Julia Johnson and her parents were part of the Redheart band.[2] They were sent to Oklahoma with Chief Joseph. She had a sister, La-et-ha-how, who was my aunt and told me about the hard time they had there; it was hard for her to talk about what all happened. I learned lots of things growing up about our history and Coyote stories—how the land was made and how salmon came to the rivers. It was all the Creator's plan, just like it says in the Bible although they didn't have it. The Indians knew these things too, just like it says in the Bible about the great flood. There was dry land then on top of Steptoe Butte. We heard their stories over and over again and the elders had us repeat them just like we heard so we got it right. Our history is our stories, and you can see them in the rocks.

In spring and summer we fished everywhere—Snake River, Clearwater River, Spokane River. Salmon and Coyote are wise and taught us how to live. Our elders said to respect them and learn and never hunt or fish all the animals, but there would come a time when they would disappear. Damming up the rivers is just like cutting off the blood to your arm or leg. You can live for a while without some parts of your body; but keep cutting off the flow and sooner or later you'll die. That's how it is with the rivers and salmon.

I didn't learn the English language till I was older. Grew up talkin' Palouse and Nez Perce. It's a good thing to study and share knowledge to help others. But nature is our teacher. You can see God in

His creation and we should watch and learn. Scientists try to know about nature, but to know nature is something different. The plants, the animals, the rocks, are all there to teach us if we watch and listen and respect them—this is what the Seven Drums mean.[3] The books say that these Coyote stories [are] from people who imagined, but to me these things are true to fact.

I have seen for myself where things happened in Coyote's time, the shape of rocks and rivers and lakes. The history of my family and people has been told by my uncles and other elders and is written in the ancient rocks. You can't read it all in a book or understand it all; you can only see it. The drums, the Seven Drums beating and the words of the song, speak the same truths as are in the Bible. Listen, you can hear them. Truth is the same everywhere.

The dams have covered many places but when the kingdom comes all the people who were turned into rocks will come to life to face judgment. The Bible has the same words like Coyote taught. But today Coyote is unwanted, unrecognized, unprotected—a victim of wanton destruction by "civilized" man. Yet God made Coyote; he had plenty to eat without sheep or cattle. He had no worries until the white man came and destroyed the rabbits, sage hens, prairie chickens, and other fowls of the sage[lands]; even destroyed the vegetation. These are the reasons for Coyote's wrath.

We lived with the seasons like God planned. Early spring [March-April] was *Aha-mi*—"Crows Acomin';" then *Hish-hush* [May-June]—"Bugs Coming," when you dig roots, then *Shih-tash*, "Movin' Out" [July-August]. *Yaka-tash* was "Fishing Time" back on the river in fall [September-October], then *Yaku-kela* when the sun comes back. Winter [January-February] is *Tzinbuk*.[4]

We also have names in Nez Perce for the seasons. Spring is *El-weth*, summer is *Ti-yum, Sek-nihm* means fall, and *A-nihm* is winter. There are also the twelve months:

Lah-tee-tahl is March, the Moon of Blossoming Flowers.
Keh-khee-tahl is April, the Moon of the *Keh-Kheet* Root.
Ah-pah-al is May, the Moon of *Ah-pah* Bread.[5]
Toos-te-ma-sah-tahl is June, the Moon of Mountain Roots.

Koi-ya-ahl is July, the Moon of the Summer Salmon.
Tah-ya-ahl is August, the Moon of Hot Weather.
Pe-khoon-mi-kahl is September, the Moon of Fall Salmon.
Hope-lul is October, the Moon of Shedding Tamarack Needles.
Sekh-le-wahl is November, the Moon of Falling Leaves.
Ha-oo-koy is December, the Moon of Deer [Embryo] Forming.
Wai-lu-poop is January, the Moon of Cold Weather.
Ah-la-tah-mahl is February, the Moon of Swelling Buds.

Our memorial ceremonies honor the past. Sometimes non-Indians come and are respected. We hold the *Wáshat* here in the [Yakima] Valley, and along the Snake and Columbia, and on into Idaho. These ceremonies are done for the new foods that are to bloom so we can dig them, and for the salmon to return to the mountain streams. We pray for this new, fresh food to be processed for the coming year. At the dinner we first honor the clean water, and give then thanks for the Creator's foods, starting with salmon and deer meat, and the roots and berries. Lots of work for everyone to prepare! All are welcome to show respect for these gifts, and so the children and everyone can learn the sacred ways that give life.

Notes

1. Smith L. George's (Ta-harts, Hay-hay-tah) date of birth is shown variously on censuses as 1867 and 1870. He was raised by relatives from a young age on the Umatilla and Nez Perce reservations. According to an interview in the 1920s with historian W. C. Brown, he was related to Chief Tilcoax of the Lower Palouse. In 1937 he is listed as being married to Emma Wilpocken with children Elsie Comedown (1905-1937) and Frank George (1912-1968). He was also the father of Andrew, Mabel (b/d. 1910), and Ruby (Williams) by his first wife, Julia (Redheart) Johnson.
2. Julia (Redheart) Johnson was the daughter of Palouse band exiles in Indian Territory, Ip-na-mat-we-kin and Ah-na-ne-mart (Dick and Fannie Johnson). Julia Johnson's siblings were La-et-ha-yow ♀ and Mark Johnson.
3. For the Seven Drums religion, or *Wáshat*, see Robert H. Ruby and John A. Brown, *Dreamer Prophets of the Columbia Plateau: Smohalla and Skolaskin* (1989); and Eugene Hunn (with James Selam), *Nch'i-Wana: The Big River, Mid-Columbia Indians and Their Land* (1990).
4. Andrew provides the Northeast Sahaptin seasonal terms known to the Lower Palouse and Wanapam peoples.
5. *Ah-pah* bread was made from dried kouse root.

Oral History

Chief Cleveland Kamiakin/ Pyúpyu Kównot

Interviewed by Nat Washington, October 1956, Ephrata, Washington; translation (Northern Sahaptin) by Carrie Jim Schuster (2008).

The following narrative is excerpted from two recordings during research for the book, Finding Chief Kamiakin. *The first recording is from an October 1956 interview conducted by Nat Washington with Cleveland Kamiakin, Billy Curlew, and interpreter Harry Nanamkin (Nánamqan). The other is from a presentation made the same week by these three elders at a meeting of the Grant County Historical Society in Ephrata. Washington's interview questions generally relate to place names and local history of the Moses Lake-Ephrata-Soap Lake area. Because this region was part of the Moses-Columbia Band homeland, many of the questions were directed to Billy Curlew who spoke in Moses Columbia Salish. The interview likely took place on Monday, October 8, 1956.*

Washington periodically directed questions to Cleveland through Harry Nanamkin, whose native language was Yakama Sahaptin. Cleveland replied in Sahaptin, distinguished by slightly different pronunciations of some words and Cleveland's occasional use of Nez Perce suffixes. The interview was originally recorded on a reel-to-reel tape recovered by Michael Finley and staff members at the Colville Confederated Tribes Office of History and Archaeology. The recording of the historical society presentation (KIT-79-117) was found by historian Barbara Owen in an uncatalogued Ellensburg Public Library collection of oral histories and kindly made available by librarian Milton Wagy. David Wicks and David Rither at Seattle Pacific University transferred the original recordings to a digital format.

Because Nanamkin tended to provide general summaries rather than literal translations of the two chiefs' words, copies of both recordings were shared with native Sahaptin speaker Carrie Jim Schuster of the Yakama Reservation who provided a literal translation of Cleveland's remarks. Carrie noted that the tone of Cleveland's voice suggests the bittersweet nature of his visit to landscapes of his youth. Carrie remembered seeing Cleveland in the 1950s when she traveled to Nespelem to attend family gatherings and special Longhouse events.

Colville Confederated Tribes History and Archaeology Office recording

Chief Cleveland Kamiakin: This is how it was. Spilyaí (Coyote) made everything. Whatever he said, he did it just like that. We came to know such things through stories. He was very smart and brave. He went around, he made this sweathouse. He bent over and hollowed out the rock and then he sweated. He was skillful and gifted. He had power and was cunning. He was someone to be reckoned with! It was awesome, and he finished it wonderfully… He finished it so my children can see it and they will. This is Spilyaí's work. They will tell the story, then tell other stories, and then they will know he did it.

I will tell the story of the sweathouse he made out of rock. That is where he made the sweathouse, he made it out of rock and I have seen it. My friend was skillful, intelligent, and masterful, and whatever he said, he made it. That is how it was, how Spilyaí was. Now I have seen it. He made it that way, where he went and sweated and where he made the water to go in. This is where he dipped and that is why the water is there, why the swimming hole is there. I am so happy I have seen it with my friends and I am going to go back and tell stories, tell everybody that I have seen it. It is made out of rock and that is how he made it. It is awesome, just awesome. It will be a good story, a really good story. That is all I have to say. I am glad that you boys brought me here, that you called this old man [Billy Curlew] and he wanted this old man [Cleveland] to come along. What I am telling you is good so we have told you.

They called it [the camp at *Sēolokun*] *Khahún* [in Sahaptin].[1] The white people called them "suckers," and then others say it a little differently. They used to just call it *Awnut'*, plentiful as mosquitoes. They called it *Khawúnus* because of the suckers. They called

Billy Curlew, Harry Nanamkin, and Cleveland Kamiakin, Ephrata, Washington, 1956. *Cull A. White Collection, MASC, WSU Libraries, Pullman.*

it *Khawúnus*. That is what I know. They used to bring their dip nets. They used to get the suckers. They used dip nets. It was good food because of the supply. Others would come and they would use gunnysacks and it was wonderful. Good food, good to eat and that is how that food took care of us. They did it and used nets and then they used the hemp and they got them that way. That is how they got them here. They used to come from Nespelem. "Let's go get suckers!" Then they used to come here. They would bring what was needed to catch them. That is what this place was for a long time back. That is how they used to get the food.

[I came here today because] Billy Curlew is from here and said, "You better come here with him and we are going to tell the history, how the elders used to roam across this area and gathered food here, how good this land was and how they lived here safely." But I am not strong like I used to be. I was telling him that I am an orphan [ánot'atnushwa] from everywhere. I am separated from all my homelands. I am not helping him because I am not strong and

I am full of concerns so I cannot. This is the elders' land. They used to go all around here… My father's name was K'amáyakun.

We used to go up to the right and then come down. That is why it is called *Indupasnuwít*. They used to go there to get caught up on the news. Now I do not know anything about that—about [traders] coming from the east. I do not know about it so cannot speak about it. I know where that place is. That is where there is a sheer drop. I know that place. [Question asked about trading for cow hides.] I do not know about the trade there and I am not going to tell about it. I can only tell you that when my uncle was a boy, his father told him to go to *Indupasnuwít*. That is when there were lots of Indians. That is all I know and I am not going to go this way or that way and tell something untrue.

ELLENSBURG PUBLIC LIBRARY RECORDING

Interview with Cleveland Kamiakin and Billy Curlew, Grant County Historical Society Meeting, Ephrata, Washington, October 1956

Moderator [unidentified]: The first man here is Mr. Cleveland Kamiakin, now of Nespelem, formerly of the Palouse Country where his father had a great empire until we deprived him of it. He was the head of the Yakama and all the confederated tribes. He was supreme chief of all the Northwest. He organized the rebellion of 1858…Our next man is Billy Curlew, the horseman I was telling you about. Billy was born right here…in 1862 and knows about this country, Moses Lake, Vantage, and the Wenatchee country. The next is Mr. Harry Nanamkin. Harry, if you will tell them a few things about the trip.

Harry Nanamkin: First I want to say that we are glad to meet you people here, that you invited us to come, that you invited my chiefs who have been our leaders for a number of years. They are trying to work out the problems of our tribes. There are several tribes in the Colville Reservation which they represent and they work for the people, not for themselves. They just work for the people, that's the way they work and lead. We call them our "chiefs" and they're both original chiefs of the Colville Reservation…

We are from the Colville Reservation which I was born in Colville [Reservation] and I am sixty-nine years old…We have been moved from this country a number of years ago. So the purpose of this trip now, [with] Billy Curlew and Chief Kamiakin, is to try to locate the old campsites which they had the names for each camp and each draws and springs and different things is unlocated now. But the future is comin' but in their heart, that is this country will soon to be settled thicker, and the country where we was today and the day before is unnamed in the map. But in their work now someday the country will be thickly settled, settlers come in or towns or something be built…

Moderator: If you will just ask Cleveland to say just a few words about the people, about how he feels and this trip and the historical society.

Cleveland Kamiakin [stands]: We are gathering here at a special place and it still holds it sacredness (*ahtow´*).[2] I am not here to speak a lot, but he [Billy Curlew] will speak about the sacredness of this land and how it provided all our needs. I came along to be an encouragement to my friend and he can tell of this place. That is all I have to say now. [applause]

Billy Curlew: Now you heard my friend Cleveland address himself to the people. The record shows that I was born right in this place we called *Tacht-ti-hai* [Cottonwood Place]. [A]nd I want to say we have carried on our leadership for three generations. Moses' father—he was a leader in this country. When he went away, Moses became a chief. Now he is gone and left; now I'm appointed chief. I'm the third leader and we call the tribe Sin-ki-yous.[3]

Our people of Sulkstalkscosum's time, they were trying to protect their rights. They knew this country was sacred, that they made their subsistence and living for every person who lived in this country. There have been certain changes in just a few years. Now that I see you people here and I'll be glad to see that you progress here and make your living in this rich country. The two leaderships—Kamiakin and Sulkstalkscosum—had covered a lot of territory. It went clear in to the Palouse and to what is the Big Bend country now. I want to advise you to carry on taking care of the country, to go ahead and protect the country for your children are comin' and the population that is comin'. You should take my advice and try to work in the best interest you can to protect the country [interrupting applause]…

Nat Washington: As I learned from them and I didn't know it before, this was a large camp area…in the area of the [Ephrata] Harvell Addition…Cleveland Kamiakin went up there with us yesterday and of course the whole thing is changed. In his day there were a large grove of chokecherry trees—the largest grove of chokecherries in the area—hardwood, and the trees grew in a grove in a more or less easterly-westerly direction and the creek came right down from where the Episcopal Church is….

There were trees on both sides and this was a large camp. They said the tribes came from every direction because this was the best spot in the whole area for the camas that they dug. And the Palouse, the Nez Perce, the Yakamas, the Wenatchis, the Okanogans, the Methow, San Poil, and the Nespelems, the Wanapums, Sinkiuse [Moses Columbia], they came here and they camped for about a month or six weeks every spring to gather the camas…

Each tribe would camp in various places but they all lived together in almost complete harmony although the Sinkiuse with Chief Moses, this was their territory, yet they had the best camas country, so they allowed all the rest of the tribes to come in. They had a real peaceful, intelligent way of living, and all the tribes came in peacefully. Then we went up to the canyon to back towards where the Schimps live, and there are little flat places all the way up. And they said in the olden days there would be tipis on both sides of the creek all the way up and many tipis all out in the flat along the creek here. The Indians came from all over Eastern Washington, gathered in a great big camp. He said, "a big camp"…

Moderator: [Recent death of Wanapum leader Pakáyatut (Johnny Buck) noted.] Smohalla, the leader of that group, had many, many thousands of Indians that he controlled and not through force. He never signed a treaty or indulged in any military engagement or resistance, but he simply ruled them as Christ or Mahatma Gandhi or as some of these spiritual leaders did, which of all we have is the strongest leadership in the world. That, after all, is what Billy meant when he said we want to take care of the country…

If you will ask him [Cleveland] if he remembers any battles his father told him between these Indians here—say the Columbias and the Palouse.

Harry Nanamkin: I can ask but can answer that question pretty well [myself]. You see, these battles wasn't the Palouse because the Palouse people had been with our people; same thing. But it was the Eastern people over in the Rocky Mountains which had attacked this area. But they don't come only certain times; maybe might take two or three or four years. Then all the family, what I want to say, we had to live *in the group*, to protect the people, the growin'-up children, the womenfolk, the children. That is why that man talked and showed that people traveled *in the group*—that was the purpose of it…

A group of people lived and they had one leadership. As we call these tribes here, we had about six or seven tribes here, we called "groups." They were awful careful in their marrying in the people. It had to be a royalty family[4] to marry 'cause they might lose the work that the people had tried to protect the future of the country…And that is one reason why they had each family or chief has what they called a royalty family, and these people married…

Moderator: Let Cleveland speak [in closing].

Cleveland Kamiakin [stands]: I will say a few things. I am happy that we have gathered here. It is good that we are having good fellowship because we must live together on the same land; one people to another, face to face. We have families, communities, in friendship on this land. I will not tell [you] how to manage the land, but my food is also here and I hope we can continue to gather it. You use this land for your needs as we have ours. May we live together.

I finish by saying that I have been here to support my friend [Billy Curlew] and I have already shared what is important about maintaining a sacred way with the land, and all creatures, so all of us can dwell here.

NOTES

1. Near the Rocky Ford Creek crossing in Grant County between present Moses Lake and Ephrata.
2. According to translator Carrie Jim Schuster (2008), the Northern Sahaptin term *ahtów* may be rendered "sacred" in English but also implies spiritual recognition of the "covenant" established by the Creator to provide sustenance to humankind, plants, and animals. (*Tamánwit* and *tamálwit,* respectively, are the Northern Sahaptin cognate terms for "law" and "custom.") In the context of Cleveland's parting words to his Ephrata audience, Carrie observes, "He doesn't tell the farmers not to cultivate the land, but he implies this is not his way. He asks that they respect the Indians' recognition that the land's natural resources are to be protected as a sacred obligation in order to sustain the Indian people. The desire to get something more than we need and are provided leads persons, families, and even countries to do things that are harmful to the land and to life. This is what Chief Kamiakin and our elders meant when they spoke about the "law" to [Governor] Stevens and others who wanted to make the treaties. For the sake of our children and in accordance with these sacred ways we must respect the land and water and not pollute it as is happening now." She further relates that the stories of the Animal People handed down over generations provide "lessons" (*sikwána,* from *sikwa,* "teach") about this law in order to understand the world's sacred origin and obligations to creation, family, and others. Bruce Rigsby observes, "God can be called *Tamanwilá* ("Law-Giver, Ordainer") in Sahaptin," and that "Naxiyamtáma traditional-customary land title does not originate from acts of the sovereign, nor from sale and purchase, nor even inheritance… Instead, the oral literature tells us there was a time before there were human beings. The Spirit-Beings who lived on the land then are called *Wat'ítaš* in Northwest Sahaptin. Principal among them was Spilyáy ("Coyote"), who fashioned many landforms and features and instituted the norms of human law and custom—that is, culture and society. Elements of the oral literature function as paper (or electronic) deeds do for owners and nonowners alike" (B. Rigsby, "The Stevens Treaties, Indian Claims Commission Docket 264, and the Ancient One Known as Kennewick Man," in A. Harmon, 2008:252).

3. The Sinkiuse or Moses-Columbia tribe.
4. The term "royalty family" is from the expression *miyawaxu´wica*, or "chiefly class," which is derived from the Sahaptin word *miyawax*, or chief. Anthropologist Bruce Rigsby observes that "this status was not overtly claimed, but respectfully understood" (B. Rigsby, personal communication with the editors, 2009).

Wallula Spring. *John Clement*

"Salmon Man and the Wolf Brothers"

Retold by Andrew George (1980)

In the time of the Animal People
   there was a big village
      down along the river.
Salmon Man lived there.
Many maidens wanted him
   because he was strong and brave.
But Salmon liked the beautiful sister
      of the Wolf Brothers.

Salmon Man thought it over
   when the Wolf Brothers were away.
They were away,
   gathering firewood for sweatbaths.
Salmon made up his mind
   to go to their sister's lodge….
He wore a fancy headdress,
   feathers green and red.
He stood outside, and she knew.
She could tell by the sound of his walk
   and his pleasing scent.

Salmon Man waited outside.
He stood at the Wolf Sister's door for a while….
Then he decided to leave.
But the Wolf Sister knew he was there.
She pulled back the door.
"Do you want to visit me?" she asked.
Salmon told her,
    "I want you to come with me.
      If you want to come,
         then get ready to leave."

The Wolf Brothers were jealous
   of Salmon Man.
He knew they would try to get him.
The Wolf Sister gathered her things
   while Salmon Man watched outside.
Soon she was ready to go
   and called for his help
      to carry the bundles.
But one of the Wolf Brothers returned,
   came along the river with firewood.
He saw her clothing wrapped in hides.
"Are you planning to go with him?"
The Wolf Sister saw he was angry,
   so she walked over to Salmon.
"You belong with us," her brother said.
Salmon Man says,
   "She is coming downriver with me."
And they loaded the bundles in a canoe.
"They will not get far!"
   the Wolf Brother told the others.

The Wolf Brothers made plans,
   they wanted to kill Salmon Man
      for taking their sister….
They ran to Old Lady Spider,
   all of them, and said to her,
"You can do anything;
   your poison can kill Salmon."
But the old lady said,
   "How can I do this to my friend?"
So they went to Grandfather Coyote.
They said, "You must help us,
   Salmon Man took our sister."
"You are all my relatives," he said.
"How can I hurt anyone in my family?"

The Wolf Brothers went on,
   they traveled far away
      to Rattlesnake's lodge….
"You can kill Salmon Man
   with a single bite," they told him.
He thought it over, he told them,
   "Why hurt someone
      who does not bother me?"
The Wolf Brothers told Rattlesnake
   that Salmon had wronged them.
They told him, that is why.
They offered him warm furs
   for winter, and other goods.
He agreed to help.
The Wolf Brothers put Rattlesnake
   in the front of Salmon's canoe
      where it rested by large rocks.
Salmon Man did not see.

Salmon Man stepped into the canoe.
He was carrying a bundle
   of the Wolf Sister's belongings.
He felt a sharp sting,
   the pain of Rattlesnake's bite.
Salmon Man turned around;
   he fell onto a flat rock.
A Wolf Brother drew his bow.
He shot Salmon Man in the head.
The others fell upon him,
   cutting with flint knives,
      and threw the pieces onto the sand….
That is how a tiny piece
   fell in the water,
      and floated away.

When Rattlesnake and the Wolf Brothers
   had killed Salmon Man,
      they decided to travel back upriver.
The brothers were jealous
   if anyone else was interested,
      and wanted their sister.
She did much of the work.
She worked around their camp.
Rattlesnake had killed Salmon Man,
   and did not return to his lodge.
He found a cave on a rocky cliff,
   high above the river.
This became his home.

Rain fell for five days and five nights.
The little piece of Salmon Man
   that fell during his death struggle
      floated down the river.
Life soon moved inside.
A smolt grew and began to swim.
Faraway it went and became stronger,
   faraway beyond the mountains.
Young Chinook grew in the ocean.
One day he was ready to return home.
He brought the warm air of the great water.

Young Chinook became strong
   and made a bow and arrows;
      carried them toward the mountains.
He knew his father had been killed.
He swam past Celilo and found
   the familiar waters of the big river.
Sometimes he walked along the shore,
   and then returned to the water.
He came to the lodge of Old Lady Spider
   and saw her spinning in the corner.

"What are you doing there?"
"Just making clothes," she said.

Young Chinook continued upriver.
He heard a noise and found
   Coyote sitting on a rock.
He was splitting *kaamúukii*.
"What are you making?"
Coyote said, "I'm making a net
   to catch lots of fish
      when they pass by here."
Young Chinook remembered
   to avoid that place.
And he kept on going
   along the river.

Young Chinook reached
   his father's old home.
He stepped ashore and
   onto Sandpiper's nest.
He broke Sandpiper's leg.
"Tell me where the Wolf Brothers live;
   I will fix your leg."
Sandpiper told him
   and warned of Rattlesnake
      living in a high canyon cave.
Young Chinook fashioned a leg
   from a twig for Sandpiper.
He traveled a long time
   and saw Rattlesnake's home.

Young Chinook made his way
   up the rocky slope.
He saw Rattlesnake
   sunning himself nearby.
Young Chinook aimed an arrow.

Rattlesnake pleaded for his life.
"Don't hurt me, Nephew;
   I know why you have come."
"I have power you need
   to defeat the Wolf Brothers."
Young Chinook put down his bow.
Rattlesnake kept his word.
He took out some of his teeth
   for Young Chinook
      to put into his mouth.

Young Chinook traveled
   to the river's faraway headwaters.
He saw smoke coming up
   from the Wolf Brothers' camp.
Their sister cried as she worked.
They only went outside
   to drink from the river.
Young Chinook hid in the water.
One by one, he bit them
   on the mouth as they came.
Rattlesnake's poison
   worked its power.
Before one could howl,
   pulled beneath the waters.

Young Chinook, powerful and brave,
   yelled his victory song! "Oweee!!!"
The Wolf Sister heard the shout
   and ran from the lodge.
She recognized his voice
   and went to greet him.
Young Chinook took her as his wife
   and they returned together
      to his father's home.

"Why Coyote Made the Palouse Hills"[1]

Retold by Andrew George (1980)

The Animal People gathered
   on *Pik'úunen*[2] long ago.
Coyote challenged anyone
   in a race to the Spokane River.
Coyote boasted,
   "Nobody can outrun me!"
Blue Jay, Marmot, and others stepped away.
Only Magpie and Turtle said,
   "We will race."
The others laughed;
   Turtle in race with Coyote and Magpie!

At that time the land beyond Snake River
   was broad prairie.
Coyote could not believe
   that anyone could be faster.
But he wanted to be sure.
The other creatures danced and sang all night.
Coyote went onto the prairie
   and pushed all that land into hills,
      and danced across the land.
Turtle would go up and down each one.
Magpie would tire of the long way
      and slow down before the end.
But Turtle called his three brothers.
"Coyote has been away;
   he has changed the land!

---

[1] A similar version of this story involving the Turtle Brothers and Eagle is found in Eileen Yanan and Cecelia Timentwa Condon, eds., *Coyote and the Colville* (1971:71-74).
[2] A Nez Perce word for the lower Snake River.

So Turtle sent his brothers onto the hills.
They lined up on top of hills before dawn
   between the rivers.
In the morning Coyote, Magpie, and Turtle
   line up on near the river's edge.
Blue Jay signals to begin.
Coyote leaps high over the hills nearby.
Turtle slowly crawls behind
   and Magpie flies by.
Coyote jumps again
   and sees Turtle
      walking over the hilltop ahead.
Coyote goes on
   but finds Turtle right there.
Coyote leaps as far as he can,
   and Turtle is there again!
Coyote begins to tire.
Magpie flies fast from the river,
   and sees Coyote and Turtle far ahead.
He knows Coyote changed the land;
   knows the Turtle Brothers are on the hills.
Magpie screams and still complains today!
Coyote jumps ahead with all his strength
      and falls worn out at the finish.
Turtle finished just ahead of him!
See who is most clever!

The Kamíakin Family

Chief Kamíakin (K'amáyaqan, Kamiahkin, Kamiakun, Kamaiyah), 1800?-1877[1]
Parents: T'siyiyak (I) (Ci-iah [TK], Si-yi-yah, Ki-yi-yah) and Com-mus-ni (TK) (Ka-mosh-nite, Kah-mas-night, Ka-e-mox-nith [AJS], dau. of Chief Weowicht), *Yakama-Wenatchi* (?)[2]
Brothers: Showaway (Ice on the Water); Skloom (Šklú·m [BR])

1st wife: Sunk-hay-ee (Shan-kia-haw, [SW]; Tsan-kah, [AJS], dau. of Chief Teias), *Yakama*
   1. Yamnaneek[3] (Yannaneck, Yum-monik [CR], Catherine), 1837-1907 (EP)
      A. Hattie? (CAC)

2nd wife: Kem-ee-yowah (SW) (To-me-ye-ou-wauk [TK], Timeoch [MK], dau. of Chief Tenax, *Klickitat*), d. 1901? (MK)
   1. We-yet-que-wit (Wee-at-kwal Tsick'-en [Talking Hunter], Young Kamiakin [SW, CAC], Umatilla Kamiakin [SHM]), 1840?-1886 near Palúus m. (1st) Agatha?[4] (SHM)(dau. of "Yellow Head" [MK] [Husishusis Moxmox]) (2nd) Tallas (Theresa) Koltsenshin (dau. of Gabriel and Theresa Koltsenshin),[5] d. 1905?, *Coeur d'Alene*
      A (1st m.). Joseph?, b. 1869 (SHM)
      B (2nd m.). Ellen Chamayakan (Helen Kamiakin), b. 1874 m. Louis Pe-ell (Pierre), b. 1874, *Coeur d'Alene-Colville* (SHM)
         (1). Catherine m. Samuel Meshell (son of Antoine Meshell), *Kalispel*
         (2). Raymond, 1910-1968 m. Mildred Nick (dau. of Moses Nick), b. 1918
         (3). Teresa, 1913-1917
         (4). Mary, b. 1918
         (5). Samuel, b. 1921

   2. Yumasepah (Chamesupum [SW], Mollie, Mary), 1845-1920[6] m. Peopeo-hy-yi-toman (Whistling Bird, "a first cousin to Young Chief Joseph," [SW]), d. 1898 (near Colfax, WCB), *Palouse-Nez Perce*
      A. Pe-nock-ton-my, 1880-c.1908 m. Johnnie Pe-el, b. 1879
      B. Sophie Kamiakin (Atwice), b. 1889 m. (1st) Tipyahlahnah Elassanin (Roaring Eagle, George Comedown, son of Wa-ya-mas-ta-kekt [Hiteyehmistaket, Charley Comedown[7]], 1856-1918? and Pomowtonmy (Pe-me-qui-nt), 1863-1936? [CAC]), b. 1882, *Nez Perce, Joseph Band* (CAC) (2nd) Isaac Wak-wak (son of Sam Wak-wak), b. 1895, *Umatilla* (UAC)

(1, 1st m.). Ned Comedown, 1909-1968
(2). Kes-les-tum (Elva Gould?, b. 1913)
(1, 2nd m.). Martha, 1916-1918 (UAC)
(2). Joseph, b. 1917 (UAC)
(3). Nancy, b. 1921 m. Matthew Goudy, b. 1921, *Yakama*
(4). Walter, b. 1925

C. Ta-lats Ton-my (Telestonmy, Susie) m. Ko-san-yum (E-yu-mah-klt, Luke Wilson [SR], son of Koh-sauh [Wolfhead, JD] and Pe-not-ye-et-yakt [SW]), b. 1870?, *Nez Perce*
(1). Hattie, b. 1890
(2). Henry, 1896-1943 m. Sadie Paul (Moses/Wilson/Williams, dau. of Tiscosarkowkow [William Paul] and Tom-quin-wit [Lucy Moses]), 1898-1977, *Nez Perce*
(3). George
(4). Helen

3. Tespaloos (Tespalúus, Tesh Palouse, Tish?), 1858-1933, Nespelem m. (1st) Pas-as-pam (Annie Kentuck, sister of Moses Kentuck?), d. 1890, *Palouse* (2nd) Me-a-tu-kin-ma (Im-a-to-i-kin-my [CAC], Mary, dau. of Tee-wa-tee-na-set [Waughaskie, Charley "Chief" Bones, 1827?-1915] and Me-a-tat, b. 1844), 1859-1931, *Cayuse* (3rd) Elizabeth (Eliza) Skumsit, b. 1865 (NA/GC)

Tesh Palouse Kamiakin. *McWhorter Collection, MASC, WSU Lbraries, Pullman.*

A (2nd m. [JD]). Mul-mul-kin[8] (Kos-al-ich-kin, Cooselican, Sam Tespaloos), b. 1891 (CAC) m. (1st) "a coast woman" (CW) (2nd) Annie (dau. of Pee-chee and Que-matk, *Wenatchi*, later married Billy Yellow Wolf [Homas], son of Yellow Wolf, 1856-1935 [LVM]), 1886-1966
(1, 2nd m.). Jeanie (Jenny), b/d. 1910
(2). Alexander, 1910-1917

B. Kay-yee-wach (Peter Gibson, Pete Bones, Hiyouwath Kamiakin), 1895?-1954 (MF) m. O-in-ta-tot-mi (Lucy)

3rd wife: Wal-luts-pum (MK) (Why-lats-pam [LVM])

1. T'siyiyak (II) (Williams, T'si-yi-ach [MK], Siyiyah, A-pas-teem-na? [TK]), 1854?-1901? at Moses Lake (WCB) m. Ni-ka-not, 1859-1937 (granddaughter of Chief Slowiarchy the Younger, Silpimkin) *Palouse*

A. Charley Kamiakin Williams (Te-meh-yew-te-toot), 1879, near Starbuck-1969 m. Alalumti (II) (Susie Chief, dau. of Koots-koots Tsom-ya-whet [Little Man Chief],[9] b. 1847 and Iatotkikt, b. 1837), 1888-1971, *Nez Perce* (AA)
    (1). Edward (Its-i-ya-ya-et-in), 1908-1966
    (2). Ida (Timentwa/Grant/Desautel), 1910-94
    (3). Walter, 1912-1961
    (4). Virginia, 1918-96 m. Albert Andrews, *Palouse-Nez Perce*
    (5). Abel, 1920-1944
    (6). Clayton (Tu-we-ni-e-cum), 1922-76
B. William, b. 1881 (CAC)
C. Mary (Ka-mosh-nite), b. 1888 (CAC) m. Smith L. George[10] (Tah-harts [NPC], Hay-hay-tah [WCB], Heheestah [FA]), b. 1870?, *Nez Perce*
    (1). Frank George, 1912-1968 m. Annie (Cleveland, dau. of Cleveland Kamiakin), 1910-1997
    (2). Winnie, b. 1914
    (3). Delia, 1917-1986 m. George Covington (son of Alex Covington and Lucy Hawk), b. 1924
D. Gilbert (Na-ta-quen-et), b. 1893 m. Sadie Paul (Moses/Wilson/Williams, dau. of Tiscosarkowkow [William Paul] and Tom-quin-wit [Lucy Moses]), 1898-1977 (JD)

2. Lukash [EP] (Luke, Neu-Cass (MK), Lo-keest´ [WCB], Locos [RR], Kee-yow-ah-kin [TK]), 1858?-1886 m. Sinsinq't (III), 1855?-1888 (Shim-shin-kt, dau. of Chief Moses, 1829-1899), *Columbia-Yakama*
    A (2nd m.). Qu-qua-la-que ♂, drowned in infancy (RR, CW)
    B. Nellie Kamiakin Moses (Sinsinq't [IV]), 1883-1958 m. (1st) Louis Friedlander (son of J. H. Friedlander), 1879-1912 (2nd?) Antoine Francis, 1888-1934
        (1). Emily (Kamooli), 1902-1984 m. Walter Peone, 1904-1971, *Coeur d'Alene*
        (2). George, 1904-1977 m. Celeste Minthorn (dau. of Grover Minthorn and Minnie Wak-wak, *Umatilla* [GG]), 1913-1976, *Umatilla*
        (3). Thomas, b. 1908
        (4). Lucy (Sinsinqt), 1910-1982 m. John Covington, 1915-1958, *San Poil-Columbia*
        (5). Louis Jr., b. 1913-1998 m. (1st) Eileen, *San Poil* (2nd) Helen Stewart

3. Sk'ees (EP) (Sk'eec, Petescot? [MK])[11]

98 *River Song*

    4. Skolumkee (Its-ka-lum-key, "Snake River"), 1867-1949, Nespelem m. Pe-malks (Annie Shumkin, sister to Teshpaloos's third wife), 1861-1957 (no children)

4th wife: Hos-ke-la-pum (CK) (Aus-kil-ah-pum [MK], Oskalappam [AM]), d. 1877? buried at *Palús* (CK)

    1. **Kiatana (Ka-you-to-nay [SW], Ki-ow-tan-nee, Ka-za-ta-ni [LVM], Lucy), 1862-1946, Nespelem m. (1st) Palouse (2nd) Ben Awhi (Owhi), 1854-1927 (son of Kluckni, d. 1861 and Sque-malks [Mary Hyockpal, dau. of Chief Owhi, EP]),** *Yakama-Palouse,* **(3rd) Que-em-le-ke (John Hayes), 1867-1941,** *Nez Perce*

        A (2nd m.). Harry Awhi (Owhi), 1894-1955 m. (1st) Mary Mocton, 1896-1951 (dau. of Wa-non-no Ilpilp [Charlie Mocton], b. 1869, *Nez Perce, Joseph Band* [CAC]), (2nd) Annie (Chuweah) (U-pa-pi Paween, dau. of Tom Paween), 1893-1989, *Palouse* (CAC)

            (1, 1st m.). McKinley, 1912-1916

            (1, 2nd m.). Rosville (Roscoe), 1919-1976

            (2). Martha, 1922-1941 m. Peter (Agapith) Judge, 1911-1970, *Wenatchi*

            (3). Dora (Francis), 1924-1971

            (4). Bertha (Williams), 1926-2001

            (5). Harry Jr., b. 1926

    2. **Pyúpyu Kównot (Bird of the Morning, Cleveland, Peter) 1870-1959, Nespelem m. (1st) Yup-cha-sin (Annie Billy, Wa-hem-pum [BR]), 1867-1965,** *Palouse,* **(2nd) Wah-pah-tan-mi (Peo-not-ah-neo-his-kin?, b. 1885 [CAC]),** *Nez Perce,* **(3rd) Alalumt'i (III), 1885-1977 (dau. of Tom Paween),** *Palouse*

        A (1st m.). Henry, b. 1899 (CAC)

        A (2nd m.?). Peo-peo-la-om-neet, b. 1907 (CAC)

        A (3rd m.). Clara, b/d. 1911

        B. Annie (Cleveland), 1912-97 m. Frank George, 1912-68

        C. Thomas, b. 1914

        D. Ruth, b. 1920

        E. Ned, 1922-1983 m. (1st) Naomi (Circle) (2nd) Inez (Andrews, dau. of Tom Billy Andrews), b. 1925

        F. Alfred Abraham, 1928-1953

Chief Cleveland Kamiakin, c. 1920. *McWhorter Collection, MASC, WSU Libraries, Pullman*

5th wife: Colestah (TK) (Kohlstiat [MK]), d. 1867?, died at Kamiak's Crossing (TK)

Part II / *Nápt* 99

Tomeo Kamiakin and family, 1905. *Frank Fuller Avery Collection, MASC, WSU Libraries, Pullman.*

1. Tomeo (Ta-mull Mox-mox [TT]), 1862[12] **(CAC) near Desmet-1936, Nespelem m. Ot-wes-on-my (At-wash-shun-my, Mattie), 1877 at Wawawai-1957 (sister of Tom Paween, 1864-1940),** *Palouse*

    A. Theodore (Teddy Tomeo, Wal-quin-a-tow-al-at), 1896-1936 m. Mattie (dau. of Jim Dick, 1906-1953, *Columbia*, and Annie [Annanypum Powulpills], *Yakama*) (TT)

        B. Arthur (Py-un-ka-tut-kit), 1906-1991 m. Josephine (Lucei), 1916-1984, Yakama (TT)

        C. Mamie, b/d. 1911

        D. Mary, 1912-1920 (TT)

        E. Cato, 1916-1974 m. (1st) Helen (Jackson) (2nd) Ruby (Miller) (TT)

2. Tomomolow (Tomolio), 1865?-1871? (EP)

NOTES

1. Kamiakin's place of birth is variously recorded as taking place in the Yakima Valley and at *Hasutin* (Asotin), his father's native village. Order of birth among Kamiakin's children given by Emily Peone to Richard Scheuerman (1981), and Mary Kamiakin (1916). Oral traditions within the Kamiakin and Joseph families attest to an undetermined kinship between the two chiefs (e.g., see

Arthur Tomeo Kamiakin interview, 1971). Historian Alvin Josephy's reconstruction of Chief Joseph's ancestry based on interviews with the Halfmoon, Blackeagle, and Red Wolf families offers insight to this possibility. Joseph was born about 1830 in the Wallowa Valley but his father, Tuekekas (Twitekis, Old Joseph), son of the Cayuse headman Wilémutkin (Wallamatkin) and his Nez Perce wife, Khapkhaponimi, was born at the Palouse village of Wawawai about 1790. This suggests his mother may have been of Nez Perce and Palouse ancestry (Josephy, 1965). Furthermore, according to T. Stern (1994), Tuekekas's half-brother, Wilémutkin (II) was the father-in-law of Peopeo Moxmox (Piupiumaksmaks), which may provide insight to Kamiakin's close association with the Walla Walla chief. "Kamiakin" as a family surname was often dropped in the generation of his grandchildren; thus the family of Tomeo Kamiakin perpetuates the surname "Tomeo" (e.g., Arthur Tomeo), Cleveland Kamiakin the surname "Cleveland" (e.g., Ned Cleveland), etc.

2. Although little is known about Chief Weowicht's wives, Arthur Tomeo Kamiakin (1972) stated that Tsiyiyak's first wife, Weowicht's daughter Com-mus-ni, was of Wenatchi background.
3. The earliest written reference to one of Kamiakin's offspring is Father Pandosy's poignant description of "Kamiakin's little girl, Catherine," in 1853. She and her young daughter were residing in Tomeo's household in 1900.
4. Although Mary Kamiakin (1916) identified We-at-que-wit's first wife only as the daughter of the Palouse Chief Húsis Moxmox, Sacred Heart Mission records show the marriage of "Xavier and Agatha Chamayakan" on June 21, 1869, and elsewhere "Xavier" is listed as godfather to several of Chief Kamiakin's younger children as early as 1861. Of the Kamiakin sons listed in all family accounts, only We-at-que-wit would have been old enough to marry at this time.
5. Theresa Koltsenshin Kamiakin's second marriage was to Andrew Saichan (SiJohn) in 1890 of the Coeur d'Alene tribe. Information supplied by Father Thomas Connolly, S. J. of Desmet, Idaho's Sacred Heart Mission, suggests that Andrew and Theresa had a son, Nicholas, who was called Chamayakan by the Coeur d'Alenes. Andrew SiJohn's paternal grandfather, Victor Lmena, was killed at the 1858 Steptoe Battle.
6. By several accounts Mary Kamiakin was a half-sister to Tesh Palouse as they had the same mother but different fathers (e.g., EP). Tesh Palouse stated that Phillip Andrews was "my sister's son" and that his father had been with Joseph in the 1877 war (Bates file, 1911, Colville Agency History Office). According to a 1935 interview with Tom Paween, "Peo-peo-hi-tum-nah killed himself by accident near Colfax 75 or 80 years ago" (WCB). The date of death would considerably precede the reference to Mary Kamiakin's Nez Perce husband but the name and geographic details seem more than incidental. Paween and Brown's Peo-peo-hi-tum-nah were prominent horse raisers among the Upper Palouse and Nez Perce from the Wawawai area.
7. Charley Comedown's wife, Pe-me-que-nt (Mary Too-quers-sin) was Looking Glass's half-sister. She was about eleven years old during the 1877 war and buried the Nez Perce chief at the Bear's Paw Battlefield. According to W. C. Brown informant Robert Johnson (Pee-hit-pa-laykt?, Joseph Band [1928]), "She put

To-hool-hool-sut in the middle, Ollicott on right side, and Looking Glass on left side." Her brothers were Red Thunder and legendary 1916 World Rodeo champion Jackson Sundown (We-yat-ta-nat-tseets-kon). Johnson was the son of Nez Perce war veterans Lame John (Yo-ho-ta-mo-set) and Estonwenahwe.

8. Mul-mul-kin is variously listed as a son of We-at-kwal Tsik'-en (MK) and Tesh Palouse (CAP), but his age (19) on the 1910 Colville census indicates he was born several years after We-at-que-wit's death (1886). His surname and family accounts (e.g, TT) explain how he remained for a time with his mother at *Palús* after his father relocated to the Colville Reservation.

9. Little Man Chief and his wife were veterans of the Nez Perce War and were also the parents of a son, Jessie Chief, who later married Hatats (1864-1964). Their son was Edward Chief (Chu-kumpts, 1907-1967), husband of Maggie Weipah (JD).

10. Smith L. George was also the father of Andrew George (1905-1989), Mabel (b/d. 1910), and Ruby (Williams) by his first wife, Julia (Redheart) Johnson (dau. of Palouse band exiles in Indian Territory, Ip-na-mat-we-kin and Ah-na-ne-mart [Dick and Fannie Johnson]), b. 1883, Nez Perce (AG). Julia Johnson's siblings were La-et-ha-yow ♀ and Mark Johnson. Smith L. George's date of birth is shown variously on censuses as 1867 and 1870 and is listed in 1937 as married to Emma Wilpocken with children Elsie Comedown (1905-1937) and Frank George (1912-1968).

11. This is the only known reference to a son by this name being buried at Rock Lake (TK). However, in a conversation with L. V. McWhorter in 1939 at *Palús*, Sam Fisher stated that "Skees, a fine looking man" of dark complexion was buried at Rock Lake. It may be that Pebescot and Skees, also mentioned by Emily Peone, are the same person. In a possible reference to this boy, Coeur d'Alene Mission records list the baptism of Kamiakin's six-month-old son Moses on June 17, 1869.

12. Although census records indicate Tomeo's year of birth as about 1862, some family accounts give 1856.

Part III/*Méted*

Gordon Fisher/Yoosyóos Tulikécin (Blue Man)

Gordon Fisher and Susie Weaskus at Palouse Falls, 2008. *Richard Scheuerman*

Gordon Fisher. *Richard Scheuerman*

Oral History

"Take Care of Mother Earth"

This account is compiled from our interviews with Gordon Fisher at Lyons Ferry on June 16, 2006, and at his home in Lapwai, Idaho, on June 19, 2006, July 24, 2008, and December 28, 2009. Richard first met Gordon at a reburial ceremony that Dr. Robert Ruby and he were invited to attend in June 2006 at Lyons Ferry State Park on the Snake River. Some 150 people assembled that morning, representing the Palouse Indian community on five area reservations, in order to reinter the remains of individuals taken from the ancient Palús village burial ground during archaeological work in 1964.

While waiting for our shovel work to proceed, an older man came over to speak with an elder who had been working nearby. The man Richard had been working alongside introduced himself to the other fellow as Gordon Fisher, and said he was the grandson of Sam Fisher. They quietly conversed for some time and when the other one left, Richard turned to Gordon and introduced himself. Gordon offered a kind smile, expressed thanks for the Renegade Tribe *book, and began telling about the visit during his youth to this sacred place where we were now assembled. We wish to acknowledge the valued assistance of his niece and great-nephew, Susie and Jarvis Weaskus, whose kindness facilitated our relationship with Gordon, who passed away in 2011. The text includes minor edits for fluency.*

Gordon Fisher: I grew up near Lapwai in the 1930s where we have a place up the road several miles from town. As a boy we would come down the Snake River to see Sam and Helen (Fisher). The Fishers and Yoosyóoses are buried in our plot there at *Palús*. The (Charley Kamiakin) Williams family was from there. Charley's boys all fought in World War II. There's a plaque telling about it in Nespelem. I knew Pete (Kamiakin) Bones. That big rock there in the river was

Ehpelútpa, it means "Above the Water." The word *"Pelús"* probably came from that. The people called themselves *Nahúumpúu*. It means "Downriver People." That was the original Palouse people's name for themselves. They never wanted to give up that land. They'd say, "Keep your land. When the white man takes something you'll never get it back."

Sam was one of five Yoosyóos Tulikécins. They go in a line all the way back to when they were fighting those mountain people [Shoshone] down on the Grand Ronde. Helen was Nez Perce. She lived here but wasn't Palouse. She was Nez Perce from Imnaha. Her mother was Ilstúulkt. Helen was just seven years old when they went with Joseph (in the 1877 Nez Perce War). She spent a long time as a young girl back in Oklahoma [Indian Territory or *Eckish Pah*], then they let them come back here. My dad was raised by Sam and Helen. His father was with those who froze to death.[1] My grandma wasn't with them. They brought them back to be buried (at *Palús*). The Fishers had their own cemetery up just around the way. That's where they are.

Folks lived around there a long time. Cleveland (Kamiakin) said the people were there when ash fell [from a volcanic explosion] and it was dark for three days. Animals just staggered around, like elk and them, they were disoriented. You could have walked up and clubbed them. It was like the world was comin' to an end. Now think of how long ago that musta' been. Three days. That's probably what made Crater Lake, maybe something like ten thousand years ago. We were here before that, and they just kept talking about it. Steptoe Butte here was used to find a spirit. *Yámuštas*, a sacred mountain. An Indian prophet told the people a flood was acomin'. He told them to climb *Yámuštas* and be safe. That's when that flood came through here ages ago, and they were safe, because that prophet knew.

The water is really deep at Rock Lake. They had stories about a monster in there, a holdover from the time of the Animal People, and they did find enormous bones over there. Cleveland said he once saw a leg bone of something that was about as high as a man.[2] They called the monster *Papúmus*; it means like "sea creature." But

Cleveland said it was really a big sturgeon. He was out fishing once and looked down and saw this thing swimming underneath. Course he was afraid at first but saw it had white stripes down one side, something like fifteen feet long. Sturgeon can get that big. Somebody must have brought one up and it just grew there.

Touchet comes from *Túuse*, it means "Roasting Place." There by Dayton, Grizzly was fishing by the river but accidentally stepped on Coyote. He didn't mean it but Coyote got mad and argued. He said, "That was no accident!" So he dug a hole and lined it with fir branches and put elk meat on top and down he went in the hole. Coyote killed him there and roasted him so that's how it got its name. Before then bears used to be our friends, but from then on they were enemies and coyotes chase them. Grizzly Bear is *Xáaxach*, and Coyote is *Ic'yéye* (Nez Perce), or *Spilyaí* (Palouse).

Once when I was a boy I was with a friend who was hunting magpies. They gather together sometimes. When they do it quite a bit that's a sign that the salmon run will be a good one. Well, he was shootin' at them, and I had a sling shot and took aim and let go. Hit one in the wing and injured it. Sure enough, an old man was called in to ask us about it. At first I lied and said, "I don't know nothing about it." But then he said, "Think about it a little more, 'Did you hurt anything in the last day or so?'" I said, "Well, maybe I took a shot at something." Still wasn't tellin' the truth. He said, "Something maybe got hurt?" I finally said, "You mean about that magpie?" And then I said what happened, and got a real lecture. They were like that to us.

Khalotas was the real chief there at *Palús* and was respected by Chief Kamiakin. That Khalotas [the first] was the one who went to the Missouri River to get the first horse—an Appaloosa colt, and he became a horse breeder. He brought a gambler with him who knew the bone game real well. They were watching the bone game, seein' the pile grow, so they played it sly. Wanted a horse with spots on the back. So finally said they'd play and when both bones were on our side and when he shakes his head they were to keep the black on the left side and the sticks on the right and lost the first time [extensive mimicking of stick and bones movement].

So next time they raised the stakes with pelts and more including women. One was a Plains White trader and six horses were part of the wager. Then they added two more so there were eight. One was an Appy [Appaloosa] female—she became the matriarch of the herd. The gambler won it for them and they brought it back. That must have been around 1750. In Palouse we call a spotted horse *tamsilpíin*. That word *máamin* is what the Nez Perce say, but that is a later thing. Probably comes from "Mormon" because they got the horse after we did from folks down to the south.

Those Bannocks, or "Mountain Shoshone" we called them, would come up and fight for horses and land. A bunch of them came up and were on one side. That first Yoosyóos had another name then. He went over to Wanapam before this happened and met with a doctor there. He said to him, "The rest of the men put red and white stripes here on the stomach and sides of the face. But your power will be blue. Put blue on your face." And when Yoosyóos was there facing all those warriors, they talked first about what to do. Those mountain fighters said, "We want to know what the Blue Man has to say about this." See, he was a good fighter, too. So they had a talk and he took that name with him, "Man With Blue," Yooyóos Tulikécin.

So Sam was one of those to carry that name. Said I could have it when I was young, but you had to fight in battle first. My dad fought in World War II so he could take that name. Fought in the Pacific, Corregidor. I hadn't fought when I was young so I couldn't take it, but I did later in Vietnam. When I was a kid, Sam said I could get power from the rattlesnake like him. He had a pit dug right back here and would get down in there with them. They would crawl all over him [laughing] and wouldn't hurt him a bit. He said, "You need to lay down there and get their power." I thought, "You must be crazy, there's no way I'm steppin' in there [laughs]!" So I didn't; I was just a kid.

In my junior year of high school there [c. 1952] a fire burned the building during the summer and it wasn't going to open in the fall. So Dad said I should go up to Nespelem and live with our relatives and continue my education. So I moved up to live with Cleveland

[Kamiakin] and Alalumt'i.³ They had a place there and their kids were older. I stayed in the upstairs. Douglas Andrews also stayed there sometimes and Frank and Annie [George]⁴ often came to visit. Cleveland was a leader in the Longhouse, very spiritual. Some called their old ways "heathen," but it was not. The native religion was not just for Sunday; it was a daily faith: Take care of Mother Earth. Never destroy anything wantonly. The elders told us kids, "All creatures have a purpose in this life. Don't ever harm of them needlessly. Make use of them respectfully."

Cleveland had a big eagle feather headdress. Not the kind from around here. Like the Plains people had, went way down to the floor. He didn't wear it often. Those people went to buffalo so they knew that country. He also had an old long-barreled musket—a big thing! Would have knocked down a buffalo with one shot! Probably belonged to [Chief] Kamiakin. He also had a big pipe, probably from Dakota, tan and red color with a very long pipestem [motions about two feet]. Wasn't one of those high narrow ones. It had a cup for holding the tobacco. Cleveland's favorite horse was a paint. The name "Kamiakin" means something like a head or skull.

Cleveland told me lots of things. I listened and I wrote a lot down. I knew Cleveland was Yakama. I said, "Hey, I know you're from Yakama, not Palouse." But he told me Kamiakin's father was from Asotin. Cleveland said, "Yea, he [T'siyiyak, Chief Kamiakin's father] took a left turn at that horse race!" They had two big rocks they rode around at that big racetrack down there by Pasco. On the north side just across from where they built that dam.⁵ He took off in the lead and when he passed that second rock just kept on goin' [to Yakama country]!

There's a mountain over there in Montana where they went. They would go over there to find a spirit. Kamiakin wanted to take Cleveland to Mount Rainier to find a spirit power, but there was way too much snow. Couldn't get up there. So they went to Montana, over by Hamilton. They knew that area because after all that fighting [in 1858] Kamiakin had to go over there. [Col. George] Wright had long-range rifles and weapons when they fought. Chief Kamiakin said they had to do something different, too. He advocated night warfare but the others were opposed to it. Hadn't fought like that before and thought they would lose too many. Cleveland said that when Wright killed all those horses it crushed the Indian people's spirit.

After the war Kamiakin had to escape over to Montana. He came back one time but folks here told him if the army caught him he'd be killed, so he went back.[6] They lived on a broad flat along the river by Darby [Montana]. Cleveland took me there, said, "This is where Father camped." Some of them wanted to just stay there; it was a nice place. But they might have had problems there, too. They loved this land. It was home and they wanted to come back. Cleveland went on his spirit quest over there, that mountain by Hamilton they call El Capitan. Indians call it Thunder Mountain. Cleveland went over there in later years and would stay at a hotel. I don't think they charged him anything. I took trips with Cleveland. He asked me if I had a power. I said, "No, I don't." He said he would take me to a place, Pilot Rock [in the Bitterroots], and I trained to get strong by running in the sand and doing sweats. He said, "Nephew, here's what you got to do," and explained it all to me…It was a place of black crickets. I had a medicine pouch and there was a little cricket in there.[7]

Húsis Kute was from Wawawai and was in Joseph's war [1877], the only other chief to survive with Joseph. White Bird went to Canada. He [Húsis Kute] was injured in the head during the war with Wright and it made him go partly bald, so he got the name Bald Head. Lawyer said he was the elected chief, but they didn't have elections in those days [laughing]. I told some of these folks, "Show me in any document where they had an election." You have to have documentation for elections and stuff like that. Húsis Kute told them not to leave Idaho during the war, but they didn't listen. He was kind of a prophet about things. When they came back there was too much Christian influence on the [Nez Perce] reservation so he went to Colville. Their religion was not heathen; they were caretakers of the land. They had it hard back there [in Oklahoma exile]. Helen would get emotional talking about it. The whites wrote that the Indians desecrated the dead soldiers when the war started at White Bird, but the old women there said no such thing. That would be an evil thing to do.

He [Cleveland] also took me to other places like Priest Rapids and Rock Lake. They left a bunch of horses there when they moved to the reservation. He said to us, "This is the last time I'll see my old home." We went down to see old man Isku't'm[8] at Wawawai. Folks there would beckon the sunset with clapping for night activities like telling stories like "How Beaver Brought Fire to the Animals."[9] We also went along the Snake River and on down by the old places all the way to Pasco. He said in the old days there was a large village where Sacajawea Park is today.[10]

When I got ready to leave Nespelem, Cleveland said to me, "Always remember who you are, Nephew, and where you came from." That's what he told me when I went away. I think he knew the end was coming. Those old ones could tell things like that. And I went lots of places and always remembered that. Been to California and Florida and Virginia and all over the place! I did three years in Vietnam. And I always remembered that. They called me "Chief" when I was an Army Ranger. Most of the guys in my training unit washed out. They sent us to Florida [in 1962] when the Russians sent a big ship with nuclear missiles across the Atlantic. It was halfway over before it stopped and went back…

In Vietnam I was a forward observer. Got a new officer once and when I was out on patrol I told him to stop. You can tell things about how the birds sound and how the leaves look when they have been laid on. I told him, "They're a comin' and get down and wait." The guys said, "Listen to the chief; he knows things." He couldn't figure out why. Sure enough fifteen minutes later here they come walking down in a line. Of course we just had to hide in the grass and watch them 'cause we were way into the brush. I learned a lot of those things growin' up.

NOTES

1. According to Winona area pioneer oral histories, about 1914 a small group of Indians perished in a spring snowstorm near the mouth of Rock Creek. They huddled around a small boy who was the only survivor. Apparently the boy was Gordon's father, Carter Sloutier, son of Meshac Sloutier, who may have died in the incident.
2. Perhaps remains of the prehistoric Columbia mammoth which have been found in the Rock Lake area.
3. Cleveland and Alalumt'i Kamiakin were related to the Fishers through her lineage. Alalumt'i's mother and namesake, Alalumti (1845-1934), was the sister of the Palouse leader Chief Hahtàlekin (c. 1843-1877), Gordon's great-great grandfather and one of the first casualties at the 1877 Battle of the Big Hole. Hahtàlekin's son, Pahta Pahtahank (Five Fogs) was also killed that day. Another son, Epahlikt Moxmox (Yellow Cloud), died in 1916 and is buried in the Grant Cemetery overlooking Lapwai. Hahtàlekin's son, Wes-ins (Fisher), was the father of Gordon's grandmother, Taneenmy.
4. Frank George (1912-1968) was the grandson of Kamiakin's son, T'siyiak (Williams), and a prominent political leader among Northwest Native Americans. His wife, Annie (1910-1997), was the daughter of Cleveland and Alalumt'i Kamiakin.
5. Ice Harbor Dam on the lower Snake River northeast of Pasco. The broad flat on the north side of the river opposite the village of *Sumúyu* was the likely location of T'siyiyak's famous horserace.
6. See Father DeSmet's 1859 report to army officials for a similar account.
7. An account of Gordon's spirit quest appears in *Nez Perce News*, March 2003.
8. Elsewhere Gordon identified this elder as Timothy.
9. Gordon separately supplied several astronomical terms including the Northern Lights ("Bright Lights Coming"), Milky Way ("Ghost Trail"), and Big Dipper ("Creeping Bear").
10. The Snake River-Palouse village of *K'wsís* ("At the Point," Relander's "Kosith"). Also see Listening Coyote's version, "How Coyote Stole Fire," in Clifford E. Trafzer, ed., *Grandmother, Grandfather, and Old Wolf: Tamánwit Ku Súkat and Traditional Native American Narratives from the Columbia Plateau* (East Lansing: Michigan State University Press, 1998), 38-43.

"How Beaver Brought Fire"
Retold by Gordon Fisher (2006)

Long ago, before there were people,
   the Creator made fire.
He gave its power to the Conifers,
   who lived high in the mountains.
They selfishly guarded its secret,
   and kept it inside their bodies to stay warm
      while other creatures shivered
         when it was cold outside.

One winter it was so cold
   that *Pik'úunen* froze completely across.
The Animal People were suffering,
   and thought they would freeze to death
      if they couldn't get fire.
Coyote called a meeting at *Wawáwi*
   and sent out Mourning Dove, Robin, and Eagle
      to spread the word all across the land.

The Animal People came from all around
   and Coyote asked, he asked;
      "How can we get fire from the Trees?"
Finally Beaver had an idea.
"The Cedars and Pines are soon gathering
   for a great council along *Wel'íwe*.
I will hide along the riverbank
   and get their fire."

The Conifers gathered just like Beaver said.
The Cedars built a huge warming fire,
   and gathered around it after bathing
      in the icy waters of the river.

They knew the Animal People wanted their fire,
   so they posted Pines as sentries all around
      to guard their secret.
But Beaver was hiding
   under a clump of earth and roots along the bank,
      and when a hot coal rolled down from the fire,
         he grabbed it, held it tight to his chest,
            jumped up and sped away.

The Pines screamed the alarm
   and started chasing after Beaver.
He lunged back and forth to escape them,
   and then raced straight ahead,
      so the Grand Ronde River is crooked in some places,
         and straight in others.

The Pines chased Beaver along the river
   until they became exhausted,
      and gathered in dense clumps still
      scattered along its banks.
Strong Red Cedar had joined in the pursuit
   and continued running until he reached *Léewikees*
      at the mouth of the river.
He knew he would not catch swift Beaver
   but went to the top of the hill to see where he was going.
From this lookout he saw Beaver reach the Snake River
   and head further downstream.
"We cannot reach him now,"
   he shouted the Trees below.

Beaver safeguarded the fire as he swam across the river
   and gave it to a group of Willows
      who had gathered along the shore.
He continued downstream and shared it
   with other trees and creatures.

When Beaver returned to the council grounds at *Wawáwi*,
    Coyote took two pieces of wood from a willow.
He put the flat one on the ground
    and twisted the sharp point of the other into it,
        which caused the one below to flame up.
All the Animal People were amazed
    to see fire made this way,
        and Coyote and Beaver gave each of the
        visitors pieces of the wood to take home.

Today Old Man Cedar still keeps watch
    where he stopped on the hilltop
        overlooking the confluence of the rivers.
The closest stand of cedars is far away upstream.
That shows how far he ran from the Conifers' camp
    when Beaver stole their fire.

"The Origin of Palouse Falls"
Retold by Sam Fisher (1936)[1]

Palouse Falls (*Apútaput'*/Falling Water), 1941. *R. R. Hutchison Collection, MASC, WSU Libraries, Pullman*

Four giant brothers and their giant sister once lived not far from the Palouse River. They were proud of how they looked, and were especially proud of their hair. They kept it sleek and shining with oil from beavers' tails.

One time they ran out of oil and wondered where they could get some.

"There's a big beaver in the Palouse River," the Wolf people told the giants. "Why don't you get some from him?"

So the four giant brothers looked for Big Beaver. They found him in the river, above where the falls are now. At that time there were no falls; the water ran smoothly and calmly all the way to the Snake River.

One of the giant brothers wounded Beaver with his spear. Beaver started down the river as fast as he could run, the four giants chasing him. At the first bend in the river, they caught up with him, and the second brother speared him.

But Beaver kept on going. Angrily, he turned to the left, away from the river, and made a new and deep canyon. Again the brothers caught up with him, and the third brother speared him. Beaver shook the spear off and plunged back into the river. As he turned south toward the Snake River, he shook his tail very hard five times. Thus he made the five little falls at that place.

There the fourth brother speared him, but Beaver kept on. He plowed out a deep canyon ahead of the brothers, until they caught up with him and fought with him. In the struggle, Beaver made the rapids you can see there today and turned the canyon sharply to the left.

Again Beaver rushed on down toward the Snake River. At the next bend in the Palouse, he was speared a fifth time. He turned on the four brothers and fought them, in the biggest fight of all. There Beaver tore out a big canyon. The river came over the cliff in a big rush and formed Palouse Falls. The marks of Beaver's claws can be seen all along the canyon walls, even to this day.

But again Beaver escaped the giants. Soon he reached the Snake River and plunged downstream, sure he was now free. Perhaps he would have been free if it had not been for Coyote. Coyote was watching from the hills on the south side of the river.

When he saw Beaver escaping, Coyote stood with one foot in the short grass and one foot in the long grass and sang his power song. His power made Beaver turn around and go back up the Snake to the mouth of the Palouse. There the four giant brothers speared him again and killed him.

You can see Beaver's heart today. It is the big round rock on the west side of the Palouse River, where it joins the Snake [now under the water].

NOTES

1. This popular Palouse story was related in 1936 to longtime Hooper resident John (Maurice) McGregor by Gordon Fisher's grandfather, Sam Fisher. The elder Fisher lived at *Palús* near the confluence of the Palouse and Snake rivers and was a prominent Appaloosa horse breeder. See Sam Fisher File, McGregor Collection (C 16), MASC, WSU Libraries, Pullman. A similar creation myth, recorded in 1841 by Lt. Robert Johnson of the Charles Wilkes' United States Exploring Expedition on his travels along the Snake River, adds that the division of Beaver's body gave rise to the region's tribes (C. Wilkes, 1844, IV:495-96).

Part III / *Méted* 119

Alice and Annie Billy, c. 1910. *Colville Confederated Tribes History Office, Nespelem, Washington*

Carrie Eneas, c. 1910. *Susie Weaskus collection*

Annie Chuweah, c. 1910. *Colville Confederated Tribes History Office, Nespelem, Washington*

The Póyakŭn/Billy Andrews and Páween Families

1. Póyakŭn[1] **(Five Times [TA], Poyahkin, from Wawawai), 1830?-1894 (WCB, TA) m. ♀,** *Yakama* **(TA)**

A. Wiyukshenéet,[1] (Jim Billy Andrews, We-yuk-sha-net, We-yuck-son-nut [FA]), b. 1846? (CAC), *Palouse-Nez Perce* m. Hiyómatway[2] (Old Lady Grizzly Bear, Eyomotwy, Yu-ma-tway [WCB], Yúmatway [NR], [dau. of Istéʼmetiʼn (TA)]), 1849 (CAC)-after 1936, Cayuse and ♀, *Nez Perce-Palouse, Alpowa Band*

    (1). Annie Billy (Yup-cha-sin, Wa-hem-pum, Annie Billy) 1867-1965 m. (1st) Cleveland Kamiakin, 1870-1959, (2nd) Wi-yu-kea Ilpilp (Red Elk), *Nez Perce* (FA)

        (a, 2nd m.): At-wa-la-tak-it, b. 1906

        (b). Matilda (Tillie Bob [FA]/Pakotas [JD]), b. 1909

    (2). Alice Billy (Alpiato, Elpiato, Wash-e-tone-my), b. 1878 (CAC) m. (1st) Charlie Wilpocken, 1852?-1927 (Yat-ah-mo-set, son of Showaway), *Yakama Palouse* (2nd) Tom (Joe) Waters (son of Tam-mop-sea-hia-kia, b. 1833 and We-at-ton-na, b. 1838 [CAC]), b. 1880, *Nez Perce*

        (a, 1st m.): Art Wilpocken Circle, 1900-1974 m. (1st) Suzanne (Kah-ni-ta, dau. of Michel Ustah), *Methow* (2nd) Annie Moses, 1905-1989 (dau. of Peter Dan Moses and Si-la-kia-mont)

        (b). Redford (Yal-pi-la-ket), 1904-1911

        (c). Iva (Tam-a-yet), 1905-1911

        (a, 2nd m.): Elsie, 1906-1922

        (b). Tom (Joe), b. 1913

        (c). Nancy, b. 1914 m. Tom Broncheau, *Nez Perce*

    (3). Thomas (Tom) Billy Andrews (Wiyukshenéet (BR), Ukshanat), 1887-1964 m. Alice (Tamaawalí, dau. of Little Wolf Moies [Moyese] [AMA] and Wéetes Ilpilp [Red Earth], *Nez Perce, White Bird Band*), 1891-1975 (FA), *Nez Perce*

    (4). Frank Andrews, b. 1897

B. Peopeo-hy-yi-toman[1] (Pew-pew-hi-tum-un, Whistling Bird [WCB]), d. 1890s near Colfax? (WCB), *Palouse-Nez Perce* m. Yumasepah (Mary Kamiakin), 1845?-1920

    (1). Sophie Kamiakin (Atwice), b. 1889 m. (1st) Tipyahlahnah Elassanin (Roaring Eagle, George Comedown, son of Wa-ya-mas-ta-kekt [Hiteyehmistaket, Charley Comedown], 1856-1918? and

Pomowtonmy (Pe-me-qui-nt), 1863-1936? [CAC]), b. 1882, *Nez Perce, Joseph Band* (CAC) (2nd) Isaac Wak-wak (son of Sam Wak-wak), b. 1895, *Umatilla* (UAC)

    (a, 1st m.). Ned Comedown, 1909-1968

    (b). Kes-les-tum (Elva Gould?, b. 1913)

    (a, 2nd m.). Martha, 1916-1918 (UAC)

    (b). Joseph, b. 1917 (UAC)

    (c). Nancy, b. 1921 m. Matthew Goudy, b. 1921, Yakama

    (d). Walter, b. 1925

(2). Telestonmy (Tooli Tonmie [JD]) m. Ko-san-yum (Luke Wilson [SR], son of Heminish Húsis, Wolfhead [JD], and Pe-not-ye-et-yakt), b. 1855, *Nez Perce*

    (a). Henry, 1896-1943 m. Sadie Paul (Moses/Wilson/Williams, dau. of Tiscosarkowkow [William Paul] and Tom-quin-wit [Lucy Moses]), 1898-1977

2. Ip-nah-ghah-lae-yown (Pe-nock-kah-low-yun, The Player [WCB], Pe-nock-a-law-apum)[3]

A. Chief Hahtálekin (Hetelexkin, Hatálĭkĭn, Italican [APC/AO], Taktsoukt Ilpilp [Red Echo], "a buffalo hunter and warrior of ability" [LVM], from Wawawai), 1843?-1877 at the Battle of the Big Hole

    (1). Pahta Pahtahank (Five Fogs, [LVM], Husispot? [APK/AO]), 1847?-1877 at Big Hole

    (2). Wes-ins (Wes-sence, Fisher), d. 1893? m. Nan-ne-me-nicht, d. 1916 (SF)

        (a). Ich-yich-whel-ek (Sam Fisher I), d. 1886 (SF)

        (b). Pah-ot-wal-ak-is-it (Bill Fisher), d. 1912 m. Wa-we-not (SF)

        (c). Yoosyóos Tulikécin (Yoh-yoh Too-le-cas-sat, Jim Fisher), d. 1898 (SF)

        (d). Taneenmy, d. 1901 ♀ m. Meshac Sloutier, b. 1874 (son of Sloutier, b. 1834), *Yakama* (SF) son: Carter Sloutier (Enna-quellers), 1900-1954 (adopted by Sam Fisher) m. (1st) Emma (Pinkham), b. 1897, *Nez Perce*, (2nd) Ilstúulkt (Lucy Paul, dau. of Tiscosarkowkow [William Paul] and Ee-yah-to-ton-my [Carrie Eneas], 1881-1962 [SW]), 1911-1938, *Nez Perce*

        (e). Chuck-louse (Sam Fisher II), 1866-1944 m. (1st) *Umatilla*, (2nd) Not-ta-mo-le-kaset (Helen Waters, dau. of Yetocown [Omy Waters], b. 1845 and Illslahtkit, b. 1844 [CAC], Nez Perce), 1881-1945[4]

    (3). Epahlikt Moxmox[5] (Yellow Cloud), d. 1916

        (a). Ip-na-ta-ma-we-na-my (AR) ♀

        (b). Tah-kah-tam-mal-lah-sah (AR) ♂

122 *River Song*

B. Ka-si-at (AR) ♀

C. E-yu-pa-ti (AR) ♀

D. Alalumti (I) (APK/AO) (Alilintai, Alla-leen-ti, [WCB], Pi-pi-ne-tsa, Kietq?), 1845-1934 m. Tenoo Paween, d. 1880?, *Palouse*

    (1.) Ah-kis-kis (II)[6] (Ar-kish-kish) m. (1st) Hal-a-mish (Helawish, Angry Woman), b. 1865, *Palouse* (2nd) Ana-chous, b. 1864?

    (2). Tom Paween, (Húsis Paween [II]), 1866 (CAC), Almota-1940 m. (1st) Skispum (dau. of Lew-los-le-wit [E-los-ti-at], *Nez Perce-Umatilla* and At-ta-tow-wis, d. 1861? [CAP]), 1860-1913 (2nd) Pe-yo-ots-on-my (3rd) I-yu-to-tum (Iatonmy, Ah-tot-ta-tat-min-ya [RR], Minnie [Yellow Wolf, d. 1935, his widow]), 1870-1955, *Nez Perce*

    (3). Metina (Amelia [RW], Milly [RR], At-pa-loh-wa-ween-non-mi? [RR]), 1869-1961 m. (1st) Tuktena-tuk-hayakt, Wyleem-lex (Black Eagle, Daniel Jefferson Green, son of Wottolen), 1868?-1943, Nez Perce (2nd) Robert Johnson (Pit-peliakt, son of Lame John), b. 1869, *Nez Perce*

        (a). Katherine (Katie, Kittie), 1894-1965 m. (1st) Waite Nan-pooya, b. 1918 (2nd) Charlie Moses (son of Peter Dan Moses), 1895-1957

    (4). We-ah-non-my (We-nam-mi [RR]), b. 1876 m. Hin-mot Ilpilp (Red Thunder [CAC]), *Nez Perce*

        (a). Joe Red Thunder, 1907-1996 m. (1st) Addie Quiltenenock (JD, dau. of Joe Moses) (2nd) Lucy Weipah, 1915-1985

    (5). Ot-wes-on-my (At-wash-shun-my, Mattie), 1877-1957 m. Tomeo Kamiakin (son of Chief Kamiakin), 1862?-1935

1. Chief Húsis Paween[7] (I) (APK/AO) (Shot in the Head, Husis Pa-ouyen [LVM], Husishusis Owyeen [CW], Shush-poween, [WCB]), d. 1890? (APK/AO) m. Teek-ton-nay, *Nez Perce, Timothy-Red Wolf Band* **(WCB)**

2. Tenoo Paween[7] (Poween, Towiltoklee?), 1846 (CAC)-1880? m. Alalumti (I) (Alilintai [APK/AO], Alla-leen-ti [WCB], Pi-pi-ne-tsa, sister of Chief Hahtalekin), 1845-1934, *Palouse*

    A. Ah-kis-kis (II)[6] (Ar-kish-kish) m. (1st) Hal-a-mish (Helawish, Angry Woman), b. 1865, *Palouse* (2nd) Ana-chous, b. 1864?

    B. Metina (Amelia [RW], Milly [RR]), 1869-1961 m. (1st) Tuktena-tuk-hayakt, Wyleem-lex (Black Eagle, Daniel Jefferson Green, son

of Wottolen), 1868?-1943, *Nez Perce* (2nd) Robert Johnson (Pit-pelaikt, son of Lame John), b. 1869, *Nez Perce*
    (1). Katherine (Katie, Kittie), 1894-1965 m. (1st) Waite Nanpooya, b. 1918 (2nd) Charlie Moses (son of Peter Dan Moses), 1895-1957 (RW)
        (a). Ruth m. Paul T. Wapato Jr.

C. Tom Paween (Húsis Paween [II]), 1866 (CAC), Almota-1940 m. (1st) Skispum (dau. of Lew-los-le-wit [E-los-ti-at], Nez Perce-Umatilla and At-ta-tow-wis, d. 1861? [CAP]), 1860-1913 (2nd) Pe-yo-ots-on-my (3rd) I-yu-to-tum (Iatonmy, Ah-tot-ta-tat-min-ya [RR], Minnie [Yellow Wolf, d. 1935, his widow]), 1870-1955, *Nez Perce*
    (1, 1st m.). Youch-youch-pouch (Bertha Carter), 1881?-1918
    (2). Alalumt'i (III), b. 1885, Almota-1977 m. Cleveland Kamiakin, 1870-1959
    (1, 2nd m.). Tu-kar-sey-i-yet ♀, d. 1924
    (2). Hat-a-mo-whil-i-ken (Hattie Paween), 1891-1980 m. Willie (Red Star) Andrews[8] (Cool Cool Smool Mool (Powder Horn?), Whits-see-you Ilpilp [RR], son of Kul-kul-kal-w-kin and Taw-mas-low-tah-kikt [AA], and adopted son of Chief Joseph), 1865?-1948, *Nez Perce, Joseph's Band*
        (a). Ruth, 1911-1912; Albert (Sr.), 1912-1951; Isaac, 1921-1968; Agnes (Davis), b. 1923; Ida, 1926-1960; Felix, 1928-29; Douglas, b. 1933; Rose Marie (Piatote), b. 1935
    (3). U-pa-pi (Pe-not-ah-me-hah, Annie), 1893-1989 m. (1st) Percy Chuweah (son of Chuweah[9] 1865?-1912, *Umatilla-Palouse* and Tan-en-my, b. 1870? [CAC]), 1892-1956; (2nd) Harry Owhi (Sr.), 1894-1955, *Yakama-Palouse*
        (1st m.). Mary, 1910-1911; Alfred, b/d. 1911 (CAC)
        (a, 2nd m.). Rosville (Roscoe), 1919-1976; Martha (Judge), 1922-1941; Dora (Francis), b. 1924; Bertha (Williams), b. 1926; Harry, Jr., b. 1926

D. We-ah-non-my (We-nam-mi [RR]), b. 1876 m. Hin-mot Ilpilp (Red Thunder [CAC]), b. 1870, *Nez Perce*
    (1). Yo-huny-we-talick ♀, b. 1896
    (2). Hal-ah-kala-keen ♂, b. 1902
    (3). Joe Red Thunder, 1907-1996 m. Lucy Weipah, 1915-1985
        Morris, Alvin, Soy, Sabe, Kenneth, Joanne

E. Ot-wes-on-my (At-wash-shun-my), 1877-1957 m. Tomeo Kamiakin (son of Chief Kamiakin), 1862? (CAC)-1936

3. Atuskis (Ah-kis-kis I) (APK/AO), b. 1849 (CAC) m. Mary, b. 1854 (CAC)

A. Wayayentutpik ♂

Notes

1. Wiyukshenéet (Jim Billy Andrews) and Peopeo-hy-yi-toman as sons of Poy-ahkin based on interviews by Bruce Rigsby with Tom Billy Andrews (April 1964), and W. C. Brown with elderly "Alla-leen-ti" (see 2.d, Alalumiti [I]) at Nespelem (April 1930). Alalumti further stated that she was "the daughter of Pe-nock-kah-low-yun who was one of the brothers of Poy-ah-kin," and was herself among the herders of the horses captured by Wright in 1858. Her date of birth is listed variously on agency records as 1846, 1849, and 1852.
2. "Tom's [Billy] mother's *ála*, her father's mother, was from *Palús*. She was named Sawíchwi, and she was said to have been a daughter left at *Palús* by Sacajawea, the Shoshone woman who accompanied Lewis and Clark's party. Tom said she was about two years old when left. I think it more likely that she was instead the daughter of a Shoshone captive, rather than of Sacajawea. In any case, Sawíchwi spoke Palouse" (Bruce Rigsby, based on Tom Billy Andrews interview, 1964). Hiyómatway's sister was Ic'ísayn who married (1st) Tom Beall Sr. and (2nd) Charlie White Sr. (BR).
3. Pe-nock-kah-low-yun as father of Hahtalekin and Alalumti I is derived from Verne Ray's remarkable May 1971 interview in Nespelem with Mrs. Cleveland (Alalumt'i Paween) Kamiakin and Mrs. Harry (Annie Paween) Owhi which recorded that "Italican was a chief of one of the villages. He was a brother of my grandmother Alilintai."
4. Helen Fisher's age in the 1930 census is listed as 58 indicating an earlier birthdate of about 1872. The 1892 Colville census for the Moses Band lists a "Chuck a Louse" (26) and "Ellen" (22) with daughter Jennie (2).
5. While Hahtelican likely had several wives, the mother of Epalikt Moxmox was Pilch-la-ya, and she had sisters Sah-ka-sine and We-ni-pots (AR).
6. Ah-kis-kis II as nephew of Ah-kis-kis I and brother to Tom Paween (Húsis Paween) is inferred from an 1891 letter from Ah-kis-kis "to his brother" (Húsis Paween) and 1910 Colville tribal census in which Ah-kis-kis and his wives are listed with other Palouses as members of the Moses band. Since Tom Paween's father is known to have died shortly before the family's relocation to Colville prior to that time, the 1891 letter had to have been written by a relative bearing the same name.
7. Húsis Paween and Tenoo Paween as brothers recorded by Annie Paween Cleveland and Cull White. Húsis Pa-ouyen's widow married Peter Wolf (Tilcoax the Younger). L.V. McWhorter records an eyewitness account by the Nez Perce historian Wottolen that a "Koosouyeen," headman at Wawawai, was killed about 1870 by the son of Henry Spalding "in the presence of many witnesses, and among the village tepees" when he intervened to prevent the arrest of a member of his band. This Koosouyeen had a brother named Tsatsikath "who

died some years afterward" (LVM, HMMC, 1952). The similarity of sound in the Sahaptin names "Koosouyeen" and "Husis Paween" (W.C. Brown's "Shush-paween") with both being from the village of Wawawai strongly suggests a relationship.

8. Willie Red Star Andrews was orphaned following the death of his father in Oklahoma while his mother died in 1885 at Fort Spokane where the exiles awaited arrangements for their travel to the Colville Reservation (AD). A Nez Perce warrior named Red Star, possibly Andrews's father, is mentioned by McWhorter's Nez Perce informant Wottolen as fighting with the Palouse Luke Andrews (Kosooyeen, He-kah Koo-sow-een) at the Camas Prairie battle. Luke Andrews escaped to Canada but was captured after recrossing the border and sent to Indian Territory. Red Star's half-brother was the warrior Ip-nas-sap-to-ka-lipt-on-my (Stephen Reuben) (AA). Willie Andrews, a nephew of Chief Joseph, returned as a boy to the Colville Reservation where he was raised by Joseph after the loss of his parents. He eventually had four wives: (1st) Yow-wan-pum, *Nez Perce*, (2nd) Annie Billy, *Palouse*, (3rd) Annie (Ca-tal-pi), *Moses-Columbia*, and (4th) Hattie Paween, *Palouse*.

9. Chuweah, 1865?-1912, was the brother of Loom-oo-lit (Charlie Scott), b. 1849?, whose parents were We-low-kee and Was-som-nok-nu-it (MF). Chuweah relocated to the Colville Indian Reservation in the late 1870s with Tatshama and other Umatillas. Charlie Scott's son was Wil-la-hom-et (Abbott), b. 1871?, whose children were Peter Scott Abbott, b. 1895; Katherine (Wilson-Sturgis), b. 1898; Annie, b. 1899; and Johnnie, b. 1902.

Part IV/*Pínapt*
Emily Friedlander Peone/Q'uomolah

Emily Peone, Nespelem, Washington, 1982. *Richard Scheuerman*

Emily, Lucy, and George Friedlander, c. 1915. *Frank Fuller Avery Photographs, MASC, WSU Libraries, Pullman*

Oral History

"Too Many Memories"

We began making regular visits to the Colville Indian Reservation in 1979 through a public school program introducing area teachers and students to tribal elders of the Moses-Columbia, Wenatchi, Nez Perce, and Palouse bands. Through these experiences we met venerable Isabel Arcasa of Nespelem, a centenarian in Washington's 1989 Centennial Year, who told about her early life at Camp Chelan as the daughter of frontier trader Joseph Friedlander and his Moses-Columbia wife, Elizabeth (Skn-wheulks).

During one of our fieldtrips to see Isabel, she excused herself several times to check on someone working in the kitchen nearby, and after the second or third time we overheard Isabel address her guest as "Auntie." Upon inquiry about the visitor's identity, Elizabeth laughed and led us into the kitchen where spry, diminutive elder Emily Friedlander Peone (1902-84) was taking a berry pie out of the oven. As we shared about our special interests in the culture of the Plateau peoples, Emily informed us matter-of-factly that she was a descendant of both Chief Kamiakin and Chief Moses through her mother, Nellie Kamiakin Moses. In this way we were introduced to the marvelous legend of the Star Brothers, from whom it was said the Owhi-Kamiakin clan descended.

A few moments in the presence of this humble, unassuming elder acquainted us with the special deference traditionally accorded the Plateau miyawaxpamáma, *or "chiefly people," who sought to guide and protect their people through the cataclysms of Euro-American settlement conflict and exile to area reservations. Emily was remarkable not only for her fluency in Sahaptin and Interior Salish dialects and family connections, but as a vital tribal historian. She had grown up in the household of her beloved maternal great aunt, Mary Owhi Moses (1830?-1937), Chief Moses' wife and daughter of famed Yakama Chief Owhi. Through Mary, Emily, and her siblings George, Lucy, and Louis, we were regularly transported to the days before the war period when the Columbia First Peoples ranged widely across the Plateau and over the Rockies to Buffalo Country.*

Emily safeguarded these stories and knowledge of the complex lineages of miyawaxpamáma *families. Her kind and generous spirit, uncommon knowledge, and berry pies kept us returning to Nespelem for many years, and allowed us to host Emily on visits to our classrooms where she shared the history and myths of her people. She also strongly supported the dedicated efforts of her sister, Lucy Covington, to oppose federal efforts in the 1950s and '60s to terminate the Colville Reservation. Lucy was profiled in the film,* Lucy Covington: Native American Indian *(Encyclopedia Britannica, 1978). The following account is taken from interviews with Emily in Nespelem on April 4, 1981, November 5, 1981, and April 30, 1982. It is followed by a portion of a remarkable interview done by Okanogan historian William C. Brown in 1918 with Mary Moses. We encountered this manuscript while conducting research at the WSU archives for our book,* Renegade Tribe, *and told Emily about its existence since it opens with a credit to a young girl residing with Mary who helped translate the account for Brown, which contributed significantly to his 1961 book,* The Indian Side of the Story. *"Oh, yes," Emily told us, "I remember his visit well. I was that little girl."*

Emily Peone: Kamiakin seems like a Spokane [Salish] word; it has something to do with the skull. They lived in the Yakima Valley but traveled around a lot. He liked to go to Kettle Falls to fish because the salmon were especially big there. Kamiakin's wife, Colestah, was a warrior woman who fought alongside him during the war. Colestah had power and could cure people. She wore tight braids around her hair and her best clothes into battle and used a war club to fight. Kamiakin wanted them to die in their burial clothes.

Colestah wore a red felt dress and tied something around her waist. Her mother would mourn for her when she went away to fight. An-sás was Tenas's wife[1] and lived with Kamiakin during the war years. He told her, "Get her ready. Tie her braids tight." Then Grandma was off to war with the braves. He gave everything—horses and guns and blankets for the fight. They wondered what kind of person he was.

After the war [1858] they first lived over by Coeur d'Alene where Kamiakin knew Chief Seltice. One of his sons [Wee-at-kwal Tsick-en] married there. His first wife, Sunk-hay-ee, went back to her people when he married his younger wives. They came here [to the Colville Reservation] not because they wanted to, that I know. There were older brothers and sisters, too. Folks down below didn't want them and the army would have killed them. They came with their cattle and horse herds. Our aunt used to tell us all kinds of things about her father when she'd stay with us, and about how they moved up here for fear of their lives.

Yam-na-nyék[2] and the family hid their possessions in caves and pits wrapped in buffalo robes. They had great big root bags—big as a sugar sack, made out of hemp. After the war most all of it was lost or destroyed. They lived for a while over by Coeur d'Alene because nobody wanted them, and then to Montana. They had no home and were afraid for their lives. He had his own land in Palouse so they came back but the white people took it later too.[3] My power mountain over there is Steptoe Butte; it was also my grandfather's [Lukash Kamiakin's] power mountain.

Colestah's son, Tomomolow, drowned in Hangman Creek when they were up there digging roots. He was only about six years old. One of the wives was supposed to be watching the children but was busy with something else. Kamiakin banished her for a while. They all lived first after the war at the place on the Palouse River where the boys had a big racetrack. A rival medicine man was jealous of her [Colestah] and stole her power and she died. She could help others but not herself. She died at the Palouse place. He [Kamiakin] wore rags and mourned for months afterward. Only Sophie's mother [Chamesupum] could talk to him then. She was a stout Catholic. Some of them later went into the *Wáshat*, but they knew our prayers when we ate. They all also talked in Coeur d'Alene and Spokane, probably because they lived close to them.

There were just too many memories there on the Palouse place so Kamiakin's children convinced him to move to Rock Lake where they also had a camp and race grounds. Kamiakin used Skolumkee to herd his horses. He lived off the land and remained single for a long time, until his sixties. He'd graze the herds by himself, following the grasslands and then meet the family at whatever camp.

Not long before he died, Kamiakin told his sons and daughters to move to the Colville Reservation. A priest from Desmet baptized Kamiakin's children and came to baptize him just before he died. His name was Caruana.[4] Chief Moses lived here on the reservation by then. He was younger than Kamiakin and one of his [Moses'] daughters [Sinsinq't] married Chief Kamiakin's son, Lukash. Kamiakin was also very close to Chief Seltice of the Coeur d'Alene, who was asked by the priests to keep peace during the war years. Wee-atkwal T'sicken married a Coeur d'Alene woman. They had a daughter whose last name was Pierre, and they later moved over to Cuisik.

The Kamiakins came to the reservation about the same time Chief Joseph's Nez Perce people came here [1885]. They sent the Christians to Lapwai and the others came here. One of their leaders was Húsis Kute.[5] He lived by himself in a little house here in town. We were scared to look at him. He's buried in that little cemetery on the road to Keller. Tomeo married Tom Paween's sister and had Theodore, Art, and several children who died. Williams had Charley Williams and Mary George. Cleveland married Tom Paween's oldest daughter, Alalumt'i, and they had Ned and Annie George and others who died young. Lukash was killed and his wife was Shen-Shen, a Yakama. They had one daughter, Nellie. Chamesupum had Sophie and two other daughters.

Notes

1. An-sás and Tenas were the Klickitat parents of Chief Kamiakin's wife, Colestah.
2. Yam-na-nyék (1837-1907) was Kamiakin's daughter by his first wife, Sunkhay-ee, daughter of Yakama Chief Teias.
3. Possibly a reference to Kamiakin family Indian homesteads established along Lower Palouse River Canyon in the 1880s.

4. Father Joseph Caruana was the Jesuit priest at the Desmet Mission near present-day Tensed in the 1870s.
5. The prominent Palouse *Wáshat* leader who surrendered with Chief Joseph at Bear Paws and led the Palouse band during the years of exile to Indian Territory in present Oklahoma.

Oral History

Mary Owhi Moses (Sanclow)

Transcribed by W. C. Brown, Nespelem, Washington, August 1, 1918, W. C. Brown Collection, C196, Box 1. Folder 4, Manuscripts, Archives, and Special Collections, Washington State University Libraries, Pullman. (Minor edits have been made for fluency.)

"I found Mary on Sunday afternoon, July 28th at the old Chief Moses ranch situated on the broad flat river bottom of the Big Nespelem. A more beautiful mountain valley would be hard to find. The wooded mountains rise up from the wide flat hay lands through which the river winds, its course marked by a heavy fringe of cottonwoods and willows along the tracks. All the women folks and children of the immediate household we found ready to start out on an extensive trip into the mountains to pick huckleberries.

We waited till after the departure of the huckleberry bunch…but she could not tarry. She was getting ready to make one of her periodic visits to her native home and the ancestral home of her family in the vicinity of Ellensburg in the Kittitas Valley. She was going to make the trip alone with her saddle and pack horse and declared it would take her only "three suns" which would be good traveling for a hardy cowboy or prospector. This was my first surprise for I had expected to find an old woman. Finally, however, we induced her to go only a few miles on her journey and camp near the agency. We found her the following morning according to agreement at the home of her relative, Kee-lee-kah-low." — W. C. Brown

Mary Owhi Moses: I am the daughter of Chief Owhi. We-ow-wict was the father of Owhi. We lived in the Ellensburg country. That was our country and my people lived there longer than anybody knows. We-ow-wict lived there and was chief. I had three brothers—Qual-chan, the oldest, next Lo-kout, also named Quo-to-we-not, and my youngest brother, Les-high-hite. He also had the name Pe-noh. The whites usually called him Seven Mountains. The names of my sisters were Way-yah-ton, the oldest, Quo-mollah, Say-may-yas, Si-en-wat, Sanclow (Mary Moses), and Yan-num-kt.

Sack-pose-un-al-an-at was the grandfather of Moses. He died about a hundred years ago. The father of Chief Moses was Sulk-stalk-scosum. He was chief of the Indians called Columbias, or Isle de Pierre Indians…Old Sulk-stalk-scosum used to go to the buffalo country east of the Rocky Mountains and he finally lost his life there. I was along at the time. I was a little girl not over ten years old. Our family went to gather and found a band of Kalispel Indians that were going to hunt. There was father and my brothers, Qualchan and Lo-kout, who was just a little boy. Young Moses was also along. He was a very young man…

We had been hunting for quite a while in the Moas-Mons-Illihee (Buffalo Country on the Plains) and had killed a lot of buffalo and were about ready to start back when we ran on to a camp of Blackfeet Indians. We had a talk with them and it was agreed to smoke. We were going to camp together when a Kalispel Indian was killed by Blackfeet and then the fighting began. It lasted for seven days, but we finally got away. But during the fighting the father of Moses got cut off from the main body and was hit in the arm with a bullet. He was along with a nephew at the time. He told his nephew to go in and clean him as there was no hope for him and the old chief was killed. The nephew got away. I know where the Great Falls of the Missouri are, and where Sulk-stalk-scosum was killed was a long way on this side of the Great Falls. It was in the summer time that we went.

[Discussion of events related to the Wright campaign against the Northern tribes in the summer of 1858 and Chief Owhi's flight from the Yakima Valley to a camp near the mouth of the Spokane in September.] The Spokane Indians came and told us that Colonel Wright had called a big council of all the Indians and had sent for all of us to come in. I don't know who these messengers were, but they were Spokanes and they said everything would be all right and we know they believed what they told us for they were our friends. Owhi went over to Wright's camp by Spokane on account of all these things the Spokanes were telling us as coming from Colonel Wright. Then Qualchan decided to go over and he took his wife and Lo-kout with him. Moses came back to our camp shortly after Qualchan had left but he had missed him on the way back. The next we heard from the Spokane Indians that Qualchan had been arrested as soon as they got to Wright's camp and that the soldiers had hung Qualchan. Lo-kout soon came back to the camp and Qualchan's wife.

Lo-kout went out in the hills with his folks and hid themselves. Moses went down towards the Moses Coulee country and kept himself concealed, for after the soldiers did those things we were all very much afraid. About ten days after Qualchan was hanged we were told that the soldiers had left the camp where they hung Qualchan, and my sisters Quo-mo-lah and Sah-me-sah-pan returned over to the campground and found where the soldiers had buried Qualchan by digging a shallow grave and covering the body with dust, grass, and sticks. Part of the face was exposed and something had chewed the nose off. The soldiers had taken his war bonnet and all his clothes away. My sisters dug a deeper grave and took up the body, wrapped it in a blanket and put moccasins on the feet and buried it again, and put some shells on the grave…

A few days after Qualchan was hung, we heard that the soldiers had killed Owhi who they had taken along with them. After we heard that Owhi was killed, my mother and my sisters and I made our way back to the Ellensburg country. It was hard traveling, for we were much afraid and only had a few good horses. Our good horses had been stolen by other Indians and by whites and soldiers. All our land was also taken away from us in the Ellensburg country and we have never had any land there since.

…The soldiers tried to catch and kill all our good fighters. We never went to buffalo country after the war. After Owhi and the rest of our great men were dead or too old we never could go to the buffalo country for that meant fighting with the Blackfeet.

Steptoe Twilight. *John Clement*

"*Yámuštas*—Elk's Abode at Steptoe Butte"

Retold by Emily Peone (1982)

In the time of the Animal People
    there was a big rack of antlers lying along Snake River.
Coyote decided to have a contest of strength,
    and called for anyone to break them apart.
Cougar and Eagle tried but couldn't do it,
    and neither could the Wolf Brothers.
Coyote tried with all his might
    but he couldn't break them either.
Finally Elk stepped forward.
He grabbed both sides and pulled and pulled,
    and with a great crack broke them in two!
So the Animal People celebrated in honor of Elk's strength.

Now the Wolf Brothers lived along the river
    with their beautiful sister.
The jealous brothers did not allow her to leave.
She wanted to see the country.
She saw Elk's strength
    and heard his stories of other places.
Elk noticed the beautiful Wolf Sister.
Her brothers were too busy.
The two left to be married upriver.
When the Wolf Brothers found that Elk
    had taken their sister away,
        they were very angry.
"We will kill him!"

Elk's wife saw her brothers
    and warned Elk to hide on an island.
He took a pair of fur gloves she made
    and used his power to make them look like an elk.
He went with his wife
    toward the mountains.
The Wolf Brothers found only gloves….
They spread out to hunt Elk;
    too far to reach the mountains.
Elk pushes up the earth
    and he and his wife hide behind *Yámuštas*….
They escaped the Wolf Brothers.
Elk's bones can be found in this place, giant bones
    near the power mountain, *Yámuštas*.

"The Two Sisters and Star Brothers"
Retold by Louis Mann

The Star Brothers myth is well known among Northwest tribes and various versions have been passed down in tribes across North America. Some Owhi-Kamiakin family members say that Little Si, a rocky bluff near Mount Si in Snoqualmie country east of present North Bend, is the stone remnant of the rope that came down to earth, and that an outcropping of shiny rock on Cowiche Mountain west of Yakima is the place where the Star Child was born. Emily Peone pointed out ancestral names that may be associated with this story, including that of her great-great uncle, Yakama War veteran Lesh-hi-hite (Líšxayxit, Paul Owhi/Awhie [1830-1914]), whose name is variously translated "Shooting Star" or "Light Above." Paul Awhie died on July 10, 1914, in Boston while working with an Eastern affiliate of the Pantages Theatre circuit, probably in a Wild West Show. He is buried in an unmarked grave in Mt. Benedict Cemetery in West Roxbury, Massachusetts.

The account given here was related to historian L.V. McWhorter in 1918 by Emily's relative, Louis Mann, a grandson of Chief Owhi's brother, Teias (Tiyáyaš b. 1815?), and is found in the L.V. McWhorter Collection, C55, Series 6, Box 44, Folder 431, Manuscripts, Archives, and Special Collections, Washington State University Libraries, Pullman.

Louis Mann: Tah-pal-lough and Yas-lum-mas[1] were the girls, two sisters. Their mother used to send them out every day for *char-kom*, a root which was used for their food. One morning they were told by their mother, "Go out this time and camp tonight. In the morning go digging the roots again, so in two days you get more *char-kom*." So the two sisters started out, going to the place where they always went digging. They came to the place, and they dug all day down there.

Evening came along, and well after supper the girls went to bed in an open space with no tipi. They looked above at the blue sky. The youngest, Yas-lum-mas, saw two stars and she began to talk. She said to her sister, "I wish those two stars could be our husbands. That red-looking, small star could be my husband, and that bright-looking star (Has-lou)[2] could be your husband." The older sister told her to keep quiet and sleep. So the girls went to sleep.

Those two stars heard the girl's wish and came down while they slept soundly. They took the two sisters above while they did not know it. When the morning came, both of the girls were in a different place. Both were sleeping with a man apiece. Yas-lum-mas woke up first, and her eyes were full of matter from the old man star. When Tah-pal-lough woke up, she was with young man star. The young man told her, "This is your sister's wish. We heard what you said, and you are with us now. You are our wives here."

So the women cooked breakfast, and their men sent them to dig roots. Their men told them not to dig too deep in the ground, and the oldest girl, Tah-pal-lough studied what was meant by not digging too deep in the ground. One day she happened to find a big, long *char-kom*, and she wanted all of it. She dug deep. Finally she ran her digger deep and she opened a hole in the ground. A big wind came through, and she looked down below and knew it was their home. She plugged the hole and told her sister, "We must get away sometime."

Their husbands on a hunt noticed the wind blow, and they hurried to find what was the matter. They came to where the women were digging roots. When they arrived, they asked their wives where this big wind came from, and the women told them they did not know. They concealed this.

Now when they went out to dig, the oldest planned how to get down. She told her sister to get the hazelnut bush, and they twisted that. They tied it together for a rope to reach down to the ground below. They worked many days, and they tried to let down the rope, but they could not reach the bottom so they hid it. Their men asked why their roots were very few. They said most of the roots were very hard to find so they could not get more *char-kom*. But they concealed their plan to get away.

The sisters continued twisting hazelnut bush. Finally they succeeded. They let down their rope, and it reached. The youngest girl, Yas-lum-mas, started down on the rope, and when she reached the ground she gave the sign by pulling on the rope. Tah-pal-lough had already had a baby, a golden boy baby. Now when she descended down on this rope, she arrived safely.[3]

When the women came back home to their mother, they told her what had happened. The runners were sent abroad to tell the news that Tah-pal-lough and Yas-lum-mas had come back home. So there was a big gathering and a feast, and a big time swinging on this rope. The swing lasted for many days…There is a class of Indians at Snoqualmie today who are descendants of the star.[4] One of these women, Josephine Yermount, lives at the Ahtanum and she is my mother-in-law.[5]

NOTES

1. The name of the youngest sister, Yáslams ("Yas-lum-mas"), is Yakama Sahaptin for the Morning/Evening Star (Venus).
2. Xaaslú ("Has-lou") is identified by some family members as the North Star.
3. In a Yakama variant of this tale in which the child, Miy'áwax (Chief), is born at Cowiche Mountain, the story concludes: "When you need something really bad, you can take an offering to Miy'áwax and ask him for help. Lay it down there beside him and call his name, 'Miy'áwax, I need help. I am offering you this gift. Help me.' State whatever it is you need, and you can call his mother's name and his father's name and exchange a gift for whatever it is you take from the mountain—a blade of grass, a branch off a tree or bush, or a small stone. This will be your good luck piece for whatever you ask for. If you want to be lucky in your ventures in life, you must take sweat baths for five days until your body is clean. Then you take your gift to him and exchange with him. You can be lucky in anything you want, but you have to lead a clean life and have a clean body, and have good thoughts!" See "Miy'áwax: Chief Mountain," in V. Beavert, ed., *The Way It Was: Anaku Iwacha (Yakima Indian Legends)*, 1974:188-93.
4. A detailed version of what may be a Snoqualmie antecedent version of this myth was related by Snoqalmie elder Siátxtid ("Snuqualmi Charlie") as "Moon, the Transformer" (A. Ballard, 1929:69-80) in which the older sister, Yáslibc, marries the red star and the younger, Tukwiyé, marries the white star. Their father is Suwáblko and the mother Tupáltxw ("Leave Without Blemish," "Clean Up"). They lived at the village of Toltxw (Tolt) and were digging bracken fern roots on the prairie above Snoqualmie Falls before being taken up to the "Sky Country" (*sxó-lgwad*) where the older sister conceived the child, Moon

(*Slokwáleb*), or Transformer. They returned home by descending a ladder rope they had fashioned of twisted cedar boughs which was then used as a great swing (*yadóad*) on which the people enjoyed swaying from *Kelbts* (Camping Place) north to *Dáxcdibc* (Footprints), or from Rattlesnake Mountain across the Snoqalmie River to Mount Si. The Dog Salmon People then stole the boy and when his mother and aunt washed out the cedar bark diaper from his cradleboard, Moon's younger brother, Sun *(Lokwál)* was born to console them. Moon grew up to marry a Dog Salmon woman and he then returned to his mother's people for the first salmon migration and "to begin his work of changing things upon the Earth." Moon met others along the way and transformed one group at a time into sandpipers, sawbill ducks, mallard ducks, clams, deer, beaver, and various plants "for the people about to come," and made Snoqalmie Falls where the people had a fish weir. Rat later climbed and gnawed on the rope and it fell to the group in a great heap. Anthropologist Ken Tollefson (2010) relates that some Snoqualmie elders identify the rope as Little Si. Then, before ascending to the sky, Moon "created the various peoples" by placing "a man and a wife" upon the rivers…"the Puyallup, the Nisqually, and the other rivers…Each people had a name, as Skagit, Yakima, Lummi, Puyallup, and others." Ballard notes that the Snoqualmie had extensive interaction with the Yakama so were generally bilingual in both Lushootseed and Sahaptin, and that Snuqualmi Charlie's parents "were predominately of Sahaptin stock." Myth dispersion and variation took place over time since marriage "outside the group was the common if not universal practice." Further, some Yakama bands regularly wintered on upriver meadows west of the Cascades and "according to tradition, the greater part [of the Naches River people] migrated to the head of the Cowlitz Valley, becoming the Taitnapam, or 'Klickitat' tribe of eastern Lewis County" (A. Ballard, 1929:39-40). A Cowlitz version related by elder Mary Iley to anthropologist Thelma Adamson in 1926 also identifies the older brother as Moon and the younger as Sun, although Moon returns from his exile only after his people pledge to provide a wife from each of the "five king-countries"—the Taitnapam, Chehalis, Cowlitz, Wishram, and Yakama (W. Seaburg, 2009:269-71).

5. Josephine Yemowit (1843-1936) was the daughter of Yakama Chief Teias. She traveled in August 1855 with her father, Chief Owhi and his warrior son, Qualchan, and others to the Spokane Valley where they participated in the Battle of Spokane Plains. Several days later Qualchan surrendered to Colonel Wright and was executed at Hangman Creek; Owhi also surrendered and was subsequently killed during Wright's return to Fort Walla Walla while crossing the Tucannon River near present Starbuck. In 1912 Josephine Yemowit related her account of these tragic events to L. V. McWhorter, which is found in the McWhorter Collection, C55, Series 6, Box 45, Folder 435. In this version of the Star Brothers myth, McWhorter footnotes Louis Mann's reference that, "There is a pile of white rocks near Snoqualmie where the swing [rope] was located. Lash-high-hit, Chief Owhi's mother, and her grandmother, are descendants of the stars." Bruce Rigsby (2011) notes that the name of the prominent nineteenth-century Nisqually leader Léšiay (Leshi, Leschi), a nephew of Chief

Owhi, appears to derive from the same Sahaptin term (*líshxayxit*: shooting star, hazy comet, Northern Lights) for which one of Chief Owhi's sons was named. Hudson's Bay Company trader Edward Huggins at Fort Nisqually sometimes spelled Leshi's name as "Lushchyuch."

The Sulkstalk'scosm/Moses Family

Chief Sulk-stalk-scosum (son of Sack-pose-un-al-an-at), d. 1848?, Columbia-Sinkiuse[1]

1st wife: Kanitsa (Karneetsa), *Spokane-Columbia*
 1. Patsk'stiway ♂, d. 1849?
 2. Q'uetalican (Loolowkin, Chief Moses), 1829 Wenatchee Flat-1899 m. (1st) Silpe, *Flathead* (2nd) Q'uo-mo-lah (Ka-mo-la, dau. of Chief Owhi), d. 1864?, near Moses Lake (RR) (3rd) Sanclow (Mary, dau. of Chief Owhi), 1830?-1937, *Yakama* (4th) Hi-o-ha-hle-ka (SW), (Hi-o-let-saw? [RR]), *Wanapum* (5th) Peotsenmy (Tamatsatasmy, Ts-mah-tsa-tsau), d. 1902?, *Nez Perce*
  A (2nd m.). Qu-qua-la-que ♀ (RR, CW)
  B. Sinsinq't (III), 1855?-1888 m. Lukash Kamiakin (son of Chief Kamiakin) 1858?-1886 (CAC), *Yakama-Palouse*
   (1). Nellie Moses (Sinsinq't [IV]), 1883-1958 m. (1st) Louis Friedlander (son of Joseph H., 1855-1899, and Elizabeth Friedlander, d. 1944?), 1879-1912 (2nd) Antoine Francis, 1888-1934
    (a, 1st m.). Emily (Q'uomolah, Kamooli), 1902-1984 m. Walter Peone, 1904-1971, *Coeur d'Alene*
    (b). George, 1904-1977 m. Celeste Minthorn (dau. of Grover Minthorn and Minnie Wak-wak, *Umatilla* [GG]), 1913-1976, *Umatilla*
    (c). Thomas, b. 1908
    (d). Lucy (Sinsinqt), 1910-1982 m. John Covington, 1915-1958, *San Poil-Columbia*
    (e). Louis Jr., b. 1913-1998 m. (1st) Eileen, *San Poil* (2nd) Helen Stewart
 A-F. (3rd m.). Three sons and three daughters by Sanclow died in infancy (EP).
 A. (4th m.). Tom-quin-wit (Lucy Moses [I], Iam-han-way [WCB]), b. 1862-1948 m. (1st) Kol-kil-le-tsa-kas-nim (Kolkolleksanim [RR], Johnson), *Nez Perce* (RR) (2nd) Tes-ka-sar-kow-kow (Kis-sko-sho-kow-kow [RR], William Paul, son of Tiska [Estookas] SW), 1867-1915 (SW), *Nez Perce* (3rd) Ben Awhi (Owhi), 1854-1927, *Yakama-Palouse* (CW) (4th) Luke? Wilson, *Nez Perce*
  (1, 2nd m.). Sadie (Sihl-pulks, Hots-a-lo), b. 1898-1977 m. (1st) Gilbert Williams (son of T'siyiak [Williams] Kamiakin and Nikenot), b. 1893 (2nd) Henry Wilson (son of Luke and Susie Wilson), 1898-1977

(a, 2nd m.). Thomas Paul Moses Wilson, 1914-1970 m. Catherine Francis (dau. of Antoine Francis and Mary Pakootas), b. 1923

(2). Edward Moses, b. 1911? (CAC)

(1, 4th m.). Thomas Moses, b. 1914 (CAC)

A. (5th m.). Quiltlay, d. age 10 (EP)

3. Sinsinq't (I), (Shim-tat), b. 1840s? (RR)[2] m. (1st?) Qualchan (son of Chief Owhi), d. 1858, *Yakama*[3]

A. Chillileetsa, 1842-1885[4] m. Ku-nullix (Connulux, Nettie, dau. of John C. "Virginia Bill" Covington [RR], 1825-1901)

B. Charley Qualchan (Sah-ku-lah [WCB], Socula [CW]), Kwalkan?, 1845?-1916? (CAC) m. Mary (Com-yuan-lal-ix ? [CAC]), b. 1850 (CAC)

(1). Sah-ku-lah (WCB) (Sam Sokula), 1862-1950 m. (1st) Chu-chu-walx (Cho-cho-wahlikcs [RR], Lizzie), (2nd) Kist (Kitsq), 1870-1954 (dau. of Nahanoomed), *Yakama*

(a, 1st m.). Harry, b. 1885 (CAC)

(b). Sit-sim-te-tock, b. 1897 (CAC)

(c). Willie, b. 1906

(a, 2nd m.). Christine, b. 1916

(b). Matilda (Madeline), 1917-2004 m. Adam Bearcub Sr.

2nd wife: Sipitsa, *Columbia-Sinkiuse*

1. Quiltenenock (I) (Qŭltnínak [EC], d. 1858 m. (1st) Tisaqt, *Wenatchi* (dau. of Chief Tecolekun [BG]) (2nd) *Blackfoot*

A. Quanspeetsah (Quin-spe-cha) m. Wee-ash-i-wit (son of Chief Tilcoax, *Palouse* [SM])

(1). Peter Dan Moses (Weashuit), 1861-1962, m. (1st) Katherine (Si-la-kia-mont), b. 1938 (2nd) Margaret Nellie Pakotas (his sister-in-law, after Joe Moses' death [SM], dau. of Peter Kolockan and Nellie Sam)

(a). Charley Moses, 1895-1910?

(b). Wapati, b. 1898

(c). Annie Moses, 1902?-1989 m. Art Circle (son of Charlie Wilpocken, *Yakama* and Alice Billy [Alpiato], *Palouse*), 1900-1974

(d). Lucy Moses (II), b. 1905

(2). Joe Moses (Quiltenenock [III], Spell-li-kulix), 1876-1935 m. (1st) Quin-ho-peetsa (Mary Ann, daughter of Swawilla?, d. 1929), 1879-1966 (2nd) Margaret Nellie (Pakotas) (SM]), b. 1889

(a, 1st m.). Albert, b. 1906

(b). Mary, b. 1908

(c). William, b. 1911

(d). Addie, b. 1913 m. (1st) Joe Red Thunder (JD), 1907-1996, Nez Perce, (2nd)? Thomas
   (e). Edward, b. 1915
  B. Quiltenenock (II) m. Clotilda Sam (Judge), 1851-1935 (BG)
   (1). Louis Judge (Nahcox), 1874-1912 m. Baptistine (dau. of T'quatas ["Doc Jim"]), *Wenatchi*
    (a). Matthew, 1907-1914
    (b). Julianne m. Noel Ustah
    (c). Sam Peter Agapith

 2. Kwee'tsa (Kwayitsa, Qui-et-sa, Crasam, Louie, Blue Robe [J. Teit]) ♂, 1839?-1913 m. (1st) Sah-shat (Mary Antoine, dau. of Okanogan Antoine and Louise), 1846-1933 (2nd) We-tu-we (Wa-ta-we), c. 1845-1908
  A. Si-sitk (Mary Louie), 1876-1922 m. (1st)? Beardon (2nd) Ed Haines (3rd) Arthur Parsons, 1861-1938 (SS)
    children: (1st m.). Louisa (Friedlander), (2nd m.). George Haines, (3rd m.). Annie, Millie, Agnes, Nancy
  B. Harry Louie, c. 1880-1911 m. Angeline (Arcall), b. 1876
    children: Matilda, John, Francis (McCragie)

 3. Shimtil (See-um-tat-quat) ♀, d. 1893
  A. Sam
  B. Yos-o-soken (Jack O'Socken) m. Minnie (Yellow Wolf), 1870-1955, *Nez Perce* (RR)
   (1). Jim Jack m. Nancy (dau. of Joe and Lucy James [RR]), *San Poil*

3rd wife: Nkiyapitsa, Spokane-Columbia
 1. Paq'uin ♂ (Keelpucken, Puckheim), d. 1858 (WCB) m. Sen-sint-qua (CAR)
  A. Ceepetsa (Ceep-peetsah)[5] m. Chief Skolaskin, *San Poil* (RR)
 2. Panekstitsa (Pan-ek-steesah, Louis), 1821-1896 (WCB) m. (1st) ?, (2nd) Q'ue-matk (Kwe-mat) (RR)
    a (1st m.). Joe Moses, 1866-1925 m. Mo-yet-at, 1872?-1941 (AB)
     (1). Madeline (Moses), 1898-1969 m. Harry Jim, 1894-1968 (AB, CJS), *Palouse*
     (2). Peter, b. 1901
     (3). Nancy, b. 1903
    A (2nd m.). Madeline ("One-Arm," Kenam-Petsa, Kekimetsa), 1884 in Moses Meadow Valley-1930 m. Robert Covington (Wa-has-to-mena, son of John C. "Virginia Bill" Covington, 1825-1901), 1870-1961 (CAC)
     (1). Eva, b. 1911
     (2). William, b. 1914

(3). John, b. 1915
(4). Eddie, b. 1916
(5). Rose, b. 1920 m. Isaac Wak-wak (CW)

4th wife: Pohamatku (Tah-k'matq [BG]), Wanapam (BG)
1. T'cher-man-chute (Cermncut [MP], Shpowlak (Spawelk) m. (1st) Nahanoomed, *Yakama, Kittitas Band* (MP), (2nd) Sk'nwheulks (Elizabeth [IA]), 1885-1940[6]
    A. Kist (Kitsq [WCB]), 1870-1954 m. (1st) Leo Thompson, (2nd) Sah-ku-lah (WCB) (Sam Socula), 1862-1950, (3rd)?
        (1, 1st m.). Harry, b. 1885
        (2). Sit-sim-te-tock, b. 1897
        (3). Willie, b. 1906
        (4). Margaret (Wash-waeik [WCB]), 1906-1987 m. David Piatote, (son of Tom-sos-tocken [David Sr.], 1870-1944, *Palouse* and Luch-a-mon [Tinsaat], b. 1876 [CTC], *Umatilla*)
        (1, 2nd m.). Christine, b. 1916
        (2). Matilda (Madeline), 1917-2004 m. Adam Bearcub Sr.
        (1, 3rd). Mary m. Charley Skaminsky (BG)

Notes

1. Order of marriages and children's birth given by Mary Moses to W. C. Brown, 1918, although Sque-malks is not listed; and to Richard Scheuerman and Clifford Trafzer by Emily Peone in 1982.
2. According to Nellie Moses, Chief Moses' sister Sinsinq't (I) died "at the river camp" near the mouth of Moses Coulee (CW). This was historic Skil-il-leet ("Viewing Place") where she could "watch her people." The site was a historic crossroads and a monument to her memory was erected there in June 1957 (JB from Billy Curlew) at a ceremony attended by Nellie Moses Friedlander, Frank George, Cleveland Kamiakin, and others. Moses' daughter, Sinsinq't (III) was his venerable sister's namesake as was his granddaughter's, Nellie Moses Friedlander (Sinsinq't [IV]).
3. As Qualchan had several wives, the affiliation of his son is not certain. One of Qualchan's guardian spirits was Otter (EP).
4. Chillileetsa, Chief Moses' nephew and intended successor, drowned while fording the Columbia River near Barry in 1885. John C. "Virginia Bill" Covington came west from Virginia in 1849 and settled in the Willamette Valley. In 1854 he relocated to the San Poil area and married a local woman, Smil-keen (Smeimollax?, 1840-84). For many years, Virginia Bill and his family operated the post store at Fort Spokane.
5. Madeline Covington stated that Ceep-peetsah's sisters, perhaps not all by the same father, included Gin-na-mon-teesah, Yat-peetsa, and Cheepat (Sally Whistocken) (RR, 1961).

6. Following the death of her husband, Elizabeth married frontier merchant Herman Friedlander who had established a trading post at Camp Chelan about 1879. One of their children was Isabel Arcasa.

Part V/*Páxad*

Landscapes of Beaver and Coyote

"The land was our religion; given to us by the Creator."
—Mary Jim

"I postulate they carried within their cultures some institutional essence of what made and maintained them as peoples. Some things that prescribed how they should live and what were their sustaining ideals as people. By contrast, modern peoples, secular and unanchored, come to feel the double-edged sword of freedom from tradition; this includes the freedom to lose one's identity and to assimilate into the dominant culture."
—Noel Pearson

At the dawn of the nineteenth century, perhaps 2,000 Native Americans lived in the lower Snake River-Palouse region for much of the year, frequenting various favored places to hunt, gather roots, pasture horses, and fish. Their numbers are difficult to estimate given the fluid nature of Plateau Indian culture; however, numerous winter villages along the lower Snake River were occupied by the Sahaptin-speaking Naxíyampam and Nez Perce tribes, while Coeur d'Alenes and Spokane Interior Salish speakers made extensive use of the northern region.

The Northern Sahaptin Snake River-Palouse language is a member of the Macro-Penutian superlanguage family and is more closely related to Coastal Chinookan and even Mesoamerican tongues than to Spokane and Coeur d' Alene Interior Salish. Linguistic analysis has led some anthropologists to propose that Sahaptin speakers may have descended from some of the earliest American Indian populations that migrated southward along the western Rockies at least 15,000 years ago, before dividing into groups that continued farther south and west. Others chose to remain in the vast realm of the Inland Pacific Northwest where, according to tribal myth, humans emerged from the parts of Giant Beaver and the land was prepared for their occupation by the Animal People.

The Naxiyamtáma "Downriver" Snake River-Palouse tribal territory, generally understood to have been their area of "exclusive occupancy," covered the Palouse River basin from the Bitterroot Mountains to the Snake River as well as adjacent lands characterized by a rolling terrain of fertile soils. This greater Palouse bioregion covers approximately 4,000 square miles and lies largely in Washington's Whitman and Spokane Counties, the eastern third of Adams County, and Idaho's Latah County. The land is composed of deep deposits of rich but fragile topsoil covering immense layers of basalt. This bedrock shield is up to 10,000 feet thick, born of successive lava flows through fissures across the Columbia Plateau between six and seventeen million years ago.

The Palouse geographic region is bounded by the Snake and Clearwater Rivers on the south, and Idaho's imposing Bitterroot and Clearwater Mountains to the east. The evergreen forests of these eastern uplands extend across the northern half of Spokane County. The Cheney-Palouse lobe of the Channeled Scablands comprises the region's western boundary, extending from the timber line near Tyler, Washington, south to the mouth of the Palouse River. Annual rainfall increases from an average of fourteen inches in the western Palouse prairies to eighteen inches in the central Palouse hills and up to twenty-two inches in the foothills of the eastern mountains.

Looming above the panoramic Palouse near the heart of the region stands a promontory known today as Steptoe Butte. To the Palouse Indians it was *Yámuštas* ("Elk's Abode"), a sacred high place of spirit quests and the abode of mythical Bull Elk. An honored figure in tribal folklore, this creature was said to have found sanctuary during the time of the Animal People in the cleft of the butte's eastern face. Its majestic antlers stretched toward the summit and remain visible today. To the area's first European-American explorers, who dubbed it "Pyramid Peak," the butte served like a mariner's landmark, a strange island in a rolling ocean of native wheatgrasses and fescue. With its summit at 3,612 feet often shrouded in purling clouds, Steptoe Butte is the highest and most ancient formation in the Palouse hills. Similar formations create an inland atoll that includes Stratton, Granite, and Kamiak Buttes and Moscow and Tekoa Mountains.

ANCIENT FLOODS—*WALSÁKWIT*—AND THE "ANCIENT ONES"

In anticipation of lower canyon flooding expected with the completion of Lower Monumental Dam on the Snake River, Washington State University archaeologists led by Richard Daugherty, Roald Fryxell, and Carl Gustafson began excavations in the summer of 1962 at the mouth of a cavernous rockshelter on property along the Palouse River. The artifacts, and human and animal remains found at Marmes Rockshelter, located approximately a mile from the confluence of the Palouse with the Snake River, gave evidence of early human occupancy of the area.

In July 1996, a nearly complete skeleton, dubbed "Kennewick Man," dating to approximately 7400 BC, was discovered near the confluence of the Snake and Columbia Rivers. Kennewick Man and the individuals found at the Marmes Rockshelter are among those reverently referred to by Plateau peoples as the "Ancient Ones." Tribal governments of the Inland Northwest's reservations have been embroiled in protracted legal struggles in federal courts fighting for their reburial as a sacred responsibility.[1]

Based in large part on Indian oral traditions describing massive floods, people, and creatures of these past ages, Secretary of Interior Bruce Babbitt in 2000 ruled in favor of the tribes, ordering the repatriation of the remains of Kennewick Man under the Native American Graves Protection and Repatriation Act. Though still contested in court by scientists who contend that the cultural affinity of groups separated by such great time is unlikely, Babbitt's landmark decision affirmed that these stories—such as Andrew George's tale of ancient floods, known to the Palouse Indians as *walsákwit*—provide valid ancestral links between these prehistoric people of the Columbia Plateau and those living here today.

The archaeological record indicates that few humans probably lived in the region 10,000 years ago, but a thousand years later, seasonal human occupation had spread throughout the Columbia Plateau, from The Dalles to Hell's Canyon and from the lower Palouse River Canyon to Kettle Falls. These early residents ranged widely along Pacific shorelines and inland waterways to gather plant foods, hunt small and large mammals, and to find favorable salmon fishing sites after the great ice sheets melted. The beginning of a significant warming trend some 7,500 years ago, continuing until approximately 2000 BC, was accompanied by the appearance of fishnets and tackle assemblies along the Columbia and Snake Rivers. The availability of salmon as a reliable staple of the native people's diet brought about more seasonal and regional migration patterns, with pit-house villages appearing on the lower Snake River around 3000 BC.

An abundance of nephrite and diorite pestles along the lower Snake River and at the Marmes site dating from 3000 BC suggests that the milling of roots and berries also came into widespread use at that time. Finely flaked projectile points show a gradual transition from use for hunting large prehistoric mammals. Enormous Clovis spearpoints are associated with the earliest occupation sites. Beautifully crafted smaller arrowheads appeared with the introduction of the bow around 500 AD. The projectile points were knapped into exquisitely symmetrical shapes and made from the widely assorted colors of semiprecious cryptocrystallines—yellow opals, banded agates, milky chert, blood red jasper, obsidian, and translucent chalcedony.

The Channeled Scablands, Rock Lake, and Palouse Falls

Twenty miles west of Steptoe Butte is an alien landscape showing evidence of unimaginable cataclysm. But the term "scablands" is an unkind name obscuring the area's remarkable geological past. The terrain was formed after the repeated failure of a massive ice dam near the mouth of the Clark Fork River in northern Idaho and the cataclysmic draining of enormous glacial Lake Missoula some 15,000 years ago. The ice dam's failure released volumes of water larger than in any similar event indicated on the planet. The onslaught of Ice Age flooding tore across the soft rolling grasslands, which were violently "scabbed" or cut to bedrock, and formed three major drainages across the Columbia Plateau. The easternmost is the Cheney-Palouse lobe which contains mammoth boulders lying as ancient monuments carried from the Rockies.

In prehistoric times, large mammals lumbered throughout the region seeking seasonal forage along grassy bottomlands. Camel, giant sloth, antelope, mastodon, bison, and bighorn sheep have been excavated at a dozen sites along the western tier of the Palouse hills from Washtucna to Rosalia. Images of bison and sheep appear in red and yellow pictographs and chipped petroglyphs believed to be hundreds of years old at Buffalo Eddy near Lewiston. A fascinating array of four mammoth skeletons, spearpoints, and other artifacts were unearthed a short distance south of Latah in 1876.[2]

To the native peoples, Rock Lake, a deep, basalt-surrounded lake in the western Palouse, was known as "Fawn Place" and "Never Freezing Water." Submerged there are said to be the remains of a great reptilian monster that terrorized both humans and animals long ago. In response to the people's prayers for deliverance from the pestilence, the Great Spirit slew the creature with a huge stone knife which then was used to tear the ground open for a grave. The dismembered creature was cast to the bottom and the chasm filled with water. Although tranquility to the region was restored, Indian legend held that the monster's tail did not die and periodically thrashed to the surface in menacing fury. For this reason Rock Lake was rarely fished by Indians who deemed it a fearful place, and their

Rock Lake (*Mupícpe*/Fawn Place). *R.R. Hutchison Collection, MASC, WSU Libraries, Pullman*

stories of its creation may explain why pioneer travelers through the Palouse referred to it as "Specter Lake."

Located five miles above the mouth of the Palouse River, *Taqa·palé'le* ("Falling Water")—Palouse Falls—is a deafening cataract throughout the spring, cascading down nearly two hundred feet into a spectacle of rainbowed spume. The Palouse Indians knew the lower river as a favored fishing area and had several seasonal camps amid the quiet copses of Osage orange and hackberry. The tribe's namesake, which was later given to the vast domain over which they ranged and knew intimately, was their principal village of *Palús* located on the bank of the river at its confluence with the Snake. The site was at the historic crossroads where the ancient east-west river route from the Columbia to Nez Perce country met a principal north-south Indian trail—still visible for long stretches in the natural rock lands, which led from the Walla Walla Valley to the land of the Spokanes and Fort Colville. The word *Palús* referred to "Standing Rock," a basaltic monolith central to Palouse Indian cosmology, located a short distance upstream.

As Palouse elder Sam Fisher related, in the time of the Animal People, four Giant Brothers armed with spears attacked Beaver who peacefully rested near his lodge at present Hole-in-the-Ground (a valley near Rock Lake). A terrific fight ensued during which Beaver clawed and chewed out the Rock Lake channel, one of the deepest lakes in the region with sections reaching down 325 feet. Beaver tore his way toward the Snake River and where he beat his tail along this route several times, smaller falls were formed along the lower Palouse River. He was struck again at *Apútaput* (Palouse Falls) where in futile lashings Beaver cut the castellated formations and sheer cliffs around the falls. The massive creature finally fell from his wounds where the rivers met and his heart was turned to stone. The Palouse people were said to have sprung from this part of Beaver, and Indian youth were taught to look to Beaver to affirm courage as one of the tribe's most noble traits.[3]

THE LAND AND ITS RESOURCES

Blue bunch wheatgrass, bunchgrass, ryegrass, and other mixed prairie perennials predominated on the rolling Palouse hills, providing luxurious forage for deer, bison, antelope, and the Indians' vast herds of horses that had descended from Spanish stock brought to New Mexico and New Spain in the sixteenth century. The Naxiyamtáma referred to the wild graminae (grass) species simply as *c'ɨktc'ɨk*, or forage grass.

The waters of the Palouse River were clear throughout the year and while salmon were not found above Palouse Falls, trout, whitefish, and freshwater clams were plentiful in the upper river and its tributaries. Turtles were common along the water and, along with the mythical trickster Coyote, were often featured in tribal folktales to explain the origin of the natural world. According to Indian elders, the Palouse hills were formed by Spilyái (Coyote), who "outsmarted himself" in an attempt to be more clever than the other Animal People with whom he once shared the land. He scooped the earth into the distinctive pattern of undulating Palouse hills in a vain attempt to defeat Turtle and his brothers in a race from the Snake River to

Spokane country. The story offered more than entertainment and explanation, for it taught Indian youth the futility of deception and the value of persistence.[4]

The serpentine Palouse River swims through the heart of the hills along a shallow western course beneath the base of Steptoe Butte, fed by quiet grassy streams that bore sibilant designations in the languages of the native peoples: *Mocallisah* (North Palouse Fork), *Ingossamen* (Pine Creek), *Oraytayous* (Rock Creek), and *Čherana* (Cow Creek). These verdant bottomlands host a more diverse flora, with isolated pines and clumps of willow, black hawthorn, and cottonwood brightened by the seasonal blossoms of golden currant bushes and tangled honeysuckle vines with rows of fiery tubular flowers. The fuzzy purple heads of lupine were gathered by area Indians as grave decorations.

The Seasonal Round

Like native peoples throughout North America, the Naxiyamtáma had a close relationship with the natural world. The Creator had made the deer, antelope, and elk, and these animals share the earth with the Indian people. The world of Snake River-Palouse area tribes revolved around a yearly cycle—or seasonal round—that covered an immense territory. Beginning in the early spring of each year, salmon swam out of the Pacific Ocean, fought their way up the great current of the Columbia River, and followed its tributaries upstream until they reached their ancestral spawning grounds in the Inland Northwest. Conditions were most favorable for fishing in May and from July through October.

The region's native peoples considered salmon part of the abundance given to them by the Creator. The spring renewal of life was evident in the resurgence of flow in the Snake and Spokane Rivers and their tributaries. Fed by the melting waters of the Bitterroot and Blue Mountains, the Snake began to rise and carry with it a variety of debris from the high country. The animals felt the change as well, particularly the horses that still sported their heavy winter coats.

Migration, trading, and raiding probably brought horses to the Inland Pacific Northwest by the middle of the eighteenth century, and Palouse-Nez Perce elder Gordon Fisher relates the story of how the first mare came to the Palouse people. March was a time of much activity for the Indians who busied themselves in preparation for their journey onto the Columbia Plain. "We called this *Shai Tash*, 'Time to Move Out,'" recalled Mary Jim. "Those horses that were to make the trip out of the canyon were cut out from the herds." Many of these animals had not been ridden in some time, so the men mounted the skittish ponies and rode them hard until they stopped bucking.[5] Men, women, and children alike then mounted the horses and began their journey to the root grounds, while some family members remained along the rivers for the first salmon runs in May. For children like young Mary, traveling again and seeing the animals of the land was an exciting time.

Linguistic indications of the native people's intimacy with the natural world is evident in countless Sahaptin terms for plant species used for food, as medicine, or in fashioning baskets, mats, and other useful items. Many Palouse names for birds were as much sung as spoken, in onomatopoetic mimicry of the creatures' calls—*áčah* (magpie), *mítalu* (mourning dove), *siwlalí* (trumpeter swan), and a sentinel bird, *wawyik'k* (whip-poor-will). Others were known by their behavior or other distinct qualities including "dances together" (sage grouse), "traveler" (snow goose), and the prairie falcon, "comes at you."[6]

The Lomatium family of perennial herbs includes such familiar greens as parsley, dill, and celery. The nine species native to the Palouse, nutritious staples of the native diet, favored the shallow lithosols (soils) among rocky outcroppings. The appearance of blossoming Canby's lomatium (biscuitroot)—known to the Palouse and Nez Perce as *sk'olkul*—in late February and early March signaled the beginning of spring for Plateau root diggers. Union Flat Creek was called the *Sk'olkul* because of the four major root grounds found along its course (near present La Crosse, Wilcox, Union Center, and Colton). Among the other eight important tuberous lomatiums that grew along the Snake River and in the western Palouse were Gray's lomatium, or "Indian celery," Hamblen's lomatium, and yellow-flowered kouse (*L. cous*).

More than twenty principal camas grounds covering up to several dozen acres each were located across the Palouse in vernal meadows at such places as Washtucna Lake and Rock Lake; along Latah, Pine, and Union Flat Creeks, and the Palouse River; and in the fertile lowlands near present-day Colfax, the Pullman-Moscow area, and at the southeastern base of Steptoe Butte. Edible camas (*C. quamash*) displays white or blue flowers and was gathered in vast quantities during early summer while the shunned death camas (*Z. venenosus*) presents yellow blossoms.

The rock rose, or bitterroot, also grew in the rocky soils of the western Palouse but was more abundant on the drier plains to the west. Along with the wild huckleberries that ripened in the fall on bushes clustered among the pines in the eastern Palouse, camas, kouse, and bitterroot were the four most important plant foods of the Palouse country tribes. Places favored by the Coeur d' Alenes and Spokanes for spring bitterroot and camas digging included the upper Palouse country from *Nigualk'h* (present Tensed) in the valley of the Palouse North Fork and northwesterly across the present Rockford, Spangle, and Cheney districts. Here the size of the roots and the ease of digging in the rich black loam attracted large tribal gatherings each spring.[7]

The Snake River-Palouse people gathered roots during their spring journey onto the Columbia Plain and the Palouse hills until the salmon began their movement up the Columbia River. When the bands learned of the spring run of the salmon, they returned to their permanent villages and prepared for fishing. Many varieties of fish were taken from the Snake and Spokane Rivers and streams tributary to them including trout, whitefish, squawfish, suckers, chubs, and eels. Snake River white sturgeon were also fished, although, when mature, some could reach twelve feet in length and weigh a half-ton, making them virtually impossible to capture. Three genera of the Salmonidae family of fishes were native to the

Snake River including the genus *Oncorhynchus* with five species of Pacific salmon (Chinook or king, pink sockeye, humpback, silver or coho, and white-fleshed chum). *Salvelinus* members are the Dolly Varden, or bull trout, and brook trout, while the genus *Salmo* includes the anadromous steelhead and non-anadromous rainbow and cutthroat trout.

With no major waterfalls for dip-netting on the lower Snake River, most salmon were taken by gill netting, weirs along small tributaries, or by gaffing spawning fish. Palouse area Indians also traveled to net fish at Celilo and Kettle Falls, the two largest fisheries on the Columbia River. The annual catch of salmon and steelhead by Columbia Plateau tribes prior to white contact is conservatively estimated to have been 17,000,000 pounds. Fish accounted for approximately one-third of the Plateau Indian diet, while roots and berries contributed about half. Game meat including venison and wild fowl substantially completed their nutritional needs.[8]

Salmon, however, were by far the most important fish to the Indians of the region. Besides being one of the most important sources of food, salmon held a special significance in tribal cosmology and myth. Most Plateau tribes of the Northwest held a thanksgiving (or First Feast) ceremony in honor of the salmon as soon as the first fish was caught. All fishing in the area stopped when a man brought in the first salmon. It was cooked, usually boiled, and became the center of the rites. Everyone was issued a portion of water, to fill horn spoons or wooden vessels, and after a prayer was said, the water was drunk by all present. Another prayer was sung thanking the Creator for the fish. Everyone then took a portion of the salmon, ate it, and then took another sip of water. A lengthy prayer was sung and the remaining skeleton of the fish was returned to the water facing upstream. Once proper religious rites were completed for the sacred salmon, fishing resumed.

Thousands of salmon were taken from the river, and each year thousands returned. According to the Naxiyamtáma, salmon runs began in the age of the Animal People after Salmon Man prevailed over the Wolf Brothers and a gauntlet of upriver challenges from the ocean. In a story related by Palouse elder Andrew George, a piece of Salmon Man's flesh was carried all the way to the ocean where it eventually grew into another salmon. The new salmon later ascended the river to avenge the killing and this journey began the cycle of salmon runs to the Snake, Palouse, and other rivers of the Plateau. The lanky trickster Coyote later taught the people how to catch the salmon by using nets made of milkweed hemp.[9]

After the spring and summer runs of salmon, many families left their villages to venture onto the Columbia Plateau or the lowland valleys in the Palouse hills. They would travel to root grounds and camp to dig, hunt, and relax. Summers in the region were usually mild and dry. The children played games with a hoop and a pole or a bat and ball. Men and boys would practice and hone their skill as archers. One of the most enjoyable pursuits was horse racing. The Plateau Indians became great horse people, and men and women alike could care for and ride horses. They were well aware of the qualities that made a good horse, and they bred horses that were strong, fast, and smart. Although it is unlikely that they bred horses for color alone, some Indians prized the beautifully spotted Appaloosa horses and recognized their value as a medium of trade.

The late summer and fall were also important times to area Indians for hunting and digging, as well as for gatherings with neighboring tribes of the region. This time of the year also had a religious significance as the time when young people, boys and girls alike, were sent on their spirit quests. Youth from about the age of twelve went out alone to seek a spirit in remote places like the summit of Steptoe Butte or in the foothills and meadows of the Blue Mountains, where tribal bands frequented fall hunting and berry grounds. As the brisk autumn weather transformed the mountain slopes into fiery landscapes of red and yellow, young people sought their guardian spirits on such peaks as *Watniwash* (Spirit Mountain). *Tehám-tehám* (Cloudy Mountain) was avoided since the summit was a one-way portal to the Spirit World that humans were forbidden to enter. Animal People sentries clad in blue feathers and white bear hides stood high upon its slopes to warn seekers not to continue further into the foggy heights.

During the quest, a guardian spirit might appear in a dream as a wolf, cloud, bear, eagle, hawk, or other animal or natural phenomenon like hail or thunder. Protection and guidance could then be summoned for a lifetime through a song imparted to the seeker. After the youths experienced a few days of solitude, they returned to camp, or elders of the tribe went to gather and feed them. The old men of the tribes, those of great wisdom, heard from the children about their experiences and interpreted dreams for those who had come of age. Such visions were not deemed fantasies but deeply revered spiritual experience revealed to a purified seeker through a timeless dimension. The native peoples' specific knowledge of regional landscapes and their creatures informed their mythology and spirit quests. Human beings existed within a sacred circle of life that brought together past, present, and place in a way that transcended tense and tangibility.[10]

Late summer meshed with early fall and the bands moved gradually into that part of the seasonal round that took them to favored hunting grounds. The men killed larger game animals like deer and elk as well as grouse and water fowl. They prepared the meat for the coming winter while the women gathered berries and dug the last vestiges of camas and kouse. Wild gooseberries, thornberries, service berries, and blackberries were among the favorites of Snake River-Palouse Indians. Two varieties of elderberries were also picked, one from the prairie and one from the higher mountains. Also found in the higher country was the serviceberry, huckleberry, snowberry, and fire berry, which were sometimes mixed with dried meat. The fireberry was so small that the Indians devised a small comb to pick the tiny fruit. Pine moss or bear-hair lichen was also collected in the high mountains, cooked underground like camas, and pounded into a fine treat that is still prized for its licorice-like flavor.

As winter approached, the many bands of Indians packed up their belongings and started on their journey back across the gentle valleys and rolling hills to their permanent villages along the

Snake, Clearwater, and Spokane Rivers. They were heavily laden with prepared meat, berries, and roots. During the winter months family lodges became the center of activity; people spent much time inside or gathered around a communal fire along the river. While the women mended baskets and men repaired hunting and fishing gear or knapped new points, children listened to family elders share ancient tales about Salmon Man and the Wolf Brothers, and Beaver and Coyote. Around this time, the entire band usually gathered for the Guardian Spirit Dance. This was a sacred ceremony for Indians of the Columbia Plateau and demonstrated their affinity with their spirit guardians and the natural world.

Notes

1. Joe Watkins, *Kennewick Man: Perspectives on the Ancient One*, Walnut Grove, CA: Left Coast Press, 2008.
2. Standing thirteen feet high at the shoulder and with fossilized ivory tusk curls ten feet long, the Palouse mammoth skeleton is impressively displayed today at Chicago's Field Museum.
3. Clark, Ella. *Indian Legends of the Pacific Northwest*.
4. A. George, 1980.
5. M. Jim, 1979.
6 M. Jim, 1979; Hunn and Selam, *Nch'i-Wana*.
7. Piper and Beattie, *Flora of the Palouse Region*; Archer and Bunch, *The American Grass Book*; M. Jim, 1979.
8. M. Jim, 1979; E. Hunn and J. Selam, 1990.
9. A. George, 1980.
10. M. Jim, 1979; A. George, 1980.

APPENDIX A

A Naxiyamtáma Lexicon of Animal and Plant Terms

A substantial portion of this lexicon is based on linguistic field research conducted by University of Washington (UW) anthropologist Melville Jacobs (1902-1971) with Northern Sahaptin Palouse speakers in 1930. Jacobs had studied at Columbia University in the 1920s under the noted anthropologist Franz Boas and in 1928 joined the UW faculty where he taught until his death in 1971. Among Jacobs's many contributions to the field was his lifelong work documenting and preserving Native American languages of the Pacific Northwest including such works as *A Sketch of Northern Sahaptin Grammar* (1931).

Entries for this lexicon were supplied by Jacobs' principal Palouse informant, George Lucas (Páxalawasq'ísit, Five Shadows, "Star Doctor," 1850?-1938?), and found in the Jacobs Collection (UW 81/73) at the University of Washington Suzzallo Library Archives. This appendix was prepared from copies at the Colville Tribal Museum Archives at Coulee Dam, Washington. George Lucas's personal story is remarkable in its own right. Following 1877 Nez Perce War exile with the Palouse band to Indian Territory, Five Shadows could not abide life in a desolate land without the life-giving rivers and hills he had known from youth. He set out to formulate a plan to return to his homeland in defiance of his captors. His is the only documented case of someone in the group who was able to do so prior to the exiles' repatriation in 1885. Five Shadows did so apparently by walking the entire way from present Oklahoma to Washington Territory.

Other important lexicon contributors are indicated by superscript numerals and include [1]Cy Johnly with Jacobs (1930), [2]Mary Jim Chapman with Richard Scheuerman and Clifford Trafzer (1979-80), and [3]Tom Andrews with Bruce Rigsby (1963-64). The arrangement of these taxonomies is based on an extensive listing of Yakama terms by Eugene Hunn with James Selam in *Nchi'i-Wána "The Big River": Mid-Columbia Indians and Their Land*, 1990.

A. Animal Terms

MOLLUSCA (mollusks)
  Pelecypoda (bivalves)
    Eulamellibranchia
      Schizodonta (freshwater clams): šiwá·la

INSECTA (insects)
  Odonata (dragonflies[2] and damselflies): papacáki
  Orthoptera (crickets and grasshoppers)
    grasshopper (short-horned?) (*Acrididae* spp.): t'át'c
    "black locust" (band-winged grasshopper?) (*Oedipodinae* spp.): c'aac'át
    green tree crickets (*Oecanthinae* spp.): sɨlksɨlk
  Coleoptera (beetles)
    "black beetles" ("stink bugs" (*Eleodes* spp.): ti'íš
  Lepidoptera (butterflies and moths)
    Papilionoidea (butterflies)[2]: wálák-wálak
  Diptera (flies)
    mosquitoes (*Culicidae* spp): wawá
    horse flies (*Tabanus* spp.): iłč'ač'apamá
    house flies (*Musca* spp.): max̣núy
  Hymenoptera (ants, bees, wasps)
    Formicidae (ants)[2] in general: kluwisá
    Vespidae (yellowjackets and hornets)[2] in general: atníwa
    Apidae (bumblebees)[2]: lawasmuk´

CHORDATA (vertebrates)
  Agnatha (boneless fishes)
    Petromyzontiformes (lampreys)
    Pacific lamprey ("eel"): k'súyas

OSTEICHTHYES (bony fishes)
  Acipenseriformes (sturgeons)
    sturgeon: x̣ílax̣
  Salmonidae (salmon, trout, whitefish)
    "salmon" in general: waykáanaš
    Chinook or king salmon[3] (*Oncorhynchus tschawytscha*): núsux̣;
      spawning: ayx
    pink or humpback salmon[2] (*O. gorbuscha*): wak´ya

coho or silver salmon² (*O. kisutch*): sinúx
sockeye or blueback salmon² (*O. nerka*): k´halux
chum, white, or dog salmon³ (*O. keta*): čilí
"common trout" [cutthroat?] (*Salmo clarki*): wilx̣awílx̣a
rainbow trout [not anadromous] (*S. gairdneri*): t'šä·t'cä´
steelhead trout (*S. gairdneri*): šušáyš
brook trout³ ("Dolly Varden") (*S. fontinalus*): wawáłam
bull trout (*S. confluentius*): áščɨnkš
mountain whitefish² (*Prosopium williamsoni*): sɨmay
  Osmeridae (smelts)
  Cyprinidae (minnows and carp)
"chub" (northern squawfish) (*Ptychocheilus oregonensis*): luqw'áya
  Catosomidae (suckers)
"young suckers" (bridge-lip?) (*Catostomus columbianus*): suwasúwa

AMPHIBIA (amphibians)
  Hylidae (tree frogs)
    Pacific tree frog (*Hyla regilla*): aluqw'át

REPTILIA (reptiles)
  Tesudines (turtles)
    in general (including box turtles): alašík
  Squamata (lizards and snakes)
    lizards (*Sceloporus* spp.): watik'áłał
    "grey lizard" (short-horned?) (*Phrynosoma douglassi*): x̣alíłáx̣liła
  Ophidia (snakes)
    in general (excluding rattlesnakes): piyúš
    "bull snake" (gopher snake) (*Pituophis melanoleucus*): kw'ayímkw'ayim
  Viperidae (pit vipers)
    Pacific rattlesnake (*Crotalus virdis oreganus*): wáx̣puš

AVES (birds)
  Ciconiiformes (herons, storks, etc.)
    great blue heron (*Ardea herodias*): múq'a
  Anseriformes (ducks, geeses, and swans)
    Cygnini (swans)
      trumpeter swan (*Cygnus columbianus*): siwlalí
    Anserini (geese)
      Canada goose (*Branta canadensis*): ákak

Anatini (ducks)
  mallard (*Anas platrhynchos*): x̱ä´tx̱ät
  common merganser (*Mergus merganser*): táštaš
Falconiformes (eagles, hawks, falcons, etc.)
 Cathartidae (New World vultures)
  turkey vulture[3] (*Cathartes aura*): q'ašpalí
 Accipitridae (hawks and eagles)
  osprey[3] (*Pandion haliaetus*): sáxsax
  golden eagle[2] (*Aquila chrysaetos*): x̱wayamá (Eagle in myth: x̱wayamayái)
  "black hawk," "night hawk" (northern harrier?) (*Circus cyaneus*): wapɨniwɬá
  "chicken hawk" (red-tailed hawk) (*Buteo jamaicensis*): tamapčíyu
 Falconidae (falcons)
  American kestrel/sparrow hawk (*Falco sparverius*): yíitit
Galliformes (grouse, quail, partridges, pheasants)
  [blue] grouse (*Dendragapus obscures*): pə´ti
  ruffed grouse (*Bonasa umbellus*): wašwášnu
  "brush chicken" (sharp-tailed grouse?) (*Tympanuchus phasianellus*): wucwu´cnu
  ring-necked pheasant (introduced) (*Phasianus colchicus*): wáɬxus
  chicken[2] (introduced) (*Gallus gallus*): likúuk
  mountain quail[2] (*Oreotyx pictus*): patašhí
Gruiformes (cranes, rails, and coots)
  mud hen (American coot?) (*Fulica americana*): wa'áwənu
  crane (sandhill) (*Grus canadensis*): úu'u
Charadriiformes (shorebirds)
  spotted sandpiper (*Actitis macularia*): wítwit
  long-billed curlew (*Numenius americanus*): kw'áykw'ay
Columbiformes (pigeons and doves)
 Columbidae
  "turtle dove" (mourning dove?) (*Zenaida macroura*): mítalu
Strigidae (true owls)
  great horned owl (*Bubo virginianus*): miimánu
  burrowing owl[3] (*Athene cunicularia*): papú
  western screech owl (*Otus kennicottii*): wéwuntiman
Caprimulgiformes (whip-poor-wills, nighthawks)
 Caprimulginae (whip-poor-wills)
  common poorwill[2] (*Phalaenoptilus nuttali*): wawyik'k
Apodiformes (swifts and hummingbirds)
 Trochilidae (hummingbirds[2]): qmamsalí

Coradiiformes (kingfishers)
   belted kingfisher[2] (*Ceryle alcyon*): šáx̣šax̣
Piciformes (woodpeckers)
   woodpecker (Lewis's?) (*Melanerpes lewis*): wiłpux̣pux̣
   "yellowhammer" [northern flicker] (*Colaptes auratus*): aatníwa
Passeriformes (perching birds)
 Tyrannidae (tyrant flycatchers)
   "bee martin" (eastern kingbird) (*Tyrannus tyrannus*): mi´tskatat
 Hirundinidae (swallows)
   swallows ("black swallow"), in general: t'íx̣tix̣
 Corvidae (jays, crows, ravens)
   Steller's jay (*Cyanocitta stelleri*): kwáškwaš (Blue Jay in myth: kwáškwášyái)
   Clark's nutcracker[2] (*Nucifraga columbiana*): lal
   black-billed magpie[3] (*Pica pica*): áčak
   American crow (*Corvus brachyrhynchos*): á'a
 Muscicapidae (Old World flycatchers)
   western bluebird[2] (*Sialia mexicana*): yulyúl
 Mimidae
   northern "mockingbird" (Bullock's oriole?) (*Mimus polyglottus*): wawšukłá
 Turdis (robins)
   American robin (*Turdis migratorious*): wíspakpak (wíšpoxpox)[3]
 Emberizadae (sparrow family)
 Icterinae (blackbirds, orioles, meadowlarks)
   western meadowlark (*Sturnella neglecta*): x̣wiłx̣wł (xulxúl)[3]
   blackbird (Brewer's?) (*Euphagus cyanocephalus*): t'ɨt'ámx̣
 Fringilladae (finch family)
   American goldfinch? (*Carduelis tristis*): míčkatit

MAMMALIA (mammals)
 Lagmorpha (rabbits, hairs, cottontails)
   hare (white-tailed jackrabbit, *Lepus townsendii*): wilalík
   eastern cottontail (*Sylvilagus floridanus* [introduced]): áykwš
   showshoe hare[3] (*Lepus americanus*): pálxc
 Rodentia (rodents)
  Sciuridae (marmots, squirrels, chipmunks)
   yellow-bellied marmot (*Marmota flaviventris*): šɨkšɨ'k'nu
   ground squirrel (*Citellus* spp.): tátnu
   prairie dog (white-tailed?) (*Cynomys leucurus*): lamiyá
  Hystricomorpha
   porcupine[1] (*Erethizon dorsatum*): šɨšaš

Castoridae (beavers)
  beaver (*Castor canadensis*): wišpúš
Myomorpha (rats, mice, and voles)
  deer mouse (*Peromyscus maniculatus*): lákas
  wood rat (*Neotoma cinerea*): wusí
  muskrat (*Ondatra zibethicus*): paptís
Carnivora (carnivores)
 Fissipedia (land carnivores)
  gray fox (*Urocyon cinereoargenteus*): tiɬípa
  wolf (*Canus lupus*): x̱áliš
  coyote (*Canis latrans*): spílya (Coyote in myth: spilyái)
  domestic dog (*Canis familiaris*): k'usi k'úsi
 Ursidae (bears)
  brown and black bear (*Ursus americanus*): yáka (Brown Bear in myth: yakayái)
  grizzly bear[3] (*Ursus horribilis*): twatí·t'as (Grizzy Bear in myth: twati·t'asyái)
 Procyonidae (raccoons)
  raccoon (*Procyon lotor*): k'a·lás
 Mustelidae (martins, minks, otters)
  mink (*Mustela vison*): papyáw
  badger (*Taxidea taxus*): šíki
  striped skunk (*Mephitis mephitis*): tistsái (Skunk in myth: tistayái)
  river otter (*Lutra canadensis*): nukšáy
  long-tailed weasel[1] (*Mustela frenata*): c'íɬała
 Felidae (cougar, lynx, bobcat)
  cougar/mountain lion[3] (*Felis concolor*): q'wayamá (Cougar in myth: q'wayamayái)
  bobcat, wildcat[3] (*Lynx rufus*): qá·p (Wildcat in myth: qa·pyái)
Perissodactyla
 Equidae (horses, donkeys, mules)
  horse (*Equus caballus*): k'úsi
   čmuk[2] (black)
   luc'á[2] (red)
   maq'á š[2] (yellow/sorrel)
   šk'i- šk'i[2] (brown)
   tamsilpíin[2] (Appaloosa)
Artiodactyla
 Cervidae (deer, elk, moose)

elk/wapiti³ (*Cervus canadensis*) bull: wewú·kya, cow: tašípka, calf: q'ayík (Bull Elk in myth: wawu·kyayái)

deer³ (*Odocoileus* spp.) buck: yúkasi ("has horns"), doe: yámaš, fawn: mups (Deer in myth: yamašyái)

Bovidae
    buffalo¹ (*Bison bison*): cúɬɨm
    bighorn sheep³ (*Ovis canadensis*): tnú·n
    mountain goat³ (*Oreamnos americanus*): caxíšxiš

Antilocapridae
    pronghorn antelope (*Antilocapra americana*): wú·taw

B. Plant Terms

balsamroot ("sunflower") (*Balsamorhiza careyana*): pášxa
barley/oats (introduced) (*Hordeum/Avena* spp.): láwín (from French)
berries, in general: tmaanít
bisquitroot (*Lomatium cous*): x̣áwš
bitterroot (*Lewisa rediviva*): piyax̣í
blackberry, raspberry (*Rubus* spp.): šáxat
blueberry² (*Vaccinium deliciosum*): lilmúk
bulrush, hardstem (tule)¹ (*Scirpus acutus*): tk'ú
bunchgrass³ (*Festuca idahoensis*): alám
camas (*Camassia quamash*): xmáš
carrot, Indian (*Perideridia gairdneri*): sawítk
cedar, western red (*Thuja plicata*): nánk
chokecherry² (*Prunus virginiana*): tmɨ́šway (fruit: tmɨ́š)
cocklebur² (*Xanthium strumarium*): k'ak'ák
cottonwood (*Populus trichocarpa*): x̣apx̣áp
currant, golden² (*Ribes aureum*) [fruit]: x̣nɨ́n
elderberry, blue² (*Sambucus cerulean*) [fruit]: c'mit
elderberry, red (*Sambucus racemosa*) [fruit]: wɨwán
fir³ (*Abies*): pápš
"grasses" in general (*Graminae* spp.): c'ɨ́ktc'ɨk
hawthorne, black (*Crataegus douglasii*) [fruit]: šɨšnɨ́m
hemp, Indian² (*Apocynum cannabinum*): qéemu (Nez Perce loanword)
horsetail fern (*Equisetum* spp.): šaykw·šáykw
huckleberry, big² (*Vaccinium membranaceum*): wíwnu
juniper (*Juniperus*): puʔúš
kouse (*Lomatium cous*): x̄āwš

lichen, black tree (moss)² (*Bryoria fremontii*): kʼúnč,² ópop
lomatium
  Lomatium canby:² lukš
  L. cous: x̱āwš
  L. dissecttum:² čalúkš
  L. donellii:² xáti
  L. farinosum:² múx̱sli
  L. gormanii:² sasamtʼa
  L. grayi:² latít-latít
  L. macrocarpum:² púkła
  L. nudicaule:² x̱amsí
  L. piperi:² mámɨn
oats/barley (introduced) (*Avena/Hordeum* spp.): láwín (from French)
onion, Douglas³ (*Allium douglasii*): kʼwiya
parsnip, Indian (*Lomatium nudicaule*): kwʼíya
pea (introduced) (*Pisum* spp.): lapoís (from French)
pine, ponderosa (western yellow, bull)² (*Pinus ponderosa*): tápaš
pine, western white² (*Pinus monticola*): tápaš
potato, Indian (*Claytonia lanceolata*): anipä´c
potato, "white flower": sasítʼama
raspberry, blackberry (*Rubus* spp.): šáxat
roots, in general: x̱nít
sagebrush, big¹ (*Artemisia tridenta*): tawsá
sagebrush, dwarf¹ (*Artemisa arbuscula*): tawsátawsa
salmonberry (*Rubus spectabilis*) [fruit]: šapyá-šapya
serviceberry¹ (*Amelanchier alnifilia*): kula·kula (fruit: ččáa)
snowberry ("little white berry")¹ (*Symphoricarpos albus*) [fruit]: wɨwán
strawberry (*Fragaria vesca*) [fruit]: suspán
sunflower: see balsamroot
thorn apple (*Crataegus douglasii*) [fruit]: šɨšnɨm (also hawthorne fruit?)
wheat (introduced) (*Triticum* spp.): àytulú (from French)
willow (*Salix* spp.): wiwnúšway

APPENDIX B

Historic Era Naxiyamtáma Village and Place Names

The following list of principal Snake River-Palouse villages is based on interviews by anthropologist Verne Ray with Snake River-Palouse elders Harry Jim (1956) and Cleveland and Alalumt'i Kamiakin (1959), Bruce Rigsby with Tom and Alice Andrews and Oswald Tias (1964), Richard Scheuerman with Mary Jim Chapman (1979), and nineteenth-century explorers' accounts. Although informants often described the same places with nearly identical names and locations, this list is by no means exhaustive. Dozens of village sites were located on both sides of the Snake River for a hundred miles from its confluence with the Columbia to Alpáwa.

Substantial populations inhabited some of these communities year after year—places like *Samyúya*, *Palús*, and *Wawáwi* among the lower, middle, and upper Naxiyamtáma, respectively. Due to linguistic and other cultural associations, families in these areas had extensive interaction with neighboring Wanapam, Umatilla, Walla Walla, and Nez Perce peoples. In addition to these traditional fishing and winter villages, numerous other temporary campsites existed along the rivers, on the prairies, and in the mountains for seasonal root digging, berry picking, hunting, and other purposes. Summer winds and marauding animals threatened abandoned

Palús villagers and longhouse, c. 1910. *Click Relander Collection, Yakima Public Library*

homes so families routinely dismantled and stored their lodge poles and tule mats when they moved to higher areas. Wooden houses and semi-underground pit houses were also used.

The central Palouse Hills were generally unsuitable for winter habitation as the area was exposed and often snow-covered, with frozen lakes and watercourses. The Snake River Canyon and lower Palouse and Tucannon, however, afforded protection, water, and access to game. Permanent villages were not occupied at the same time given river conditions, wildlife distribution, and mere human caprice. Periodic movement from one village to another was usually congenial, although families tended to favor fishing and winter residence in the same general area.

Principal Snake River, Palouse, and Tucannon Villages

1. *K'wsís* ("at the point"): At the confluence of the Snake and Columbia rivers where the pioneer settlement of Ainsworth was located below present Pasco; variously referenced as "*Kosith*," "*Quosispa*."

2. *Samyúya*: South side of the Snake River above present Burbank, and principal residence of the Cawa-w´tiak/Jim family; C. Relander's "*Sumuya*." A famous horseracing track was located on the broad flat across the river.

3. *Twenatčus*: Both sides of the Snake River near present Ash, perhaps Mary Jim's *Tyáwtaš* ("drying shed").

4. *Wiša·wap·yes*: At Levey on the north side of the Snake River.

5. *Ákak* ("Canada goose"): South side of the Snake River above Levy.

6. *Tamáyp·la* ("wind against the river"; perhaps indicating the sound of waves): An important fishing site on the north side of the Snake River near the terminus of Herman Road.

7. *Wawyuk'má* ("poorwills"): On the south side of the Snake River at Fishhook Bend; a principal residence of the Tilqawayks/Tilcoax/Wolf family. Nearby islands included *Nch'i-'imá* (Big Island), *Šaykw·šáykw* ("horsetail fern"), and *Siipa* (piled "rubble" rock).

8. *Tásiwiks* ("whirlpool"): On the north side of the Snake River near present Page, Relander's "Tasawiks." Some accounts mention a south side location though that was likely the nearby fishing place *Mítax*.

9. *Keekíya* ("Racoon," in myth): a large village and popular north shore torchlight fishing site near Winders Ferry. Oswald Tias [1964] identifies *I·máwtaš* in this vicinity where "there used to be a ferry boat."

Appendices 173

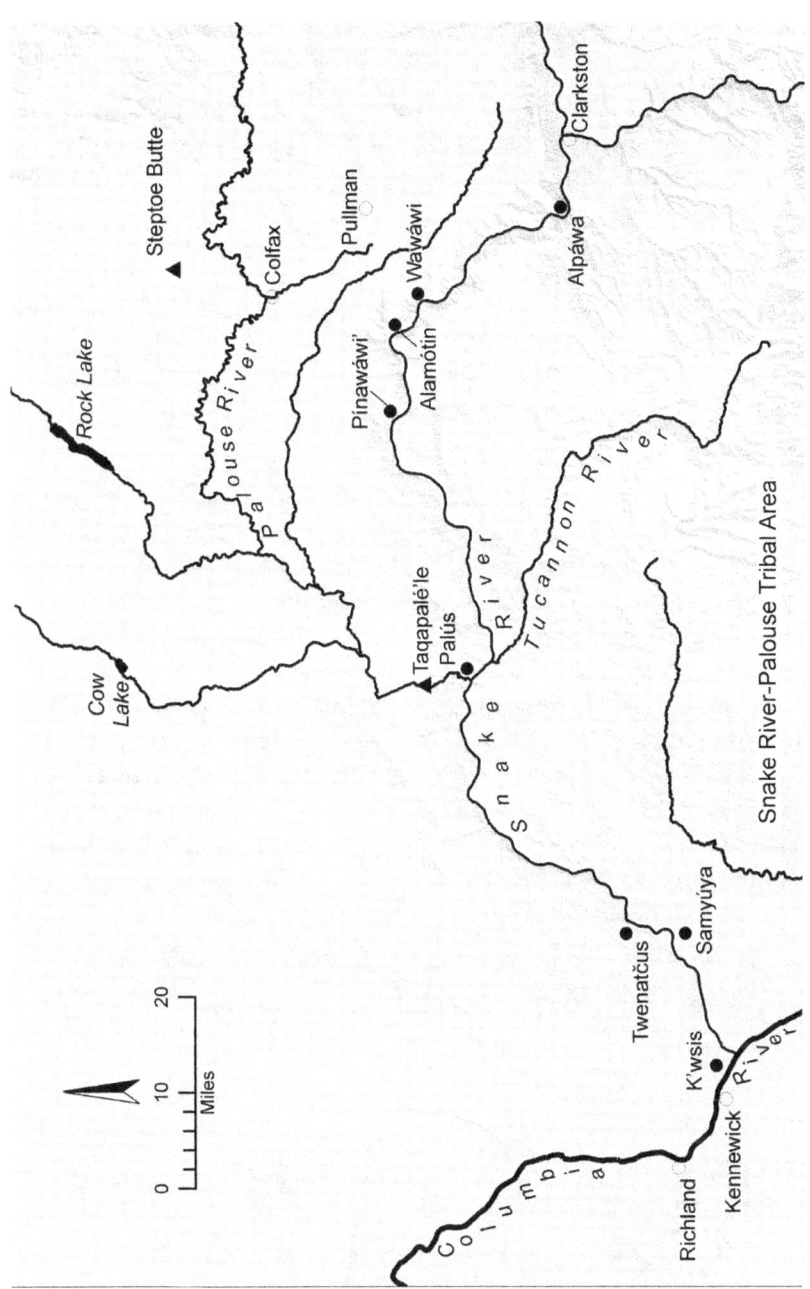

Snake River–Palouse Tribal Area. *Map by Robert Johnson, Conservation Biology, University of California, Riverside*

10. *Páyčaš* ("standing at the edge"): An important village and river crossing site on Jim Boat Island and the south side of the Snake River near present Walker; variously referenced as "Pichias."

11. *Xalótaš*: One-half mile below present Harder; also the name of a series of prominent nineteenth-century Palouse headmen. Oswald Tias (1964) identifies Kahlotus Lake with this name.

12. *Múun·pa* ("at a whirlpool"): A winter camp opposite Ayer Junction on the north shore.

13. *Samlá*: About one mile above present Ayer Junction. Harry Jim spoke of *Póotkwistot* near here; a term related to a gambling wager and perhaps associated with a mythical contest nearby between Grizzly Bear and Sturgeon.

14. *Q'ínak·pa* ("at a gorge"): A spring fishing site about 2¼ miles above present Sand.

15. *Palús* (*Palúus, Pelus*): Located at the mouth of the Palouse River and ancient crossing of the Snake River—now Lyons Ferry. This major village and namesake of the Palouse tribe, inhabited well into the twentieth century, was a principal residence of the Yoosyóos Tulikécin/Fisher, Slowiarchy/Felix, and Kamiakin families. The term is derived from the rock monolith prominent in tribal mythology near the confluence of the rivers with Palouse Sahaptin prefix *pa-* ("placed upright") with the root *–lú* ("be in water"), plus the diminutivized mediopassive suffix *–s*. "Palouse" in conventional spelling first appears in the 1855 Yakima Treaty, following references to "Peloose" in 1846 by Hale with Charles Wilkes' United States Exploring Expedition, and Isaac Stevens' "Pelouse" in an 1854 report to the Office of Indian Affairs. (See *Palótap*, #30 below, for possible earlier written associations with the word.)

16. *Liptó·pa*: The next village on the Palouse River upstream from *Palús*.

17. *Slaxó·pa* ("wash-out"): In lower Palouse River canyon.

18. *Ápatap* (A-put-top, "falling water"): At the base of Palouse Falls.

19. *Wá·pnit·pa* ("coming out"): On the Snake River near Riparia at the mouth of the Tucannon River.

20. *Téksas·pa* ("debouchement"): Several hundred feet up the mouth of the Tucannon River and namesake for the "Texas Ferry" and "Texas Road."

21. *Táimsk*: On the Tucannon River near present Starbuck.

22. *Q'ŏl·pa* ("hollow"): On the lower Tucannon River.

23. *Wétswei'*: On the south shore of the Snake River near present Ridpath.

24. *Pínawáwi'*: At the mouth of Penawawa Creek near the settlement of Penawawa; an important salmon, sturgeon, trout, and eel station; a principal residence of the Poyahkin family. Carrie Jim noted that the name may be derived from a Nez Perce word meaning "flat place."

25. *Mexmáx (má'mas)*: north side of the Snake River between Swift and Almota.

26. *Alamótin* ("torchlight"): Situated at the mouth of Almota Creek near the settlement of Almota and one of the largest Snake River-Palouse villages; a principal residence of the Paween/Billy-Andrews family.

27. *Atásas*: On the north side of the Snake River at Davis' Bar.

28. *Wawáwi* ("fishing place"): A large village at present Wawawai and principal residence of the Hahtálekin (Red Echo) and Paween families.

29. *Saxátap*: A small village on the north bank of the Snake River near present Crum.

30. *Palótap* ("green slime mold"): At present Truax on the northwest side of the Snake River. Although apparently unoccupied at the time of Lewis and Clark's expedition, the name may be associated with their use of the terms "Pallotepallows," "Palloatpallah," and its variants (e.g., Alexander Ross's Palle-to-Pallas) and misprints ("Selloatpallahs" on Lewis and Clark's 1814 map) which have influenced forms of the name "Palouse."

31. *Nuhsuema*: A small village on the south side of the Snake River opposite *Palótap*.

32. *Aiákuewi'*: A small village on the northwest bank of the Snake River at present Bishop.

33. *Toqó'p*: At Bishop's Bar on the northwest side of the Snake River.

34. *Witkís·pa*: A large village on the northwest side of the Snake River at Indian Siding. The name may derive from the Northeast Sahaptin word for alder.

35. *Keláišun*: On the south side of the Snake River opposite *Witkis·pa*.

36. *Alpáwa*: On the northwest side of the Snake River at the mouth of Alpowa Creek, and perhaps a location on the opposite side; J. Doty's "Al-pow-ow-wee."

OTHER FEATURES AND LOCALES

37. *Naxíyam* ("lower river," i.e., the Snake River): This Northeast Sahaptin name appears to be related to the Nez Perce term *lexéyu*, or "Sahaptin People" (e.g., Palouse, Wanapam) through a common ancient cognate. The Nez Perce word for the Snake River is *Pikúunen*, or "Big River," perhaps the origin of the name "Ki-moo-e-nim" for the river recorded by Lewis and Clark.

38. *Nčii·wana* (*Nch'i-wana*, "big water," i.e., the Columbia River): Known to the lower Nez Perce bands as ʔeteyé·kus ("Distant Water").

39. *Taqa·palé'le* ("falling water"): Palouse Falls.

40. *Qiqíya* (perhaps mythical "Racoon"): a falls nearby *Taqa·palé'le*, probably Little Palouse Falls.

41. *Túše*: present Dayton.

42. *Pátite*: Patit Creek valley near Dayton.

43. *Patáha*: Pataha Creek valley near Pomeroy.

44. *Qápyayn*: present Waitsburg.

45. *Tkwánanma*: Tucannon River.

46. *Mupícpe* ("fawn place"): Rock Lake, principal home of the Chief Kamiakin family following the 1850s Yakima War until many relocated to the Colville Indian Reservation in 1885.

47. *Elatsaywitsun*: Spokane Salish word for Sprague Lake.

48. *Tínatpaʔama*: present Colfax; a Nez Perce word. "Tenapanup" also shown as the South Palouse Fork by frontier topographer John Mullan. (Mullan variously identifies the main Palouse River and North Fork as "Mocalissiah" and "Ky-an-ee-mah.")

49. *Čerana*: Cow Creek

50. *Yámuštas* ("Elk's Abode"): Steptoe Butte, a destination for spirit quests and prominent in tribal legend; Mullan's "Eomoshtoss."

51. *Táqw't* ("still water"): Moses Columbia Salish for the White Bluffs area north of Pasco. (Virginia Beavert and Sharon Hargus [2009] note that an old village site is located at Hanford Reach called *Maxaxmi K'mil*, or White Clay Cliff.)

52. *Sqúten*: Moses-Columbia Salish word for Scootenay Lake, a large summer gathering and horse-racing camp.

APPENDIX C

Atinapam-Johnley Stories

The following tales were related in 1930 by Palouse-Wallula elder Ms. Atinapam and translated by Cy Johnley for anthropologist Melville Jacobs at Cayuse, Oregon, on the Umatilla Indian Reservation, and found in the Jacobs Collection (UW 81/73) at the University of Washington Suzzallo Library Archives. These versions were prepared from copies at the Colville Tribal Museum, Coulee Dam, Washington, and transcribed with minor fluency edits.

"Young Coyote, Green Cricket, and Old Lady Spider"[1]

A chief was living,
   he was the son of Coyote.
His father thought it over,
   "Now I will send him away,
     far away."
       His own son.
He made up his mind,
   and put a pole far up on a tree.
He placed a nest of young eagles[2] up there,
   and said to his son,
     "I have found good birds,
       Eagle's young ones.
          Let's go now, I'll show you."
So Young Coyote went with him.
They saw the birds, nice feathers,
   Eagle's young ones.

---

[1] Spilyáy, Sɨlksɨ́lkya, and Waxalxalí.
[2] From xwayamá, young golden eagles.

Coyote told his son,
  "Take off your shirt and leggings,
    leave them here,
      and the dentalium tied around your hair;"
        That is how you can ascend."

So he climbed
  there up the tree.
He went close to the young eagles,
  but thought, "No, I'll get to them pretty
  quick."
He ascended the pole faraway,
  and got lost,
    up there,
      in the blue sky.
Young Coyote was lost.

Coyote then went home,
  to his son's family
    in this land.
One was named Green Cricket,
  and the other woman was Duck.[3]
    Young Coyote had two wives,
      but now he was lost,
        and they were down here
          in this land.
Green Cricket's child was a boy;
  she had just one child,
    and Duck had none.

Young Coyote was lost for a long time,
  and finally found some people.
They were there afar off.
He found them,
  two old Spider Women.

---

[3] Yuxyúxya.

He went inside their house and told them,
   "I am poor, I am lost, I am hungry."
They said, "You are far away from home,
   and have arrived up here, in the sky."
They made food for him.
   He ate.

One Old Lady Spider told him,
   "You'll have to make a rope."[4]
"Where can I get rope?" he asked.
So they showed him the rope.
They gave him a knife;
   he cut the rope plant like this,
      and he packed five bundles.
He took it back to their house.
They were all glad about the rope.
Old Lady Spider said,
   "Now I'll let you down below."

She was fierce, brave, and powerful.
She tied the rope around him,
   then went outside
      and opened up a place
         where she let him down.
He paid with the rope.[5]
He finally stepped down
   and loosened himself.
He shook and pulled at the rope.
She thought,
   "He has surely now gotten down to earth,
      and is sending the rope back to me."
So she pulled it up.

---

[4] A rope of *taxús*, Indian hemp (*Apocynum cannabinum*).
[5] That is, by letting them keep the rope.

Young Coyote was very glad.
   He went to where his place was,
     and arrived at his house.
Nothing. No people there.
   They must have moved away.
His people and all his belongings were gone.
Nothing was there.
He looked around.
"Where did they go?"
He found a road eastwards they had gone,
   and he followed that.
He got to an old fireplace,
   and continued on.
Then he found the same thing.
Again he went on
   and found a fresh, newer fireplace.
Again he went on
   and found a new one.
     Oh, the fireplace was hot!
"Not very long ago
   they must have just gone."

So he followed them
   and then saw one woman packing on foot.
A child was riding on the pack.
He had found his woman, Green Cricket,
   his wife and baby.
As she went she cried.
He knew her, all of them, faraway.
They had left her behind all alone,
   poor woman.
He pulled back on her rawhide packing rope[5];
   she didn't see him.
He kept it up, pulling harder to hold her back.

---

[5] *wátisaspa*

Then she saw him.
Oh, she knew, recognized her man!

She sat right down, and told him the story.
"I was behind all the time, and they left me."
"The Chief[6] took Duck for his wife;
  he's up ahead in the lead,
    and he ran us off,
      and we are far away with different people.
He said to her, "In the evening let's follow them."
So they went on that evening.
Green Cricket told him where they stayed.
Coyote Chief arrived there with Duck
  and they also came there
    to the house.
They were all glad;
  they felt good to see each other.
They stayed overnight.
In the morning someone said,
  "Young Coyote is chief, now that he has
  arrived."
Another heard and sang,
  "Coyote, why do you not pay attention?
    Do you not hear that he has come back,
      and that you lied?"
Duck straight away hit Coyote,
  she was ashamed;
    he was not her husband.
She went out
  to the water.
She went into the water
  and flew away.
Young Coyote thought it all over,
  he knew everything,
    and told the people the story.

---

[6]That is, the elder.

"Father Coyote will travel all over the land
   to different places.
That is how it will now be for him."

"How Coyote Made the River Flow"

In olden times,
  in the beginning,
    were the people.
The One Who Plans,[1]
  he looked on this land.[2]
He put bodies upon the people,
  the right hand with his right hand,
    and put his spirit inside for thinking.
He put our bodies here in this land,
  and everything across the west toward the
  sunset;
    on the left hand side there his thought and
    spirit [were] put inside.
He let them go where the sun sets.
We were first in this land
  and then the last ones on the left hand,
    on the sunset side.

The birds and everything in this land,
  Ordained[3] with the wind.
The wind cleaned it up
  and altogether different birds came here then,
    the same ones everything from then on.
That is the same way deer[4] and different creatures
  were all different from then on.

---

[1] "The One Who Plans" is *təmyutáin*.
[2] "He looked" is from *pátamanwíya*, as if "he ordained/instituted it."
[3] Ibid.
[4] *iwínat* is collectively both deer and elk.

But the first ones,
  the wind cleaned them up,
    that same way.
Instead fire came down,
  water came down, behind it was fire,
    rain first, and there it was water.
The ones that belong here, all over;
  it cleaned them up.
But all the birds,
  they went on through and finished
    the first law.[5]
The same ones were all the birds;
  different then from now.
The fire went out,
  the fire nowhere in every river, just land.
He also found Coyote,
  far away and alive.
He was there.
"Now I'll go in every land;
  there's no water,
    no water was there.
      I'll be going."

He went far off where water first comes out.
Frog's[6] house was standing there.
Her house was holding back the water;
  She was sitting on the water.
Coyote went after her,
  then he made a law for the people,
    but there was no water and he went far away.
He went and found the house.
"She's holding it back."

---

[5] "Law" is *tamánwit*.
[6] *aluq'át*, in this story as animal without a personifying suffix (-áy, -yái, -ya, -á·ya).

Coyote got to her, he went in.
She was sitting there,
  Frog was sitting there
    with water in a small basket.[7]

He said to her,
  "I'm thirsty, Grandmother."
She didn't reply,
  so he spoke to her again.
But she didn't say anything at all.
He asked five times,
  then she gave him water.
Coyote drank from the small basket,
  he swallowed what she gave him.
She filled it with water again.
He looked at it,
  "Oh, water again; give me more water."
She gave it to him,
  then in one gulp he swallowed the water
    from the small basket.

She recognized him now, a Dangerous Being.[8]
  "He has come to me."
She feared Coyote, "A Dangerous Being has come to me."
"Grandmother, now I'll take you away."
 He's lying now,
  he planned it.
Now he heard the noise, warriors.
She sat there, she knew.
"Yes, now me; he's holding me to kill later on."
She feared him.
  Oh, Grandmother!
Now he took her by the hand.

---

[7] *taxsmí* is a hard coiled basket, as from cedar root.
[8] From *kw'alalí*, "Dangerous Being" in myth.

"Grandmother, now I'll take you home."
He got her by the hand,
   he pulled the earth and all;
      he pulled it out and so much water.

She tried to pull back.
He pulled out,
   Coyote lifted and a little more water came out.
He pulled against the door,
   and lots of water came out.
He pushed her out of the house;
   the water then started flowing,
      he pushed her behind the water.
"Now you will be just a frog,
   and if the water flows bigger and faster,
      then you will croak, *wá·x̣-wá·x̣-wá·x̣*."

You will be only a frog.
"There are many people,
and why should they be thirsty?
Why should you hold it back?"
Then Coyote came,
   he planned this river,
      and the water went far on to the ocean.
And when it got to the ocean
   then salmon[9] came upriver,
      and fish of every kind.

---

[9] *núsux̣*, salmon in general.

"How Coyote and the Foxes Tricked Each Other"

Coyote lay down and went to sleep.
They smelled it from afar.
The Wolf Brothers.[1]
  there were five of them,
    and also five Foxes.[2]
They had been gathering eggs at *Át'cwatam*,[3]
  and cooking them.
They were roasting them in the ground
  and smelled Coyote's salmon.

They ran over there;
  it was still smoking on top of the knoll.
They slowly went over to Coyote
  and took his roast.
Meanwhile he was sleeping.
Aha, they ate it all up, five, ten, fifteen,
  and left the bones piled by the fire.
The Wolves went over to Coyote
  where he was asleep.

With unwashed hands
  they smeared him
    on the mouth
      with salmon grease.
They made his ears pointed
  and his nose and his eyes,
    his narrow eyes.

---

[1] Wolf Brothers: *x̱alí·shyama*

[2] Foxes: *tɨlpayáima*

[3] "A lake near Ephrata, Washington," possibly Moses Lake which was known as a popular egg-gathering place because of springtime waterfowl migration.

They fixed Coyote,
  made him a sharp nose,
    sharp ears.
That's what they did to him
  with salmon grease smear.

They left him there
  and went to the lake
    to get the eggs to bake.
They got lots and the Wolves baked their eggs
    and the Foxes theirs.
They baked their eggs in two separate places.
Coyote awakened.
"So I went to sleep after eating too much salmon!
  Only the bones are left.
    I must have eaten everything."
He thought he ate it all up,
  though they stole it.

Coyote went on and on.
"Now I'll be going over there,"
  and he crossed from there to the other side.
He went upriver
  and became very thirsty.
Because of the salmon,
  he went down to the river, and drank.
Then he saw something.
"What is that?"
It was something fearful,
  so he went upriver.
Again he went to drink
  and again it was so.
His eyes were narrow,
  his nose was sharp,
    and his ears were pointed!

He asked his sisters,
  "What has happened to me?
    What is bothering me in the water?
      I am very thirsty but afraid to drink."
He was scared from seeing himself in the water.
"Others know it already,
  but you don't.
    The Wolves and the Foxes stole from you;
      they ate up the salmon
        and made your sharp nose
          and narrow eyes and pointed ears,
            and left the fish bones after they had
              eaten."

Coyote got angry.
"I will track them."
He then ran toward the river
  and drank,
    and drank,
      and drank.
He drank a lot and then pursued them
  far off toward the lake.
He got to a hill and looked down below.
Yes, far off they were indeed baking
  down close to the lake.
"Sleep!" he ordered,
  "All of you, sleep!!"
Then Coyote saw them go to sleep,
  the Wolves and the Foxes.

He uncovered the dirt and leaves,
  and found their steaming food.
He ate the eggs
  leaving five each time;
    one apiece for them.

He put out the fire and closed the pit
  and happily walked away.
When the Wolf Brothers awoke,
  one saw Coyote's tracks and said,
    "We tricked a notable person,
      and now we have been paid back."
Coyote continued on his way.
He created places in the river and streams
  where fish could swim so the people could eat
    where they treated Coyote nicely.

SELECTED BIBLIOGRAPHY

ORAL HISTORIES (conducted by Richard D. Scheuerman and/or Clifford E. Trafzer)

Gordon Fisher. June 19, 2000; July 24, 2008; December 28, 2009 (Lapwai, ID), June 16, 2006 (Lyons Ferry, WA).
Andrew George. November 15, 1980 (Toppenish, WA); November 11, 1981 (Wapato, WA).
Mary Jim. May 1, 1977; April 1–2, 1979; November 17, 1979; August 12, 1980; February 21, 1985 (Parker, WA).
Emily Peone, April 4, 1981; November 5, 1981; April 30, 1982 (Nespelem, WA).

MANUSCRIPT COLLECTIONS

Eastern Washington University, Archives and Special Collections, Cheney: Winans and Kingston Collections.
Federal Records Center, Seattle, WA: Colville Agency Records, Simms Letters, Yakima Agency Records.
Gonzaga University, Foley Library, Spokane, WA: Ray Collection.
National Anthropological Museum, Washington, DC: Sohon and National Congress of American Indian Collections.
National Archives, Washington, DC: Indian Claims Commission Dockets 161, 222, 224; Records of the Bureau of Indian Affairs; Records Related to Negotiations of Ratified Treaties.
Northwest Museum of Arts & Culture, Spokane, WA: Davis, Doty, Ruby, and Harder Collections.
Oregon Province Archives of the Society of Jesus, Crosby Library, Gonzaga University, Spokane, WA: Cataldo, DeSmet, Joset, and Kowrach Collections.
Spalding Center Museum, Spalding, ID: Spalding-Allen Collection.
Tamástslikt Cultural Institute, Umatilla Indian Reservation, Pendleton, OR: Treaty of 1855 Exhibit.
University of Oregon, Special Collections, Eugene: Palmer Collection, Nez Perce Agency Letterbook.
University of Queensland, Department of Anthropology, Graceville: Rigsby Papers.
University of Washington Suzzallo Library, Special Collections, Seattle: Haller, Jacobs, Stevens, and Swan Collections.
Washington State Historical Society Research Center, Tacoma, WA: Ankeny and Milroy Collections.
Washington State University Libraries, Manuscripts, Archives, and Special Collections, Pullman: Brown, DeSmet, Deutsch, Horan, Kuykendal, McGregor, McWhorter, Oliphant, Simms, Sutherland, White, and Winans Collections.
Yakama Nation Heritage Cultural Center, Yakama Indian Reservation, Toppenish, WA: Oral History Collection.
Yakima Valley Regional Library, Yakima, WA: Relander Collection.

Books and Manuscripts

Archer, Sellers G. and Clarence E. Bunch. *The American Grass Book*. Norman: University of Oklahoma Press, 1953.

Bancroft, H. H. *The Works of Hubert Howe Bancroft, Volume 31, History of Washington, Idaho, and Montana, 1845–1889*. San Francisco: The History Company, 1890.

Brown, William C. *The Indian Side of the Story*. Spokane: C. W. Hill Printing Company, 1961.

Burns, Robert Ignatius. *The Jesuits and the Indian Wars of the Northwest*. New Haven: Yale University Press, 1966.

Chalfant, Stuart A. *Interior Salish and Eastern Washington Indians*. 4 vols. New York: Garland Publishing, 1974.

Clark, Ella. *Indian Legends of the Pacific Northwest*. Berkeley: University of California Press, 1953.

Colville Confederated Tribes. "The Year of the Coyote: Centennial Celebration, July 2, 1972." Nespelem, WA, 1972.

Curtis, Edward S. *The North American Indian*. 20 vols. Norwood, MA: The Plimpton Press, 1911. Volume 7.

Creighton, J. J. *Indian Summers: Washington State College and the Nespelem Art Colony, 1937–1941*. Pullman: Washington State University Press, 2000.

Deloria, Vine, Jr., ed. *American Indian Policy in the Twentieth Century*. Norman: University of Oklahoma Press, 1985.

Frey, Rodney. *Landscape Traveled by Coyote and Crane: The World of the Schitsu/umsh (Coeur d'Alene Indians)*. Seattle: University of Washington Press, 2005.

_____, ed. *Stories that Make the World: Oral Literature of the Indian Peoples of the Inland Northwest*. Norman: University of Oklahoma Press, 1995.

Haines, Francis. *Appaloosa: The Spotted Horse in Art and History*. Austin: University of Texas Press, 1963.

Harmon, Alexandra, ed. *The Power of Promises: Rethinking Indian Treaties in the Pacific Northwest*. Seattle: University of Washington Press, 2008.

Hunn, Eugene, with James Selam. *Nch'i-Wana: The Big River, Mid-Columbia Indians and Their Land*. Seattle: University of Washington Press, 1990.

Jacobs, Melville. "Palus Dialect (N. Sahaptin)," Unpublished manuscript. MJC, UW, 1930.

Kamiakin, Tomeo. "Chief Kamiakin." LMC, MASC, WSU Libraries, Pullman.

Kuykendall, George. "Historical Essays II," n.d., MASC, WSU Libraries, Pullman.

Manring, B. F. *Conquest of the Coeur d'Alenes, Spokanes, and Palouses*. Spokane, WA: Inland Printing Company, 1912.

Miller, Christopher L. *Prophetic Worlds: Indians and Whites on the Columbia Plateau*. New Brunswick, NJ: Rutgers University Press, 1985.

Mullan, John. *Report on the Construction of a Military Road from Fort Walla Walla to Fort Benton*. Washington, DC: Government Printing Office, 1863.

Pambrun, Andrew D. *Sixty Years on the Frontier in the Pacific Northwest*. Fairfield, WA: Ye Galleon Press, [c. 1893] 1978.

Piper, Charles V. and R. Kent Beattie. *Flora of the Palouse Region*. Pullman: Washington State Agricultural College, 1901.

Reimers, Henry [Wes Lloyd]. *The Secret Saga of Five Sack* [George Lucas]. Fairfield, WA: Ye Galleon Press, 1975.

Relander, Click. *Drummers and Dreamers*. Caldwell, ID: The Caxton Printers, Ltd., 1956.

Rigsby, Bruce. "Changing Property Relations in Land and Resources in the Southern Plateau." Unpublished typescript, BRC, UQ, 2006.

_____. "Comments on the Chiefly Name 'Kamiakin.'" Unpublished typescript, BRC, UQ, 2007.

_____. "The Oral History Narratives of Thomas Billy Andrews." Unpublished typescript, BRC, UQ, 2007.

Roe, Frank. *The Indian and the Horse*. Norman: University of Oklahoma Press, 1968.

Scheuerman, Richard D. *Palouse Country: A Land and Its People*. Walla Walla, WA: Color Press, 1994.

Scheuerman, Richard D., and Michael O. Finley. *Finding Chief Kamiakin: The Life and Legacy of a Northwest Patriot*. Pullman: Washington State University Press, 2008.

Seaburg, William R. and Laurel Sercomb, eds. *Folk-Tales of the Coast Salish: Collected and Edited by Thelma Adamson*. Lincoln: University of Nebraska Press, 2009.

Sohon, Gustavus. "Records of the Walla Walla Council, 30th May 1855, Translated in the Language of the Spokan Indians," n.d., Manuscript 4306-c, National Anthropological Archives, Washington, DC.

Splawn, A. J. *Ka-Mi-Akin: Last Hero of the Yakimas*. Portland, OR: Kilham Stationery and Printing Company, 1917.

Stern, Theodore. *Chiefs and Change in the Oregon Country: Indian Relations at Fort Nez Percés, 1818–1855*. Corvallis: Oregon State University Press, 1996.

_____. *Chiefs and Traders: Indian Relations at Fort Nez Percés, 1818–1855*. Corvallis: Oregon State University Press, 1993.

Stevens, Hazard. *The Life of Isaac Ingalls Stevens*. 2 vols. Boston: Houghton, Mifflin and Company, 1901.

Stevens, Isaac I. *Narrative and Final Report of Explorations for a Route for a Pacific Railroad, Near the Forty-Seventh and Forty-Ninth Parallels of North Latitude from St. Paul to Puget Sound*. Washington, DC: Government Printing Office, 1855, 1860.

_____. *Washington and Oregon War Claims*. Washington, DC, 1858.

Trafzer, Clifford E. *Earth Song, Sky Spirit: Short Stories of the Contemporary Native American Experience*. New York: Doubleday, 1992.

_____, ed., *Grandmother, Grandfather, and Old Wolf: Tamánwit Ku Súkat and Traditional Native American Narratives from the Columbia Plateau* (East Lansing: Michigan State University Press, 1998), 38-43.

_____, ed. *Indians, Superintendents, and Councils: Northwestern Indian Policy, 1850–1855*. Lanham, MD: University Press of America, 1986.

Trafzer, Clifford E., and Richard D. Scheuerman. *Renegade Tribe: The Palouse Indians and the Invasion of the Inland Pacific Northwest*. Pullman: Washington State University Press, 1986.

Walker, Deward E., Jr., ed. *Handbook of North American Indians*. Vol. 12 (Plateau). Washington, DC: Smithsonian Institution, 1998.
Wilkes, Charles. *Narrative of the United States Exploring Expedition During the Years 1838, 1839, 1840, 1841, and 1842*. Philadelphia: Lea and Blanchard, 1845.
Winthrop, Theodore. *The Canoe and the Saddle, or Klalam and Klickitat*. Tacoma, WA: John H. Williams, 1913.
Yanan, Eileen, ed., *Coyote and the Colville*. Omak, WA: St. Mary's Mission, 1971.

ARTICLES AND REPORTS

Ballard, Arthur C. "Mythology of Southern Puget Sound," University of Washington Publications in Anthropology 3:2 (December 1929): 31–150.
Beall, Thomas B. "Pioneer Reminiscences." *Washington Historical Quarterly* 8 (1917): 83–90.
Bischoff, William N. "The Yakima Campaign of 1856." *Mid-America* 31 (1949): 163–208.
———. "The Yakima Indian War, 1855–56, a Problem in Research," *Pacific Northwest Quarterly* 41 (1950):162–169.
Brown, W. C. "Life of Owhi is Epic," *Wenatchee Daily World*, February 21, 1928.
Burns, Robert Ignatius. "Pere Joset's Account of the Indian War of 1858." *Pacific Northwest Quarterly* 38 (1947):285–314.
Chadwick, S. J. "Colonel Steptoe's Battle." *Washington Historical Quarterly* 2 (1907–08):333–43.
Clark, Stanley J. "The Nez Perces in Exile." *Oregon Historical Quarterly* 36 (1935):14–59.
Coonc, Elizabeth Ann. "Reminiscences of a Pioneer Woman." *Washington Historical Quarterly* 8 (1917):14–21.
Deutsch, Herman J. "Indian and White in the Inland Empire: The Contest for the Land, 1880–1912." *Pacific Northwest Quarterly* 47 (1956):44–51.
Elliot, T. C. "Steptoe Butte and Steptoe Battlefield." *Washington Historical Quarterly* 18 (1927): 243–253.
Fisher, A. H. "'This I Know from the Old People': Yakama Indian Treaty Rights as Oral Tradition." *Montana The Magazine of Western History* 49 (1999):468–92.
Frush, Charles W. "A Trip from the Dalles of the Columbia, Oregon, to Fort Owen, Bitter Root Valley, Montana, in the Spring of 1858." *Contributions to the Historical Society of Montana* 2 (1896):337–42.
Garrecht, Francis A. "An Indian Chief." *Washington Historical Quarterly* 19 (1928):167–78.
Gibbs, George, et. al. "Reports on the Indian Tribes of the Territory of Washington." *Secretary of War Reports of Explorations* 1 (1854):400–49.
Jacobs, Melville. "A Sketch of Northern Sahaptin Grammar." *University of Washington Publications in Anthropology* 4 (1931):83–292.
Kamiakin, Cleveland. "The Vision Quest." *Tác Titóoquan News* (March 2003):5.
Lewis, William S., ed., "The Daughter of Angus MacDonald [Christina McDonald McKenzie Williams]," *Washington Historical Quarterly* 13 (1922):107–117.

MacMurray, J. W. "The Dreamers of the Columbia River Valley in Washington Territory." *Transactions of the Albany Institute* 11 (1887):241–48.

McDermott, Paul D. and Ronald E. Grim. "The Artistic Views of Gustavus Sohon." *Columbia* (Summer 2002):16–22.

McDonald, Angus. "A Few Items of the West." *Washington Historical Quarterly* 8 (1917):188–229.

Meany, Edmond S., ed. "Historic Gardens of Chief Kamiakin." *Washington Historical Quarterly* 9 (1918):240.

Painter, Harry. "The Indian War of 1858." *Washington Historical Quarterly* 2 (1908):237–40.

———. "New Light on Chief Kamiakin." *Walla Walla Union Bulletin*. March 18, 1945.

Painter, Robert M., and William C. Painter. "Journals of the Indian War of 1855–1856." *Washington Historical Quarterly* 15 (1924):11–31.

Ray, Verne. "Native Villages and Groupings of the Columbia Basin." *Pacific Northwest Quarterly* 27 (1936):99–152.

———. "Tribes of the Columbia Confederacy, and the Palus." Plantiff's Exhibit No. 112, U. S. Court of Claims, Docket 261–70 (1973).

Richards, Kent. "Issac Stevens and Federal Military Power in Washington Territory." *Pacific Northwest Quarterly* 63 (1972):81–86.

Rigsby, Bruce, and Noel Rude. "Sketch of Sahaptin, a Sahaptian Language." *Handbook of North American Indians*, Vol. 17. Washington, DC: Smithsonian Institution, 1996.

Schuster, Helen H. "Yakima and Neighboring Groups." *Handbook of North American Indians*, Vol. 12. Washington, DC: Smithsonian Institution, 1988.

Sprague, Roderick. "The Meaning of 'Palouse.'" *Idaho Yesterdays* 12 (1968):22–27.

———. "Palouse," in *Handbook of North American Indians,* Vol. 12. Washington, DC: Smithsonian Institution, 1988.

Thompson, Albert. "The Early History of the Palouse River and Its Names." *Pacific Northwest Quarterly* 62 (1971):69–71.

Thompson, Erwin N. "Men and Events on the Lower Snake River." *Idaho Yesterdays* 5 (1961):10–15.

Trafzer, Clifford E., and Richard D. Scheuerman, "The First Peoples of the Palouse Country." *Bunchgrass Historian* 8, No. 3 (1980):3–18.

Index

Ahtanum, Wash., 141
Alalumti, 112n3
Alamótin (*Almáta,* Almota), 6, 31, 52, 56n5, 175nn25-26
Alpáwa (Alpowa), 31, 175n36
Amtalút (Wha-lits-pah), 47
Andrews, Tom Billy, 52n2
An-sás (Klickitat), 130, 131n1
Appaloosa, 3, 52, 107-8, 118n1, 160
Arcasa, Isabel, 129
Aripa, Lawrence, 7
Ash, Wash., 48, 172n3
Asotin (*Hasutin*), Wash., 99n1
Awhie (Owhi), Paul. *See* Lesh-hi-hite
Ayer Junction, Wash., 174nn12-13

Babbitt, Bruce, 151
Badger Mountain (Wash.), 49, 50, 51
Bannock (Shoshone) Indians, 24, 108
Beard, Dan, 58n14
berries and berry-gathering, 10, 51, 76, 134, 158, 160, 161
Bishop, Wash., 175n32
Bitterroot Mountains, 4, 27, 110, 150, 156
Blackfeet Indians, 24, 136
Blue Mountains, 4, 51, 156
Bones, Pete (Kay-yee-wach, Hiyou-wath), 6, 105
Bolan, Andrew J., 33
Boston, Massachusetts, 139
Brown, William C., 130, 134
Buck, Johnnie (Pakáyatut, Wanapum), 41, 83
Buck, Rex, Sr., 47

Camp Chelan, 129, 148n6
Caruana, Fr. Joseph, 132, 133n4
Cascade Mountains, 4
Cayuse Indians, 10-11, 24, 34-35
Channeled Scablands, 150, 153
Chapman, Alex Jesse, 57n9

Cheney, Wash., 158
Chinook Trade jargon, 24
Christianity, 11-12, 16, 29-30, 74, 83, 110
Clark, Newman, 31
Clark Fork River, 153
Clearwater Mountains, 150
Clearwater River, 74, 161
Cloudy Mountain (*Tehám-tehám*), 51, 62-65, 160
Coeur d'Alene, Id., 131
Coeur d'Alene Indian Reservation, 38
Coeur d'Alene Indians, 24, 149, 158
Colfax, Wash., 158, 176n48
Colton, Wash., 157
Columbia Indians. *See* Moses-Columbia Indians
Columbia Plateau Indian War of 1855-58, 20, 33-34, 80, 109-10, 135-36, 142n5
Columbia River, 87-92, 152, 156
Colville Indian Reservation, 17, 33, 38, 56n3, 81, 110, 125nn8-9, 129, 131, 132
Cornelius, Thomas, 57n6
Cottonwood Place (*Tacht-ti-hai*). *see* Ephrata
Covington, Lucy Friedlander, 17, 33-34, 129-30
Cow Creek (*Čherana*), 156, 176n49
Cowiche Mountain (Wash.), 139, 141n3
Crater Lake (Oreg.), 106
Crum, Wash., 175n29
Cuisik, Wash., 132
Curlew, Billy (Moses-Columbia), 77-82

Darby, Mont., 110
Daugherty, Richard, 151
Dayton, Wash., 56, 176nn41-42
DeSmet, Fr. Pierre, 112n6
Desmet Mission (Id.), 133n4
disease and epidemics, 30, 39, 52

195

Dominy, Floyd, 58n13
Douglas, Wash., 49

Earth Song, Sky Spirit (book), 73
education and schools, 39-40, 74-75, 84
Ellensburg, Wash., 134, 136
Endicott, Wash., 33
Epahlikt Moxmox (Yellow Cloud), 112n3
Ephrata (Cottonwood Place), Wash., 50, 77, 81, 82, 84n1, 186n3
Estama, Tom and Jennifer, 41, 47

Finding Chief Kamiakin (book), 1, 14, 56n3, 77
Finley, Michael, 77
First Foods ceremonies, 10, 27-28, 39, 50, 51, 76, 159
Fisher, Carter, 52
Fisher, Gordon, 1-3, 5-6, 8, 11, 14, 16-17, 19-20, 103-12
Fisher, Sam and Helen, 6, 12, 16, 35, 52, 105, 106, 108, 111, 116, 155, 174n15
Fishhook Bend (Wash.), 49
Fishhook Jim (Cawa-w'tiak), 12, 47, 54, 55, 57n8, 172
Fishhook Millie, 12
fishing and salmon, 22-23, 48-51, 59-61, 74, 78-79, 87-92, 106-7, 152, 156, 158-60. *See also* First Foods ceremonies
Fort Colville, 154
Fort Spokane, 147n4
Fort Walla Walla, 142n5
Frey, Rodney, 7
Friedlander, Joseph and Elizabeth, 129
Friedlander, George, 129
Friedlander, Louis, 129
Fryxell, Roald, 151
Fur trade, 29

George, Andrew, 1-3, 5, 8, 10-11, 14, 16, 19-20, 27-28, 37, 73-76, 151, 159-60
George, Frank and Annie, 109, 112n3
George, Smith L. (Hay-hay-tah), 74, 76n1

Grand Ronde River, 106, 114
grasses, native, 155
Great Falls, Mont., 135
Gustafson, Carl, 151

Hamilton, Mont., 109-110
Hanford Reach (Wash.), 176n51
Hangman Creek. *See* Latah Creek
Hatáhlekin (Red Echo), Chief, 37, 112n3, 175n28
Hell's Canyon, 152
Hole-in-the-Ground (Wash.), 155
Hooper, Wash., 118n1
Howard, Oliver O., 35-36
horses, 3, 52, 53, 107-8, 118n1, 132, 160. *See also* Appaloosa
Huggins, Edward, 143n4
hunting, 10, 51, 76, 135, 160, 161
Húsis Kute (Bald Head), Chief, 16, 17, 31, 37, 110, 132

Ice Harbor Dam, 53, 55, 57n7, 57n10-12, 112n5
Indian Homestead Act of 1887, 14, 31
Indian Territory (Okla.), 11, 37, 74, 106, 110-11, 133n5
Indian Siding, Wash., 175nn34-35

Jacobs, Melville 8, 38
Jim, Agnes, 48
Jim, Anna, 54
Jim, Annie (Liplíptkwin), 47-48
Jim, Annie (Tu-yu-tu-yet), 48
Jim, Carrie. *See* Schuster, Carrie Jim
Jim, Charlie, 47, 54
Jim, Harry (Ximtyutsá'kin), 47, 48, 49, 56n1, 56n3, 57n12, 69n11, 171, 174
Jim, Fishhook. *See* Fishhook Jim
Jim, Mary, 1-3, 5, 11, 14, 15-16, 19-20, 30, 39, 42, 47-55, 57n12
Jim, Thomas (Alíwiya), 47
Jim Boat Island (Wash.), 52n3, 56n3, 174n10
Johnson, Annie (Wów-nye-yu), 48
Johnson, Dick and Fannie, 76n2
Johnson, Julia (Redheart), 74, 76nn1-2

Johnson, Lyndon, 57-58n12
Johnson, Robert, 118n1
Joseph, Chief (Nez Perce), 16, 35-37, 74, 133n5

Kahlotus Lake (Wash.), 174n11
Kalispel Indians, 135
Kalyton, Matilda, 57n9
Kamiah, Id., 51
Kamiakin, Charlie Williams. See Williams, Charlie Kamiakin
Kamiakin (K'amáyakun), Chief (Yakama-Palouse), 12, 14, 16, 26-27, 33, 40, 80, 82, 84n2, 107, 109-10, 130-32, 174n15, 176n46
Kamiakin, Cleveland and Alalumt'i, 8, 12, 16, 52, 77-84, 106, 108-9, 111, 112nn3-4, 132
Kamiakin, Colestah, 17, 130-31
Kamiakin, Lukash and Shen-Shen, 131, 132
Kamiakin, Skalumkee, 51, 56n3
Kamiakin, Sophie (Chamesupum), 131, 132
Kamiakin, Tesh Palouse, 6
Kamiakin, Tomeo, 17, 132
Kamiakin, Tomomolow, 131
Kamiakin, T'siyak, 56n3, 112n3
Kamiakin, Wee-at-kwal T'sicken, 132
Kamiakin, Yam-na-nyék, 131, 132n1
Keller, Wash., 132
Kennewick, Wash., 18
Kennewick Man, 151
Kettle Falls (Wash.), 130, 152
Khalotas, Chief, 107
Kooatyahhen (Yakama), 58n13
Kooskooskie Canyon (Id.), 51, 62
Kotaiaqan (Yakama), 12

LaCrosse, Wash., 157
La-et-ha-how, 74
Lapwai Councils of 1876 and 1877, 35
Lapwai, Id., 105, 112n3, 132
Latah Creek, 17, 131, 142n5, 158
Latah, Wash., 153
Lawyer, Chief (Nez Perce), 110

Lesh-hi-hite (Líšxayxit, Paul Awhie, Yakama), 134, 139
Leshi (Léšiay), Chief (Nisqually), 143n4
Levey, Wash., 47, 48, 49, 59n1, 172n4-5
Lewis and Clark Expedition, 5, 20, 29, 56n2, 124n2
Lewiston, Id., 153
Little Palouse Falls (Wash.), 176n40
Lokout (Luqaíôt, Yakama), 134, 136
Looking Glass, Chief (Nez Perce), 37
Lost Mountain (*Palinywash*), 51
Lower Monumental Dam, 151
Lucas, George. See Star Doctor
Lyon's Ferry (Wash.), 105

Mann, Louis, 139, 142n5
Marmes Rockshelter, 151, 152
material culture, 8-11, 152
McWhorter, Lucullus V., 25, 28
McGregor, John (Maurice), 118n1
McGregor, Peter and Maude, 31
Methow Indians, 82
Milroy, Robert, 58n13
Moscow, Id., 158
Moses, Chief (Moses-Columbia), 17, 82, 132, 134
Moses, Mary Owhi (Sanclow, Yakama), 17, 34, 129, 134-36
Moses, Nellie Kamiakin, 129, 132
Moses, Sinsinq't, 132
Moses-Columbia (Isle de Pierre) Indians, 82, 85, 135
Moses Coulee (Wash.), 136, 147n2
Moses Lake (Wash.), 52n3, 84n1, 186n3
Mount Adams, 26
Mount Rainier (Tahoma), 26-27, 109
Mount Si, 139, 142n4

Nanamkin, Harry, 77-84
Native American Graves Protection and Repatriation Act (NAGPRA) of 1990, 57n10, 151
Nespelem, Wash., 79, 105, 111, 129
Nespelem Indians, 82
Nez Perce Indian Reservation, 34, 35, 38, 73, 74, 76n1, 110

198   *River Song*

Nez Perce Indian War of 1877, 10-11, 20, 26, 34-38, 56n4, 106, 110, 112n3
Nez Perce Indians, 8, 10-11, 24, 34-38, 48, 49, 82, 108, 149

Okanogan Indians, 82
Oklahoma. *See* Indian Territory
Old Bones (Waughaskie), Chief, 52
Owen, Barbara, 77
Owhi (Aúx̱ai), Chief, 17, 32, 134-36, 142-43n5

Pacific Ocean, 4, 90
Page, Wash., 57n10, 172
Pahta Pahtahank (Five Fogs), 112n3
Palmer, Joel, 32
Palouse Falls (Wash.), 59-60, 74, 116-18, 154, 174n18, 176n39
Palouse Hills, 93-94, 150-51, 153, 155, 160
Palouse region, 150
Palouse River, 150, 155-56, 176n48. *See also* Palouse Falls
Palús (*Pelús*, Palouse Village), 52, 56n2, 105-6, 154, 174n15
Pambrum, Andrew, 57n7
Parker, Wash., 42, 55, 58n13
Pasco, Wash., 54, 109, 111, 112n5, 172n1, 176n51
Pataha Creek, 176n43
Paween, Chief Tom, 132, 175n26
Penawawa. *See Pínawáwa*, 31
Pendleton, Oreg., 53
Peone, Emily Friedlander, 1-3, 5, 6, 11, 14, 17, 19-20, 33-34, 37, 127-32
Peopeo Moxmox, Chief (Walla Walla), 33
Pettyjohn, Jack and Margaret, 31
Pik'úunen. *See* Snake River
Pilot Rock, 110
Pínawáwa (Penawawa), 31, 175n24
Pine Creek (*Ingossamen*), 156, 158
Pinkham, Josiah, 23
Plateau Indian Wars. *See* Columbia Plateau Indian War of 1855-58
Pomeroy, Wash., 176n43

Priest Rapids (Wash.), 15, 26, 48, 55, 111
Pullman, Wash., 158

Qualchan (Qáhlchŭn, Yakama), 17, 134-36, 142n5
Quo-mollah (Yakama), 135, 136

Rattlesnake Mountain (Wash.), 26
Relander, Click, 57n9
Renegade Tribe (book), 1, 30, 130
Richland, Wash., 48
Ridpath, Wash., 175n23
Rigsby, Bruce, 47, 56n2, 84n2, 85n4
Riparia, Wash., 56n5, 174n19
Rock Creek (*Oraytayous*), 112n1, 156
Rock Lake (Wash.), 26, 33, 42, 106-7, 111, 112n2, 132, 153-54, 158, 176n46
Rockford, Wash., 158
Rocky Ford Creek (*Khahún*), 78-79, 84n1
Rocky Mountains, 83, 135
roots and root-digging, 10, 27, 39, 48-51, 82, 139-41, 157-58, 161, 169-70. *See also* First Foods ceremonies
Rosalia, Wash., 153
Ruby, Robert, 105

Sahaptin language, 6, 24, 56n2
salmon. *See* fishing and salmon
Samyúya, 6, 46, 112n5, 172n2
Sand, Wash., 174n14
San Poil Indians, 82
Say-may-yas (Sah-me-sah-pan, Yakama), 135, 136
Schuster, Carrie Jim, 26-27, 54, 77-78, 84n1
Scootenay Lake (Wash.), 176n52
seasons and seasonal round, 49-50, 70, 156-62
Seltice, Chief (Coeur d'Alene), 131
Seven Drums religion. *See Wáshat*
Shawaway, Alba and Nettie, 58n13
Sherman, William G., 35
Shoshone Indians, 56n2
Showaway, Chief (Yakama), 58n13

Si-en-wat (Yakama), 135
Sinkiuse Indians. *See* Moses-Columbia Indians
Sloutier, Carter and Meshac, 112n1
Slowiarchy (Felix), Chief, 174n15
Smohalla (Šmúx̱ala, Wanapum), 12, 27, 48, 83
Snake River (*Pik'úunen*), 3, 6, 21, 47-49, 50, 51-54, 56nn2-3, 57n8, 57nn10-12, 58n14, 59-61, 73, 87-92, 93n2, 105-106, 112n5, 113-15, 116-17, 118n1, 149-52, 159-60, 171-75
Snoqualmie Indians, 141
Snuqualmi Charlie (Siátxtid), 141-42n4
Soap Lake, Wash., 50
Spalding, Henry and Eliza, 30
Spangle, Wash., 158
Spirit Mountain (*Wátniwash*), 51, 131, 160
spirit quest, 109-10, 160-61
Spokane, Wash., 74
Spokane Indian Reservation, 74
Spokane Indians, 24, 136, 149, 158
Spokane River, 74, 161
Sprague Lake (Wash.), 176n47
Star Doctor (Páxalawasq'ísit, Five Shadows, George Lucas), 38, 52, 56n4, 163
Starbuck, Wash., 56n5, 142n5, 174n21
Steptoe Butte. *See Yamuštas*
Steptoe, Edward, 16
Stevens, Isaac I., 32, 84n2, 174n15
St. John, Wash., 33
Sulkstalkscosum, Chief (Moses-Columbia), 82, 135

tamánwit (*tamánwas*, law), 2, 5, 6, 20, 22-28, 84n2
Tehánap (Wenatchi), 26
Taitnapam (Klickitat) Indians, 142n4
Teias, Chief (Tiyáyaš, Yakama), 132n1, 139, 142n5
Tenas (Klickitat), 130, 132n1
Tensed (*Nigualk'h*), Id., 158
Texas Road, 56n5
The Dalles, 152

Thief Treaty of 1863, 34, 37
Thomash (Ish, Estamalóot), Chief, 52-53, 57n7
Thunder Mountain (El Capitan), 110
Tilcoax (Tílqawayks), Chief, 31, 76n1, 172n7
time balls (*ititamat*), 13
Tollefson, Ken, 142n4
Tolt, Wash., 142n4
Toohoolhoolzote, Chief (Nez Perce), 35
Touchet (*Túuse*), Wash., 107
Truax, Wash., 175n30
Tsiyiyak (Čiyái), 16, 109, 112n5
Tucannon River, 52, 56n5, 142n5, 174nn19-22
Tyler, Wash., 150

Umatilla Indian Reservation, 38, 76n1
Umatilla Indians, 24
Union Flat Creek (*Sk'olkul*), 157
Union Center, Wash., 157

Vietnam War, 3, 108, 111

Waiilatpu. *See* Whitman, Marcus and Narcissa
Waitsburg, Wash., 176n44
Walla Walla, Wash., 51, 56
Walla Walla Treaty Council of 1855, 14, 25, 32-33
Wallowa Lake (Oreg.), 51
Walker, Wash., 174n10
Wanapam Indians, 24, 48, 76n4, 82
Warm Springs Indian Reservation, 38
Wasco Indians, 24
Wáshani (*Wáshat*, Seven Drums, Longhouse religion), 4-5, 10, 15, 16, 18, 25-26, 27-28, 41, 50, 55, 58n13, 76, 76n3, 78-81, 84n2, 109, 131
Washington, Nat, 77, 82
Washtucna, Wash., 153
Washtucna Lake (Wash.), 158
Waterville, Wash., 49
Wawáwi (Wawawai), 6, 27-28, 31, 41, 110, 113, 115, 124-25n7
Way-yah-ton (Yakama), 135

Weaskus, Jarvis and Susie, 105
Wenatchi Indians, 82
Weowicht, Chief (Wiyáwiikt, Yakama), 134
Wes-ins (Fisher), 112n3
White Bird Canyon (Id.), 111
White Bluffs (Wash.), 56n3, 176n51
Whitman, Marcus and Narcissa, 30, 52, 56n1, 69n11
Wilbur, James, 58n13
Wilcox, Wash., 157
Williams, Charlie Kamiakin (Tamayatut), 51, 56nn2-3, 105, 132
Wilkes, Charles, 118n1, 174n15
Wilpocken, Emma, 76n1
Winder's Ferry (Wash.), 172n9
Winona, Wash., 112n1
Wishram Indians, 24
Wiyáwiikt (Weowicht), Chief, 17
Wolf, David, 53, 57n9
Wolf, Eugena, 53, 57n9
Wolf Necklace (Xáliš Wášimuxš, Tilcoax the Younger) Chief, 15, 53, 57n9, 57n12, 172n7
Wool, John, 31
Wright, George, 16, 34, 109-10, 135-36, 142n5

Xímtyutsá'kin (Fú-ta-kin). *See* Jim, Harry
Xímtyutsá'kin ("Shot in the Mouth"), 47, 56n1, 69n11

Yai-nach-shaw, 55
Yan-num-kt (Yakama), 135
Yakama Indians, 24, 48, 82
Yakama Indian Reservation, 28, 38, 47, 55, 76, 77
Yakima, Wash., 25
Yámuštas (Elk's Abode, Pyramid Peak, Steptoe Butte), 15, 26, 74, 106, 131, 137-38, 150-51, 153, 158, 160, 176n50
Yellow Wolf, Chief (Nez Perce), 8, 26
Yellowtail, Tom, 7
Yermount, Josephine, 141, 142n5
Yoosyóos Tulikécin (Blue Man), 3, 16, 106, 108, 174n15
Young Charlie (Wáptas Timani), 52
Young Chief (Taitau, Cayuse), 25, 32
Yuyúni (Wanapam), 48